CHALK TALK

AL HOBBY

CHALK TALK

ACKNOWLEDGEMENTS

This book is affectionately dedicated to my wife, Deb for putting up with me being consumed in coaching and then allowing me to take the time away from her to write this book. It's also dedicated to my son and daughter, Kelly and Todd, who did listen to me during their playing days. And to my grand kids, Dylan, Alicen, Izzy and Milez who sometimes listen to me.

I want to thank my two best friends and fellow coaches George and Eddie who after years of games and practices we would spend a great deal of time pontificating and discussing a multitude of baseball philosophies. And sometimes we didn't agree.

A special thanks to Jeff, one of the best high school coaches in this area, who shared with me some of his ideas and quotes that he, has collected throughout his coaching career.

TABLE OF CONTENTS

INTRODUCTION

Talent alone does not create success. There's more to success than just the physical part of the game. In sports there are two components for performing: the physical and the non-physical. Now, the physical component is easy to explain. In baseball it's the mechanics of swinging a bat. In football it's the quarterback's footwork. In basketball it's the crossover dribble to get by a defender. In other words it's how you control your body to complete the task at hand.

Then there is the non-physical component, which is comprised of two distinct categories: mental and emotional. The mental category is your general sports knowledge. In the baseball world it's called a player's baseball IQ, for example, knowing where to be defensively like backing up or knowing which base to throw to or understanding game situations and the importance of pitch counts, etc. There are plenty of "handbook"- type publications that can help with that.

Then there is the emotional category—your mindset. This part of the non-physical component is why I state, "Talent alone does not create success." Your mindset is the collection of thoughts and beliefs that shape what you think and how you feel—your emotions and attitude—which in turn have an effect on what you do physically—or don't do.

When I ask players if they are willing to give 100 percent of their efforts in their physical development, I get a resounding "YES!" And when I ask what percentage they think their mental attitude plays in their performance, the answers I get are usually in the 20 to 30 percent range. So there is some thought process concerning the role it plays. But the players' faces are most interesting when my follow-up question is "Knowing it's important, how much time can you honestly say you spend working on your mental game?" And you should see their faces when I ask, "As a pitcher or a hitter how successful will you be if you only bring 70 to 80 percent of your abilities to the mound or plate?"

I have been coaching youth baseball for over thirty years, twenty-four at the high school level, so I have worked with a tremendous number of players. And obviously these players possessed a wide range of abilities. While there was disparity in their abilities, they all had one thing in common—the desire to work on improving their physical abilities, especially their hitting. For example, unless he was injured, I don't think I can ever remember a player telling me at practice that he didn't want to take his "hacks."

But it's been my experience that the most difficult instructional component within the framework of coaching is convincing players of the integral part the non-physical—the emotional—part of their game plays in their development. When asked what part they think their mental part plays, they give the answer they think the coach wants to hear. So they will acknowledge the importance of the mindset, but it's hard to get them to commit to it.

This is a mistake because it's the difference between being a fair player and a good player or a good player and a great player. Or as Tom Seaver, ex NY Mets pitcher, one of the greatest pitchers in the history of the game, states, "The difference between the physical abilities of the players in the Major Leagues is not that great and the difference between the teams is not that great. So what it comes down to is that the dividing factor between the team that wins and the one that loses is the mental attitude…the mental alertness that keeps them from making mental mistakes. That's the…intangible." In other words, he is saying that to be successful you have to understand and believe that THE GAME IS PLAYED FROM THE NECK UP.

One reason why it's so difficult to get young players to grasp the importance of the mindset is that it's not measurable. It's objective. If I work on a batter's mechanics and the player's batting average goes from .250 to .300, that's objective—and measurable. But if I get that same player to focus on his mental game and his batting average goes from .250 to .300, there's no way to determine if it went up because of the player's mind improvement or his physical improvement or a little bit of both. It's subjective.

Another reason is that change does not happen overnight—it needs time. We live in a microwave society, so it doesn't take long for our patience to run out. When a player makes a change in his hitting mechanics, he works on it at practice but goes 0 for 10 in the next three games. Because he doesn't experience immediate results, he reverts back to the "old way." It doesn't matter if it's physical or mental—when an attempt at changing is made, if there aren't immediate results, people take the easy route. They fall back to what they did in the past—which was nothing.

Then we have what I refer to as the fear of the unknown. Players and in some cases coaches don't know what they can do regarding learning or teaching aspects of the mental side. "How do I get started? What should I discuss?" There are plenty of sports psychology books out there filled with suggestions. But that increases the uncertainty. "What books should I buy? Which one is considered the best one for my sport?" Then there's fear of incompetence. "What if I don't comprehend the 150-plus pages of scientific babble? I don't want to feel stupid! How do I teach it?"

There's also a fear of change. In general, no one likes change. We are creatures of habit. We are comfortable with our routine, so we have difficulty incorporating changes no matter how beneficial they may seem. It's different. It's the unknown. "I've never done it before, so why should I do it now?" "It's extra work." "Is the reward worth the effort?"

In the end it feels overwhelming. So players and coaches spend minimal or no time and effort on changing their approach in their daily process of developing their game. It's simply easier not to do it. Or as management consultant Rosabeth Kanter writes in an issue of the *Harvard Business Review*, "People will often prefer to remain mired... than to head to the unknown." This reminds me of the old expression "Better the devil you know than the devil you don't know."

Yes, players will tell you that spending time on their mental game is important and they will tell you they do or will work on it, but the reality is they don't "walk the talk." It's easy to say but hard to do, especially for the young players who have experienced success and are considered some of the better players, maybe the stars, in their minds, on top of their game. What they don't realize is that they have been on top because of their raw ability, their athleticism, and in some cases the level of competition they have faced.

But at some point this failure to recognize the importance of the mental game will catch up to them. It could happen at any time— during play-off games or while playing against elite fall teams or when they go up a level, like high school or college, and when they begin competing against players of equal ability. While some players will realize they need more than just natural abilities, many won't. While some will change their approach to their game, many won't. Remember, baseball is a game of adversity, and how you handle it will define you as a player and a person. So the real question is how do you—will you—handle the adversity?

This book is my attempt to convince you that instead of paying lip service concerning your mental game, buy into it. Don't just acknowledge it, but commit to it and have patience. Now to be clear, technically, this is not a how-to book. Instead it's a collection of "chalk talk" sessions.

"Chalk talk" refers to a talk or lecture in which the speaker uses a chalkboard to convey some thoughts or an idea. So the speaker lists points and/or issues on the chalkboard, discusses them, and invokes participation from the audience. In other words the speaker gets the audience to consider the point and/or issue he or she is trying to convey.

The high school team I coached was located in a cold weather state, so there were a lot of times, especially early in the season, when we were forced to go inside. And because it was a small school the space and time allocation to the baseball team was limited. So to overcome that problem, prior to our scheduled starting time, we would go to a classroom. Whenever we did this, because we used the chalkboard, we referred to it as having a chalk talk. Even when we eventually did go outside, we still started each practice with a chalk talk—minus the chalkboard. The players knew that this was when the coaching staff was going to "get into their heads" and work on the mental and emotional side of their development.

That's where the title of the book comes from. The book is a collection of the written version of the chalk talks. The various articles represent my thoughts pertaining to the makeup of a player's mindset like attitude, emotions, confidence, etc. The themes came from specific sports incidents, articles from sports subscriptions like *Sports Illustrated*, a famous sports figure and how they responded to certain situations from the previous game, etc., that I felt reflected the point I wanted to make. And because I'm not a sports psychologist, to give each chalk talk some expert validity, I have interjected some pertinent statements and conclusions made by the authors of the numerous sports psychology books that I have read.

As you read the various articles, there are three things you should notice. First, in many cases the message is the same but said a different way. The more an issue is discussed—issues like how to control yourself, how to handle the pressure of performing or approaching the game with confidence—the more chances the player has to grasp it. Secondly, there's more than one message in some of the articles because sometimes one message leads to and supports another. Lastly, while there are some suggestions as to how you can control your emotions and the stress of pressure situations, this is not designed to be your typical how-to book. It's an attempt to get players to become aware—to think about it.

The book *Modern Warriors* written by Pete Hegseth is a collection of inspiring stories from highly decorated service men. One of which is Senator Daniel Crenshaw who was a Navy SEAL and retired as a Lieutenant Commander. Need I remind you of the notorious rigorous training one must go through to become a Navy SEAL? A member of an elite team. The following is how he described some of those that did not make it. "The failures are more surprising than the successes. A lot of times, the most athletic, the fittest, the physically strongest candidates were the ones who quit. They should have been able to crush it, but they didn't. Part of that is because they spent too much time on physical preparation and not enough on the mental preparation. They believed that because of their physicality, their athleticism, they wouldn't be surprised when faced with failure". His statement exemplifies my message that 'There's more to success than just the physical part of the game'.

Whether you are a player or coach consider *Chalk Talk* as a primer. Instead of reading various sports psychology books, use the articles as a template of what to consider and discuss concerning the role emotions play, just like a speaker or lecturer uses chalk talk as the vehicle to get you thinking about something. I hope this makes it easier to get started. A final thought—no matter how many years you have played or coached, you don't know everything. Remember, a good coach, a good player, never stops learning.

ATTITUDE AND ENERGY— INTERNAL CONTROL

Whenever a pitching coach is working with his pitchers, he reminds the players about being efficient. The more efficient the player's pitching motion, the harder he will throw and, much more importantly, the less likely it is that he will get injured. So the pitching coach looks for physical issues that are inefficient. For example:

- Front side flies open early

- Elbow comes up over shoulder

- Forearm flies out

- Doesn't pronate

Again his intent is to get the pitcher to be physically efficient. Any good coach can spot players' physical inefficiencies pretty easily, and any good coach can teach the fixes. After all, they are right there— right in front of his face.

But how easy is it for a coach to notice mental inefficiencies? How easy would it be to teach a fix? The answer is it's not. And because of that the player needs to be the coach of his mindset. The player needs to spot—be aware—of any inefficient thinking so that he can change it to be efficient. So what does inefficient thinking mean? For example, do you:

- Spend a lot of energy on your stats?

- Tend to be overly concerned what your coach thinks?

- Need to be perfect or you're a loser?

- Beat yourself up for a mistake?

- Fear failure?

- Doubt your future success?

You need to be aware of where your head is because it's all about your energy. You need to pay attention to where and when you're having inefficient thoughts like the ones listed above. How efficiently you manage your attitude—the mental part of your game—has an effect on your energy—the physical part of your game. Realize that thoughts like the ones listed, especially during game time, are not helping you on a straight line path to success.

I believe there are two major concepts that lead to success but that cannot be taught. They are ATTITUDE and ENERGY. Coaches can encourage, reward, and cultivate but nobody can teach you to have high energy or a good attitude. They have to be taken care of internally.

Understand that attitude is not an emotion. It's a series of thoughts. Thoughts give direction and control. As defined in the dictionary, our attitude is "our state of mind as we approach our lives. The mental message (thoughts) will dictate the physical action ....the body tends to do what it hears."

Okay, so what does all this mean? It means that your attitude, good or bad, affects how your body will perform physically. If you tell yourself that you can make the play or get the base hit, odds are good that your body will function efficiently. It won't interfere with your muscle memory. But if you tell yourself that you can't make the play or get the base hit, odds are you will be inefficient. It interferes with your muscle memory. Because the body tends to do what it hears, you have a tendency to become tense and lose your fluidity. This is where positive thoughts come into play.

Attitude in playing the mental game of baseball is your state of mind as you approach each aspect of the physical game—each pitch, each game, and each practice. While there are many factors that can affect the outcome of a game, you can't control or change them all. Wasting time and energy worrying about things you can't control or change is inefficient thinking. It leads you to a negative energy level and attitude.

I haven't read anything by a psychologist or a psychiatrist who can clinically explain why it happens, but I have seen players who lock into negative thinking and usually become depressed. And when you are depressed the body tends to lose energy. You've seen people like this. They drag themselves around and appear tired. Shoulders slumped. They have a tendency to yawn a lot. They sit by themselves. On the other hand, a positive attitude triggers enthusiasm. When people are positive, their energy seems to be endless. You hear them laughing and interacting with their teammates. They have what during my days was called "swag." They act confident, even when things aren't going so well.

Now as anyone involved in sports knows, confidence is critical for a player's success. Sports psychologist Tom Hanson feels that a player needs to "project an air" of confidence—have a sense of mission and purpose. In an article titled "White Line Fever," Hanson quotes Dennis Eckersley to support his point. "A pitcher might be scared to death in a game but you can't show it. You must project confidence… If the body acts confidently, you will be confident. If you act confidence out, you begin to think it."

In his time Dennis Eckersley was considered one of the best closers who ever played. So much so, that as a closer for the Oakland Athletics, he earned himself the reputation as "The Man." He attributed his success to making sure he carried himself with confidence. Even when he went into a game and didn't feel like "The Man," he would, and I quote, "Fake it. You do. The next thing you know it works. You can't let on that you're not throwing well. There's a body language; I really believe it. You've still got to act like you're the man…give the impression that your stuff is on time."

To further support Hanson's statement that a player needs to project an air of confidence, consider the quote from H. A. Dorfman, author of the book *The Mental ABC's of Pitching*. A pitcher needs to "establish the habit of acting who you want to be rather than the person you don't want to be." This is just another way of saying sometimes you need to fake it.

Bottom line, you are responsible for controlling your attitude. Your attitude—positive or negative—is your decision. How you react—your response—your "internal control"—determines your state of mind. And your state of mind will determine your confidence—your energy level. If you have "internal control" you will have "external control."

Consider the following scenario. It's Monday morning—you have to get up early, catch the bus—you are dreading the history test you will have to take today. Your alarm goes off. As you are lying in bed, you think, *I'm going to have a miserable day.* So how do you react? What's your body language? What's the message you are sending to your mind and body? Do you jump up right away or do you hit the snooze button several times? When you do get up, do you rush to get ready or move like a slug, waiting till the last minute to leave? What's your energy level? What's your attitude? Are you positive?

Now let's flip the scenario. It's Monday morning—you have to get up early. You are going to Disney! As you are lying in bed you think, *I'm going to have a great day!* So how do you react now? What's your body language now? What's the message you are sending to your mind and body now? Do you jump out of bed or hit the snooze button? Do you rush or move like a slug? What's your energy level? What's your attitude? Are you positive?

I forget which sports psychologist told this story, but it's a great example of controlling your internal feelings. He and his wife were vacationing at the beach. They decided to go down to the beach to do their exercises and to relax. He grabbed his things and waited for his wife outside. But she didn't come out. He became extremely angry because she was taking so long. *What could she possibly be doing? Let's go!* He screamed to himself. The more he waited, the more frustrated he got. But as he was waiting he realized that he was standing under a bunch of palm trees and it was nice in the shade. So he decided to get started on his exercises. Before he knew it he started to feel good. In fact so good that when his wife finally did come out, he warmly greeted her and never mentioned his frustration. He went on to have an enjoyable day.

Consider what happened. What was his response to his wife's tardiness? Initially it was frustration, which turned to anger. His response could have been to have an argument with his wife. Instead, he took control of his response to the situation and went about his business. His response was to just let it go. It changed the course of his day.

In the 2018 NFC Championship game, New Orleans Saints versus the LA Rams, late in the fourth quarter there was what might be considered the worst missed call in NFL playoff history. After a missed obvious pass interference call against the Rams, the Saints were forced to kick a field goal instead of running out the clock. There remained just enough time, one minute forty seconds, for the Rams to move the ball into field goal range and tie the game. The game went into overtime ending with a winning field goal by the Rams.

Think about it. A game that decides which team is going to the Super Bowl is decided by the officials.

So imagine how the Saints players must have felt. After the game there were the usual post-game interviews. Read what Drew Brees, the Saints quarterback, had to say after the game: "Yeah, that's tough to swallow. I think there were plenty of times throughout the season that there are calls that go against you, or they (the officials) miss, or they didn't." However, he also stated, "Listen, you're going to play ball. Just like you would throughout the season when something like that happens, whether it goes your way or doesn't. You move on to the next play. You can't let it bother you. So it had no bearing…at least not for me." He continued, "You feel like that it was something out of your control. And I like to focus on the things I can control."

He was then asked what he was thinking in the moment of the non-call. "In the moment you obviously yell and scream, 'How did you not see that?' But again, once you come back (to the huddle) it's like there's nothing we can do about it. It's on to the next play." He ended the interview stating you have two choices. Get angry over the result or work toward a better future. "I think you have to with anything that happens… You can go one of two directions. You can either go in the tank or you can find a way for this to come together for our good. That's the mindset I take."

Speaking of going into one of two directions, consider Tom Brady's mindset in Super Bowl LI when the NE Patriots were down 28 to 3 against Atlanta. "You could look at that situation and basically quit and say, 'We have no shot of winning' or you could say, 'This is going to be an amazing comeback.' When we come back from this, this is going to be the defining moment in our life or professional career.

I think when you shift your mind to think that way it becomes very empowering, as opposed to being very discouraging. For me it's very much about 'How do I reframe it in my mind?'"

In an article written by psychologist Dr. Rich Bayer titled "Understanding Emotions," he mentions that "an initial emotional reaction usually lasts only twenty to thirty minutes. That is, our physical response to an emotional situation lasts only that long. But, if we keep thinking about the emotion or the situation, replaying the scene in our mind and re-experiencing it, the emotion can last longer." So be positive.

When I was growing up if you wanted to listen to music, you played records. Because they were made of vinyl, they would sometimes crack. And when you played a record that had a crack in it, all you would hear is the same line sung over and over. At times that line would stick in your head and you'd say to yourself, "I can't get this song out of my head." My point being that the longer you dwell—the more you play that cracked record—if it's negative—the more frustrated, angry, or disappointed you will get. If it's positive the more confident you will get. Your emotions will carry into the next pitch, the next game.

Drew Brees and Tom Brady understand this. In essence they are saying dwell on the positive. Let it consume you. If it consumes you emotionally, as Dr. Bayer stated, "The emotion can last longer." And the longer it lasts—the more times you play that record—the longer you will have a positive attitude and positive energy. Remember—no one forces you to play that negative record because you control that internally.

Oh by the way, as of 2019, Brees holds the NFL records for career pass completions, completion percentage, passing yards, and touchdown passes; he's third in regular season career passer rating, and fourth in postseason career passer rating. He holds the record of consecutive games with a touchdown pass. He has passed for over 5,000 yards in a season five times—no other NFL quarterback has done so more than once. He has led the NFL in passing yards a record seven times and in passing touchdowns a record-tying four times.

Brady's comeback is considered the greatest comeback of all time. I think I know why both players have been so successful. They know attitude is a small thing that makes a big difference.

By having internal control, you will have external control of your performance. So how efficient is your attitude and energy when you make an error? When the team is losing or striking out? After the coach discusses some mistakes you made in the last game? Or how about that shrinking batting average? Remember, the most important thing that you have complete control over is the way you feel, the way you respond to any situation, and the things you think about at any minute of the day. "Days are made of moments—and each moment you have a choice as to how you are going to respond—you choose your focus and actions." Be efficient.

BELIEF AND TRUST

There is nothing like playoff baseball. It's an emotional roller coaster! There's no running out the clock. No quarterback taking a knee. In baseball you must finish off your opponent yourself. While the following examples might be considered dated, that does not invalidate the message. Focus on the message and not when they occurred.

As the 2011 MLB season was coming to the end, there were still four teams vying for the last two wild card playoff spots. Up to this point no team had ever been down nine games in September and made the playoffs. Ever—in over 100 years. But this year, because both the Boston Red Sox and Atlanta Braves played so poorly down the stretch, it came down to the very last game of the season to determine who would make the last playoff spots. If the Red Sox and Braves won their games, they'd make the playoffs and eliminate the St. Louis Cardinals and the Tampa Bay Rays, the two teams that were down the nine games. But both lost—experiencing the worst collapse in history. In other words they did not finish off their opponent. Some would say they choked.

Then you have the 2012 playoffs. The San Francisco Giants defeated the Cincinnati Reds in the National League Division Series in five games. They lost the first two at home but won the last three on the road, thus becoming the first major league team to ever do that.

To top that off they then came back from a 3-1 deficit to defeat the St. Louis Cardinals in the National League Championship Series. Think about it. They won all six games facing elimination in consecutive postseason series, yet another first. And by doing so they advanced to play the Detroit Tigers and a chance to win the World Series.

Now I'm sure you don't remember what happened in the 2012 World Series. The series started in Detroit. For the first game the Tigers started Justin Verlander. At that time he was probably considered the best pitcher in baseball. You had the reigning American League MVP and Cy Young winner facing a very tired Giant team. All the pundits and even the Detroit players believed they had game one in hand and that they would at the very least, after the first two games, have a split situation when they went back home for Games 3, 4 and 5. They had the advantage.

But Verlander was chased after allowing five runs and six hits in just four innings. This was his shortest start that year. The Giants' Pablo Sandoval hit a solo home run to right-center on a ninety-five-mph 0-2 fastball in the first inning. On his very next at bat he hit another one. An opposite-field "bomb" on another Verlander ninety-five-mph fastball. I can still see Verlander standing on the mound, facing left field, with his mouth wide open, saying "WOW" as the ball sailed well over, and I mean well over, the fence. Even he was in awe.

I'm not going to go into the details of the remaining games, but suffice it to say the Giants proceeded to sweep the Detroit Tigers four games to none and win the 2012 World Series. They finished off their opponent! Three times!

So imagine how the losing players felt. I'm sure that in the locker room and the days that followed, every issue under the sun was mentioned and discussed as to what happened—why they did not put their opponents away. There were so many things they could point to that, in their minds, would explain just what happened. And I'm sure in those discussions that their hitting and pitching, the physical aspects, were mentioned as the reason for their downfall.

Yes hitting and pitching mechanics are important but in the end, especially in pressure situations, the driver of the success bus is something inside. "Something inside" can be explained in two words: BELIEF and TRUST. The Rays and Cards believed they could win. They were confident they could win. The Braves and Red Sox, after losing their nine game leads, had doubts. Just like the Tigers and Verlander after that first game. I can still see Verlander with his mouth wide open, saying "WOW" as the ball sailed well over the fence. Individually and as a team they lost their confidence because they questioned and didn't trust their abilities. Trust is the opposite of doubt, worry, and fear.

My point is that you need more to win than just mechanics. Can you successfully hit a ball without perfect mechanics? Yes! Or throw a strike without perfect mechanics? Absolutely. Can you hit or pitch well without believing in yourself? Maybe but maybe not. I say this because, as any psychologist would tell you, we "see" in the world what we believe to be true. Our perceptions govern our emotions and feelings and the actions we take. They mold our beliefs. Our body responds (physically) to what our mind—our emotions—mentally tells it.

In an article by psychologist Dr. Rich Bayer titled "Understanding Emotions" he explained it this way: "If we look upon ourselves as a car, our emotions would be the engine. They rev us up. They get us going. They provide raw power." Now using Dr. Bayer's car analogy, consider your mind as the steering wheel. It guides you to your emotions, suggests how you should feel, and guides you to how you respond.

For example—take two people who have an opportunity to ride a hot air balloon. One can't wait to get into the basket. He experiences a feeling of wonder or excitement at just the thought of doing this. The other person wants nothing to do with it. He experiences feelings of fear and anxiousness and is ill at ease. Both are reacting to the stimulus—the hot air balloon. The person who does not want to do it could be afraid of heights, so, staying with Dr. Bayer's car analogy, his mind steers him to thinking about how unsafe it might be and not the possible fun and excitement.

Let's talk snakes. I don't know about you, but I hate snakes. I don't know why, but I do. People like me fill with fear the instant we see a snake. Our feelings take over, and there is no thinking involved. Our gut reaction says "RUN." We get as far away as fast as we can. Not until we are safely away do we start thinking, *Maybe it was just a garden snake.* Often we can't think until we feel we are safely away.

Sport psychologists explain it the following way. When you feel good about where you are, have love-based beliefs—saying things like "I love this game" to yourself—you go into aggressive mode. You do so because you feel you have the advantage. And when you are in aggressive mode you are on offense. You are an attacker—fearless. Your physical response to love-based beliefs will show up as freedom, focus, fun, fluidity, fearlessness, laughter, joy, persistence, and acceptance of the unavoidable failure in baseball. You believe—have trust—in your abilities!

But if you feel that you are at a disadvantage and have fear-based beliefs, you go into what is called "survival mode." And when you are in survival mode, you are on defense. Going on defense usually results in a player getting away from his everyday approach. To avoid possible mistakes he plays it safe. The physical response to 'fear-based beliefs shows up on the field as poor focus, muscle tension, contraction, self-pity, anger, frustration, self-degradation, the need to be perfect, and a lack of self-forgiveness.

Let's apply this to just one of many aspects of playing the game—hitting, for example. Consider your approach at the plate when you are facing a 2-0 count versus a 0-2 count. As I'm sure you are aware, the success rate—for the sake of argument, batting average stats—with a 2-0 count is considerably better than with a 0-2 count. Now we can certainly list all the reasons and have a great debate as to why this is true, but ask yourself: With a 2-0 count do you believe you can hit the next pitch or you will get a better pitch to hit? Well, of course you do! And do you trust—feel confident—that you can handle a 2-0 count? Of course you do. That's because at this count you are the guy who climbs right into the hot air balloon! You feel good about your position—you go on offense! You are an attacker—fearless. Welcome to aggressive mode!

But what's your approach facing a 0-2 count. Let's face it, as we all know, using the same success measure—batting average—it is definitely lower than a 2-0 count. And why is that? One reason is that you believe the advantage goes to the pitcher. So you see snakes! Snakes! Your perception of the situation is that you are at a disadvantage. You become scared, non-aggressive, defensive, and move away from your everyday approach. Welcome to survival mode!

But herein lays the problem. When you are in the batter's box, you are supposed to be on offensive, no matter what the count is. As an offensive player in any sport, if you find yourself in survival mode, the chances of you being successful as an offensive presence are dramatically reduced. Why is that?

When it comes to baseball and hitting, you are allowing the pitch count to dictate how you feel. Because of your perception you have decided, for some reason, that on 0-2 or with two strikes you can't trust your abilities. You can't trust your ability to recognize a good pitch versus a bad pitch. It's as if there is a rule in the baseball rule book that states once you get a 0-2 or 1-2 count, before the next pitch, you must hand over your faith in your ability to see the ball and hand the ball over to the pitcher. For some reason once you get a 0-2 count, you must give up your confidence.

When you allow the pitch count to determine how you feel, you put yourself on defense. Thoughts like *OMG, I'm in trouble* run through your head. And when you do that, it's human nature to be afraid. Thus you put you into survival mode. In survival mode, because you are afraid, you play in fear. You are now not thinking clearly, and your body is not relaxed. You give up your confidence. You don't believe you can be successful. You do things like take pitches—pitches that are strikes—or better still, chase balls out of the strike zones.

Now while there certainly are no stats to prove it, swinging at pitches out of the strike zone is probably a primary reason why success rates—batting average stats—on a 0-2 count are considerably lower than a 2-0 count. That's a mental problem, not a physical problem. That's a mental problem that causes a physical problem.

Sometimes I find psychology terms hard to grasp. So using the KISS philosophy—KEEP IT SIMPLE, STUPID—I came up with the following analogy that shows the message being conveyed in the terms "survival mode" and "aggressive mode."

If I laid down a plank—a two-foot-by-ten-foot board—on the ground and asked people to walk across it, I'm sure you would agree that everyone would probably without hesitation just go. It's a no-brainer— no thinking, no doubts. They believe they can do it. Let's change the scenario. Take that same board and raise it ten feet off the ground. Now how would they react? Can we agree that probably most would slow down and hesitantly try to go across? Why is that?

Well, they start thinking: *I might fall off* or *If I fall, I might get hurt.* They have doubts. They are allowing the height of the plank to affect their belief system. They are allowing the height of the plank to affect their trust level. But the height of the plank is not asking them to do something they can't do. They did it when the plank was laid on the ground.

The analogy is that the board on the ground represents aggressive mode. Love-based beliefs. It's you hitting in the cage. No thinking—just go—no doubts. And the board ten feet off the ground could represent survival mode. Fear-based beliefs. It could be you up at the plate in the bottom of the seventh inning with the bases loaded. Notice I said "could." If you are allowing thoughts like *I'm not sure I can hit this guy* or *I struck out the last time* creep into your head, then you are allowing the situation—the height of the board and the stress of the situation—control what you believe. That's a mental problem, not a physical problem. That's a mental problem that causes a physical problem. Like swinging at pitches that are out of the strike zone.

In all sports, not just baseball, there is a dirty seven-letter word that no athlete wants to hear: CHOKING. I did some research on "choking in sports." Here's what I found. Let's see if there is any difference between choking and being in survival mode.

Choking in sports happens when you get in your own way mentally, or your mind prevents you from performing at your best. In most cases, athletes experience physical changes, such as tension, increased heart rate, and rapid breathing. Athletes also report mental changes, such as anxiety, apprehension, and confusion. Athletes often change their strategy when choking and often perform more tentatively. Most athletes and coaches would agree that choking happens when you are firmly in command of your performance or the competition and you lose because of a change in your mental state, which leads to a mental meltdown of sorts. You feel pressure or suddenly lose confidence.

The article went on to say that athletes who choke will lose a big lead because they are fearful of not finishing off the game, or they perform tentatively or defensively and lose trust in their skills. They might feel intimidated, or doubt interrupts their mental processes. They proceed to play scared or afraid to lose and thus can't perform with trust in their skills.

The message being conveyed is that the perception of the situation by the teams and players affects their physical response. They choke because they see snakes; they perceive that they are in a threatening situation. They choke because thoughts like *Hey, this isn't fun anymore. Hey, we can lose this thing!* start running through their heads.

They choke because they go into survival mode. They choke because they become hesitant and unsure of themselves. They choke because they start questioning themselves.

Here's a more recent football example. In 2017, Philadelphia Eagles backup quarterback Nick Foles took over for injured starting quarterback Carson Wentz. To everyone's surprise he successfully led the Eagles through the playoffs and brought the city of Philadelphia its very first Super Bowl with a victory over the New England Patriots.

Then in 2018, late in the season, with the Eagles on the brink of not making the playoffs, Carson Wentz again gets injured, and once again Nick Foles has to take over. He not only proceeds to lead the Eagles to four consecutive wins to make the playoffs but also goes on and wins the playoff game against the higher-seeded Chicago Bears.

You don't have to be an Eagles fan—or even a football fan—to appreciate Foles' accomplishments. As I'm sure you can imagine, Foles participated in many after-game interviews, and the obvious questions he was asked were how did he do it? The following is his response after winning the last four games of the season to make the playoffs: "What I learned on those stages is just how to calm myself in a chaotic moment, when there's…a ton of pressure. And just really simplifying in my head. Getting in the huddle, looking at the guys that I trust. Know that it's all on the line for us and we're just going to get the job done." He summed it up best when he said, "It's just belief in one another."

After the playoff game, he said that while he admitted that things weren't going well for the Eagles offensively—he threw two interceptions—Foles gave his defensive players credit for helping keep his team in the game. "They just kept coming and telling us: 'We got you. We got you. We're going to get you the ball back,'" said Foles. "They never turn; they never get upset."

He summed it up by saying, "It's about believing in one another—in the hard times. It's easy to pat each other on the back when things are going well. It's, hey, when things aren't going well or when I make mistakes, what's going to happen? What happened today is I…made a couple of mistakes, but the guys were there to be there for me, to lift me up. The defense said they got me. And that's what this team is about."

Foles' experience is a great example of belief and trust. Trusting and believing in yourself! Trusting and believing in your teammates that together the job will get done. And it's what can help you and your team get the most out of one another—in good times and bad. You have to bring the same mentality you have about what you can do in the batting cage out onto the field.

The expression "putting an opponent away" does not just refer to the team you are playing. It also refers to the players you are going up against. It refers to the various personal battles you face during the course of the game. In every situation you are facing an opponent. It can be the batter up at the plate when you are on defense. It can be the catcher trying to throw you out on your steal attempt. It can be facing a 2-0 or 0-2 count, just to name a few "battles."

Think of all of the possible personal battles you might face in a game or a season. So imagine the number of times, because of your perception of that particular battle, you get to decide what mode you want to get into. When faced with any individual battle, you control whether or not you are the driver of the success bus. You are behind the steering wheel of that bus. Only you control your emotions that determine the level of confidence or doubts about your ability to perform at that time.

BUMP IN THE ROAD

Imagine you are a starter on your high school team. You are the leader—the captain. You have high expectations for the upcoming season. However, your coach tells you that you cannot play the first four games of the season and gives you a reason that you feel is not valid.

Or imagine you are the star on your local travel team. You have aspirations and dreams of playing for a USA national team. In fact you get invited to try out for the USA National Junior Team. Things are going great until not only are you cut from the junior team but the coach tells you that you are not even national team material.

Do these situations sound familiar? The first one should. It made the sport headlines. This is exactly what happened to Tom Brady, quarterback of the New England Patriots, in 2016. It's famously referred to as *Deflategate*. The second situation would sound familiar if you followed the USA Woman's soccer team. It's exactly what happened to Carli Lloyd, a two-time gold medalist for the USA National soccer team.

Imagine how these players must have felt. It would be natural for them to be upset. Maybe very upset. That's human. So let's look at how both of them responded to their "bump in the road" concerning their careers.

TOM BRADY

Because of the four game suspensions, Brady was not allowed to use the Patriots' facilities or work out with any of his teammates. As described in a *Sports Illustrated* article, Brady practiced football on the same days and at the same times as his teammates at a local high school field. He ran through the same quarterback drills and agility exercises as before, performed the same resistance-band training, and had the same massage work done before and after his practices that he normally would have done if he was with his teammates on the Patriots facilities.

In the same article it mentions that Brady's favorite bit of reading is *The Four Agreements*, a spiritual guidebook by Don Miguel Ruiz. One of the four agreements is *don't take anything personally*. Ruiz feels that people tend to "fall into narratives that others create for them, that they're angry because they're expected to be angry, aggrieved because most others would be too." Which explains the following two statements in the article: "Brady never mentioned the ban, never so much as uttered Deflategate" and "Brady—at least publicly—never blamed the NFL Commissioner Goodell."

Now I'm sure I don't have to remind you about the multitude of articles about *Deflategate*. But what I can say is that Brady did not let the "noise" influence him. He maintained control of his attitude. He did so by staying with his program. He kept to his meticulous schedule as best as he could and got ready for the first game that he was allowed to play. Or as the author of *The Four Agreements* stated, "Brady has created his own truth."

Oh, by the way, the Patriots won the Super Bowl that year and guess who the MVP was?

CARLI LLOYD

In her book *When No One Was Watching: My Hard Fought Journey to the Top of the Soccer World*, Lloyd goes into detail about what she did when she was cut from the USA National Junior team.

She contemplated quitting but took her father's advice and went through an audition with James Galanis, a highly regarded soccer trainer. Galanis put her through a couple of skill work drills and a fitness evaluation, during which he constantly asked her questions. "Why do you think you were cut? What sort of teammate are you? Do you like to go on the attack? What are your strengths? Do you get back on defense?" Lloyd admits that almost every answer she gave was full of excuses or finger-pointing. She took no ownership of what happened to her.

Now it was time for Galanis to give Carli his analysis of her. "Okay, Carli, this is the story as I see it," he said. "Can you make the national team? Yes. It is going to take a whole lot of work. But if you put in that work, I don't see any reason you can't go as far as you want.

"You are very strong technically and tactically. But you are not fit...mentally...you are weak. You don't push yourself hard; you are lazy. You aren't the sort of player who's going to thrive under pressure. And your character? That's poor. You make excuses and find people to blame. You always have a reason things aren't working out, instead of *making* them work out."

He continued. "You need to stop with the excuses. You need to start treating every training session, every game, as if it were a World Cup final. You need to be the hardest-working person out there every time. Soccer needs to be number one in your life—not your boyfriend or your social life. If it's not, let's go home right now.

"If I call you at 10 p.m. on a Saturday and say, 'Meet me at the field in a half hour,' you turn to your friends and say, 'Sorry, I have to go train.' You have to be willing to train on Christmas and Easter and Thanksgiving. If you are willing to make these sacrifices, I'll work with you. I'll do everything I can to help you reach your goals. When do we start?"

Wow! The last thing she was expecting was a scathing evaluation. After all, she was the star on her local team. So imagine her response! But let's read on: "My head is spinning…this is the most detailed evaluation I've ever gotten. This coach, a man who barely knows me, has shredded me…"

Carli's meeting with James turned her whole career around. She didn't quit soccer. Instead she went into James's Universal Soccer Academy, worked harder than she ever had, and made the USA National team at the age of twenty-two. She went from someone who wouldn't make the USA National Team to a full-fledged, pro soccer player. Her bio reads as follows: She is a two-time Olympic gold medalist, 2015 FIFA Woman's World Cup champion, two-time FIFA Player of the year, and a three-time Olympian.

YOU

These two stories lead me to the following scenario. You are the star of your local team. You make the high school team but not as a starter. The coach refers to you as a role player. In essence you are going to be a part-time player. So how do you feel when faced with your "bump in the road"? We know how Tom Brady and Carli Lloyd would act but how about you? How you respond, how you control your response and your attitude about not being a starter will actually determine your true value as a player and your value to the team.

In many cases players consider being a role player a negative and will take it personally. Some athletes evaluate their self-worth and importance to the team based on their playing time. When the coach says "role player" what the players hear is "sitting on the bench," which they perceive negatively. It's demeaning. Maybe even a bit embarrassing. They don't see it as a position of value, so they take a negative attitude toward their position.

So what happens to the role player who takes a negative attitude? It goes something like this: First he gets angry. Then he focuses on how unfair the coach is. Then he thinks he should be starting instead of so-and-so and ends with "This sucks!" Again, how you respond, how you control your response and your attitude about not being a starter will actually determine your value as a player and your value to the team.

No matter how angry you are, it will NOT make you a better player or improve your chances of getting more playing time. On the contrary! Your anger and resentment will bring you and your level of play down. They will undermine your motivation, sabotage your confidence, and affect team chemistry. Put quite simply, nothing good will ever come from having a lousy attitude and selfishly dwelling on how little playing time you're getting.

WHAT TO DO

So what is the first thing you need to do when faced with this "bump in the road"? First you need to change your whole attitude about the value of a role player. To explain let's look at the primary positions of a football team: quarterback, full back, offensive end, defensive end, wide receiver, offensive tackle, defensive tackle, offensive guard, defensive guard, center, punter, place kicker, holder, cornerback, linebacker, and safety. Now rank them in order of what you would consider most valuable to least valuable.

Have you ever heard of a football player by the name of Ken Walter? To give you a hint, he played a pivotal role playing for the New England Patriots. I'm pretty sure you haven't, so I will give you a quick summery of an iconic playoff game—referred to as the Snow Bowl game—and of two Super Bowl games that he played in.

In the 2001 football playoffs, during a blizzard against the Oakland Raiders in the final game at Foxboro Stadium, Adam Vinatieri kicked a forty-five-yard field goal to tie the game 13-13 at the end of regulation and send it into overtime. The Patriots then won the game when Tom Brady drove the team down close enough to set up a successful field goal of twenty-three yards by Vinatieri. By the way, that forty-five-yard kick in driving snow is regarded as one of the greatest clutch plays (and greatest kicks) in NFL history.

Then in Super Bowl XXXVI, Adam Vinatieri kicked a forty-eight-yard field goal on the final play to give the New England Patriots their first Super Bowl victory, a 20-17 win over the St. Louis Rams. Two years later, and in an almost identical situation, he kicked a forty-one-yard field goal with four seconds left in Super Bowl XXXVIII to boost the Patriots to another championship. This time, the Patriots defeated the Carolina Panthers, 32-29.

In each game Adam Vinatieri kicked the decisive field goal. Wow, what a great player Adam Vinatieri was—the first player ever to be the deciding factor in two Super Bowl games! Imagine the great press he got after each of these games.

But wait a minute! What if the unthinkable happened? What if the holder dropped the ball before he could kick those winning field goals? Now would you like to guess who Ken Walters is? He is a guy who plays the position that you would probably rank last or close to last concerning value. That's right! Ken Walters was the holder for Adam Vinatieri! Think about it. If he drops the ball during any of those field goal attempts, the Patriots lose. Think I'm crazy? Go ask any Dallas fan if he remembers the famous Tony Romo fumble in the 2007 playoff game against the Seattle Seahawks with 1:19 left in the game down 21-20. He fumbled the snap (which has been called one of the worst fumbles in NFL history). Thus the place kicker never had a chance to kick the ball and Dallas lost the game.

Ken Walters was probably never mentioned in all of the press releases but I'm sure that the Patriot players, coaches, and Adam Vinatieri know his value as a role player. And Ken Walters knows every time he looks at his Super Bowl ring.

Okay —those are football references. What about baseball? In Game 3 of the 2013 World Series—Cardinals against the Red Sox—the Red Sox entered the bottom of the ninth inning with a 4-2 lead. But St. Louis threatened when Allen Craig singled to bring the tying run to the plate with one out. And the tying run at the plate was the ever-dangerous Carlos Beltran. Before Beltran got up the Cardinals put in the speedy Kolten Wong to pinch run for Craig. But Beltran never saw a pitch. Kogi Uehara, the Red Sox closer, picked Wong off at first base to end the game. For what it's worth, no World Series game has ever ended with a pick-off.

And then there's Quintin Berry. Outside of his parents, I'm sure no one has ever heard of him. In 2013, he started the year with the Kansas City Royals but was traded to the Boston Red Sox. He was then assigned to their Triple A team, where he hit just .191 in 100 Triple A games that season. However, interestingly, he made the Red Sox Playoff and World Series roster. Quite a feat for someone with a meager .191 batting average.

So why did the Red Sox take Berry? How did he make the World Series roster? Well, if you look into his career stats, you will find statements like: "He's been successful on thirty of his thirty-four steal attempts. He went twenty-one for twenty-one in the majors last season and forty-two for forty-nine in the minors in 2011." Quintin Berry knows he's on the Boston Red Sox roster for one reason: to be a pinch runner. Oh, by the way, Berry stole three bases in three attempts for the Red Sox during their 2013 World Series run, which they won.

But here's what's really interesting. Whenever you go on the web and look up a player's stats, the player's primary position is always listed. In Berry's stats, when it comes to his primary position, he is listed as an outfielder AND PINCH RUNNER. Imagine that—pinch runner as a primary position.

When asked about his role as a pinch runner, Berry stated, "I'm excited to do it. I'll do it my whole career if this is what they want. I'll come off the bench and run any time they need it." Now let's face it, being a pinch runner is not a glamorous role. In fact if I had asked you to rank the various baseball positions, pinch runner might not have made the list. But apparently Berry's coaches and team management realized his value as a base-stealing threat so much that Berry lasted thirteen years in the Major Leagues.

And he has a World Series ring.

What about basketball? At one time the following famous NBA players were considered reserve players: J.R. Smith, James Harden, Lamar Odem, Jamal Crawford, Jason Terry, Manu Ginobili, Mike Miller, and Ben Gordon. What do they have in common? Each one has won the Sixth Man of the Year Award—an award handed out every year since the 1982–83 seasons. This award goes to the best NBA reserve selected by a national panel of pro basketball writers and broadcasters. Think about it—an award for a role player.

Let's go back to 2017, when Philadelphia Eagles backup quarterback Nick Foles took over for injured starting quarterback Carson Wentz, led the Eagles through the playoffs, and brought the city of Philadelphia its very first Super Bowl with a victory over the New England Patriots. Imagine—a role player winning a Super Bowl.

In 2018, Carson Wentz was injured again, and again Nick Foles took over and led the Eagles to four consecutive wins to make the playoffs, going on to win the playoff game against the higher-seeded

Chicago Bears. Think about it: two years in a row a backup player—a role player—stayed mentally prepared to perform when called upon.

WHAT TO DO—SECOND

So what is the second thing you need to do when facing your own bump in the road? Change and/or control the direction of your energy. Take your anger and frustration and channel them into the only constructive direction there is: WORKING ON BEING READY! Make yourself mentally and physically ready so that if and when you are called upon, you will be more than ready. Here are some ways to put your energy toward being ready:

- Find your "winning edge" (SEE WINNING EDGE ARTICLE). Find something that could set you apart from the other role players and even the starters. For example, decide to become the best bunter or best base runner on the team.

- Visualize mental at-bats during the game while on the bench. Watch every player at bat so that you can determine pitchers' tendencies; i.e., does he throw his curveball for strikes?

- Work harder on your skills, conditioning, and strategy. At practice act like it's your game. You're not at practice—you are in the game! Force the coach to notice you.

- Demonstrate a winning, team-first attitude and let go of "my playing time" as an issue.

- Stay positive and support your team in any way that you can. Don't let yourself get caught up in bad-mouthing the coach or starters. Be mature enough to give up the "me" for the "we."

33

- Watch a baseball game at home, not as a fan but as if you are in the game.

A player's value that is predetermined at the beginning of the game can change dramatically by the end of a game. A value that is predetermined at the beginning of the season can change dramatically sometime during the season.

To illustrate, I'll use a sports analogy using comedian Chris Rock, who got his start doing standup comedy. When a comedian does standup, his act consists of three or four segments called sets. A set is made up of three or four jokes about one particular subject. At one of Rock's shows, he started a set off by saying to the women in the audience, "A man is only as faithful as his options," meaning that women should not assume their boyfriend's total allegiance is to them. Yes, right now he's faithful because you are his only option. But if another good-looking woman comes around, maybe your boyfriend now has options.

Now let's change Chris Rock's statement to "A coach is only as faithful to a starter as his options," meaning that a coach is faithful to a starter, but if a role player noticeably improves, he now has options. If his starter is not doing well—in the game or during the season—then the coach has options. And you could be one of them.

So what are some of the things a coach is looking for from his role players?

- Role players should be pushing the starters, keeping them honest performance-wise, challenging them.

- A role player must be physically ready to replace the starter due to injuries, grades, etc.

- Role players must be mentally ready to compete as well.

- Role players should be vocal—a source of support and positive feedback.

- While on the bench, role players should be in the game, an "assistant coach" who sees or senses things that the coaches or starters don't realize because they are wrapped up in the moment of the game. They provide observations that could contribute to winning the game.

Consider what legendary New England Patriots coach Bill Belichick had to say when asked what he felt his team needed to do in order to improve. Now for those of you who do not follow NFL football, Belichick is considered one of the best coaches in NFL history. He holds six Super Bowl wins as the Patriots' head coach. So he knows a thing or two about winning.

In a wide-ranging interview in 2017 with CNBC contributor Suzy Welch, Belichick stated, "This is not a game Tom Brady is going to win by himself. Every single player matters. Every single player can change the course of the game. That's why everybody, even the ones who are going to be on the sideline, have to go into the stadium completely prepared to be the person who wins the game for us."

He went on to state that there are four things he asks of his team every day in order to improve.

1. Do your job.

2. Be attentive.

3. Pay attention to details.

4. Put the team first.

This is what "we look at every day when we walk into the building," said Belichick. "Ultimately, the team has to come first even though we all have individual goals and preferences. If you pay attention, and you're coachable and you work hard, you've gotta improve."

While I have spent a lot of time on things you can do when you hit your bump in the road, there is something you absolutely cannot do, and that is to allow self-doubt to creep into your head. When this happens to a player, he has a tendency to play tentatively or to try too hard—becoming vulnerable to making mental and physical mistakes. When he does get an opportunity, it is highly likely he will worry too much about messing up and ending up back on the bench.

So how would *you* respond to your bump in the road? As you continue to play and advance in playing levels, odds are you will have to face some obstacles. Could you embrace a less than glamorous role—like being a pinch runner? A role that is perceived by most players as one of a lesser value. Could you acknowledge and accept that no matter what the others think, there's value even while, as we both know, most players won't?

No matter the level, playing time does not determine your value. Every member of a team has something to add to a team's success. I wonder how Kolten Wong felt about the value of a pinch runner before and after he was picked off in that crucial World Series game. Do you think Tony Romo has a better appreciation for the value of a "holder"? Understand that it's not the size of the contribution but the fact that you do. Teams don't win just because of the starters. Bill Belichick understands that.

The only time playing time determines your value is when you decide to let it. You decide to control or not control your response. You control whether or not the situation sucks. Will you bad mouth the coaches? Complain to anyone who will listen that it's not fair? Every player on the team—starters and role players—should emulate one of basketball's greatest players—Kobe Bryant. The following quote from him tells it all: "I'll do whatever it takes to win games, whether it's sitting on a bench waving a towel, handing a cup of water to a teammate, or hitting the game-winning shot".

CALCULATED ANTICIPATION

Ever wonder why you hit so well in practice but not as well in a game? Well, the obvious answer is the pressure. There's nothing at stake. You relax! Or you are facing batting practice pitch speed versus game time pitch speed, and you know you will predominantly see fastballs. You anticipate them. You have an "I know what's coming" mentality, so you relax and confidently think "dead red" on every pitch.

But in a game situation there is no way of knowing on every pitch what pitch the pitcher is going to throw. Now, there has been enough data collected to ascertain which counts give the batter the advantage and which counts give the pitcher the advantage. And yes, there is solid information concerning which pitch counts you will most likely see a fastball. So because of this research, on six of the possible twelve pitch counts, you should use "calculated anticipation." Assume fastball—odds are on your side. You should not be fooled.

What about the other half—the other six pitch counts? The ones where you may or may not see a fastball. Those where you simply cannot look for one specific pitch. You know—the ones that you are essentially just guessing. Call them EITHER counts. Wouldn't it be great if there was a way you could improve your odds of knowing what pitch was coming on those counts? Ever hear of deductive reasoning?

Deductive reasoning is the logical process in which a conclusion is made based on things that are assumed true. Applying this to baseball, it's the logical process to come to a conclusion on pitch counts. So when you are facing the EITHER counts you need to use logic to make a practical judgment. A byproduct of deductive reasoning is "calculated anticipation."

Getting back to improving your odds of knowing what pitch is coming… Besides knowing fastball counts and hitters' counts and pitchers' counts, there is one other important component you need to know, and that is the pitcher's tendencies. Become the pitcher's student. Get to know him. You need to figure out what floats his boat—what his habits are. Doing so will give you the edge, not him. By collecting factual data about his idiosyncrasies and habits—by using deductive reasoning—you can make a practical judgment on what pitch is coming. Remember, pitchers generally are creatures of habit—especially at the teener / high school level. They will do the same thing—especially what they have confidence in it—over and over. This way you can use calculated anticipation on the EITHER counts.

Here's what you need to know:

- On what pitch counts does he throw his second pitch—his non-fastball?

- Does he throw his second pitch for called strikes or are they "chasers"—swings at balls out of the strike zone?

- On what counts does he likes to throw a chaser—fastball off the plate or up in the hitter's eyes?

- What is his second pitch?

Let's look at whether he throws his non-fastball pitch for a strike. He either does or doesn't. If he doesn't have control of his breaking ball, he will lose faith in throwing it. So when faced with an EITHER

38

count, the probability of seeing a fastball is higher. Advantage to the hitter. But what if he does throw his breaking ball for a strike? Because he has faith and trusts that he can, there's a higher probability you will be seeing it. Advantage to the pitcher. But while it is—is it? If the hitter knows what pitch count it is—the ones where the pitcher likes to throw a breaking ball—when up at the plate facing those counts, the hitter should be more relaxed, more confident. Because of calculated anticipation you should not be guessing. Your concern should be how to handle it.

Besides confirming the tendency of the type of pitch, you also need to confirm the pitcher's preferred location. When he throws his fastball on the EITHER counts, where does he usually throw it? For example, let's say that whenever he gets a 0-2 count, the pitcher has a tendency to throw a fastball. Is it always a high or low and away? When he throws his curveball on the EITHER counts, is it always low—in the dirt—away or does he always start it right at the hitter? Not only should you know the type but also the pitcher's favorite pitch location.

By collecting data on a pitcher, you can probably change some EITHER counts into a hitters count. Now, if there is one count you absolutely should know, it's the 1-1 count. Whenever you check any charts, on any level, the batting average difference between a 2-1 count and a 1-2 count is in the 200-point range!

So using deductive reasoning I created the following Pitch / Hitter Count chart. The percentage numbers listed under the "Probability of Fast Ball" comes from a study done by the University of Delaware. I realize this is one study, but in doing research, looking at other studies, I found the Delaware numbers reflect the conclusion that the other studies came to. Knowing the percentages doesn't guarantee it will be a fastball, but they do tell you on which pitch to anticipate one. You should not be surprised if it is.

Count	Probability of Fast Ball	Pitcher's Thinking		Advantage	What the Hitter Should Be Thinking	Calculated Anticipation
0-0	68 percent	Get ahead	Throw a strike	Hitter	Fastball - my pitch - Not just any strike	FASTBALL
0-1		You're ahead	Waste a pitch	Even	Cannot look for specific pitch	EITHER
0-2		Way ahead	Waste a pitch	Pitcher	Cannot look for specific pitch	EITHER
1-0	84 percent	I'm behind	Throw a strike	Hitter	Fastball - my pitch - Not just any strike	FASTBALL
1-1		I'm ahead	Waste pitch, a chaser	Even	Cannot look for specific pitch	EITHER
1-2		Way ahead	Waste pitch	Pitcher	Cannot look for specific pitch	EITHER
2-0	93 percent	I'm behind	Throw a strike	Hitter	Fastball - Relax! Drive it!	FASTBALL
2-1		I'm falling behind	Throw a strike	Even	Fastball - unless pitcher throws non fastball pitch for strikes	FASTBALL
2-2		Still ahead	Borderline strike, a chaser	Pitcher	Cannot look for specific pitch	EITHER
3-0	99 percent	Big trouble	Must throw a strike	Hitter	Fastball - my pitch - Not just any strike.	FASTBALL
3-1	96 percent	Don't walk him	Throw a strike	Hitter	Fastball - Relax! Drive it!	FASTBALL
3-2		Oh no! Don't walk him	Throw a strike	Hitter	Cannot look for specific pitch	EITHER

I also listed what the pitcher is probably thinking and what the hitter should be thinking. So based on these factors, under the "calculated anticipation" column, I indicated fastball or EITHER. Again the EITHER counts are the "cannot look for a specific pitch" counts. I put the 0-2, 1-2, and 2-2 counts in the EITHER category even though they usually are considered pitchers' advantage counts because it's my opinion that because of pitchers' tendencies, the competition level, score, etc., you might see a fastball but you might not. You might see a non-fastball—the pitcher's second pitch—and you might not.

Remember, probability means that odds are greater it will happen than not. It does not mean 100 percent of the time. Nothing is embedded in stone. There will be times when you will be fooled by the pitcher when he goes against what the "calculated anticipation" suggests. So consider the chart as a viable reference point. It's a suggested approach that will increase your chances of bringing the same relaxed, confident feeling you have in practice into a game. It should eliminate some of the guessing at the plate.

In the introduction I mentioned that there are two components to playing sports—the mental and the physical. I also told you that whenever I ask players if they are willing to give 100 percent of their efforts in their physical development, I get a resounding "YES!" Well, here's where that mental part comes into play. The 100 percent of your effort includes paying attention on each pitch, every inning—especially early in the game or after a pitching change—so that you can use deductive reasoning, determine pitcher tendencies, and use calculated anticipation when facing the EITHER pitch counts. Reality is, if you pay attention, in a high school game, you get up twenty-one times—three up at the plate and eighteen on the bench.

You have to be disciplined. When up at the plate, before each pitch, remind yourself of the pitch count tendencies instead of thinking, *I gotta get a hit, I can't strike out*, etc. This should be a habit. When on the bench, whether you are a starter or a role player, throughout the entire game, you have to PAY ATTENTION and collect the data. You control your attention span. You control how you handle distractions, like a teammate talking to you about your science homework while you are on deck or focusing on the error you made. The level of your success at the plate is affected by the level of your calculated anticipation.

In closing, it doesn't matter what the sport—I've heard it hundreds of times. After the World Series, Super Bowl, or whatever that particular sport's big game is, the reporters will ask the players and coaches the standard "why or how did you win." At some point you hear about how disciplined the players were. So remember—we all know that players are not created equally. Players have different levels of abilities. But an ability that every player has in common is the ability to PAY ATTENTION. The ability to mentally store information.

CLUTCH PLAYERS – DIFFERENT MINDSET

After years of research, baseball analysts have concluded that there is not a definitive way to measure "clutch hitting." So whenever a player is tagged as a clutch hitter, it's purely subjective. During the research ESPN aired a show titled Major League Baseball's "In the Clutch." It was a show about players who performed the best under pressure—in the clutch. The winners were selected by coaches, players, and sports writers.

During the show they had some of the nominees' teammates, opposing players, their coaches, opposing coaches, and sports reporters explain why they felt these particular players were so successful under pressure. The following were the most commonly mentioned traits for clutch hitters:

"You have to want to be there."

"Need to be focused."

"No fear—confident."

They also asked the nominees why they felt they were successful when faced with game pressure. The following are some of the answers:

David Ortiz—"I'm not afraid. I just try to hit the ball hard."

Frank Thomas—"You can't be afraid to be in that situation."

Joe Mauer—"Just try to have a good at bat."

Carl Crawford—"Treat it as any other at bat."

Jeff Francoer—"I want to be there."

Now I realize that you may not recognize the names of some the players. But that does not invalidate their mindsets—what they said. No matter what years you play in, pressure is pressure. These are all professional players who have successfully performed under pressure.

What's interesting is that none of the reasons mentioned to explain the players' success have anything to do with the physical part—the mechanics—of the game. No mention of bat speed, arm slot, keeping hands back, etc. Rather, they are all statements concerning the mental part of the game: staying focused, being sure of themselves, accepting the pressure of the situation.

So what's going through your mind when you get up with the bases loaded, bottom of the seventh, with the winning run on third? Or when your team is up by one run and the coach hands you the ball to get the last three outs? Do any of these statements sound familiar? "I gotta get a hit! I hope I don't strike out! I wish it wasn't my turn to hit. This guy's the best hitter, I can't get him out! I haven't got a hit off this guy yet!"

Now, don't think for one minute that these statements don't go through some players' minds. They do. What players don't realize is that they give themselves away. They reveal their thoughts through their body language, their facial expressions, and their actions.

Let me tell you two quick true stories that occurred during my high school coaching years. There was a local American Legion team that had a chance to make it to the state playoffs. They needed to win one more game. The problem was that the regular season games are seven innings long, but in the playoffs, the games are nine innings long. So after playing five games in a row, going into this last game, the game everyone knew they had to win, the pitchers were stretched to their limits. Before the game, the coach held a team meeting, explained the situation, and essentially asked for someone to "take the ball." His thinking was that one of the senior pitchers, one of the team leaders, would step up and volunteer. Well, no one did.

The game started with an infielder pitching. As you can imagine it did not go well. When the game reached the fifth inning, they were down by five runs and the infielder who was pitching was getting hit hard. Finally, one of the leaders went to the coach and asked for the ball.

Why then and not before the game started? The answer is simple: the consequences or, better yet, the fear of the possible consequences. By accepting the challenge before the game he would have to accept the results. And based on their situation, it didn't look good. Odds were they were going to lose. So by accepting, in his mind, he would have to take the blame if they lost. If they lost, it would be his fault. And people do not like to be at fault—to be blamed. Imagine the finger pointing from his teammates, the coaches, or next day's tweets.

And that's why, when the team was down by five runs with only four more innings to go, in his mind, they were not going to win, so he asked for the ball. At that point there was no pressure, no consequences, and asking for the ball at that point gave him a guarantee: if they lost, it certainly wouldn't be his fault, but if they won, he could get the credit!

The second story is about a lefty on my high school team. He was a pretty good pitcher because he took lessons from an ex-major league player. If he was having a lesson on a practice day he would ask me if he could take it easy so that he would be all right for his lesson. He would then remind everyone during practice why he was taking it easy. And every time I asked him in practice how his arm felt, his answer always was "It's great!"

He always asked who the starting pitcher was going to be. If it wasn't him, he would make some comment to his teammates about how he wished it was him. There was always some specific reason why he so badly wanted to face that team. During the games he didn't pitch in, if things weren't going well, he always had the answers. And when I told him he was starting, he would tell anyone in earshot how bad we were going to win.

This is the same player who never pitched a complete game and, in fact, never made it beyond the fourth inning in his two years of varsity high school baseball. By the second or third inning, between pitches, he would start looking toward the bench—toward the coaching staff. Didn't matter if we were winning or losing. Didn't matter if he struck out the side or got them out one, two three. After each inning he would ask me if he was going to pitch the next inning, and I would ask, "How's your arm?" His answer was always the same. "It's getting a little sore."

So why is it that a pretty good pitcher could not finish a game? Because he didn't want to be out there! How do we know? Because as I stated earlier, some players reveal their thoughts through their body language, their facial expressions, and their actions. In this particular player's case, it was the despair on his face when he looked over to the bench between pitches. In between innings he would complain to his teammates that his arm was sore. And you should have seen his eyes light up when he was told he was done, especially if at that point, we were winning.

It was no coincidence that his arm always got sore during a game but felt great at practice. He did not want to be out there. So the question is why? Consequences. Blame. Fear of failure! Once he started looking over, we knew he was done. He wanted out. Even when he was having success, you could almost hear him say to himself, "When will this end? At some point I will fail."

Players usually don't admit to thinking statements like *This guy's the best hitter. I can't get him out! I haven't got a hit off this guy yet!* But what you will hear from them are excuses. Pitchers will blame the umpires, the bad mound, or "The ball was wet and it slipped out of my hand when he hit the home run." When infielders throw the ball away, it was because they have a sore arm or the first baseman should have had it. You see—excuses deflect potential criticism. Or as I heard my lefty say to a teammate one time after we lost a close game: "Hey, it wasn't my fault the coach took me out of the game!"

So what's different about the clutch player? The clutch player's mindset is positive while the others are negative. The clutch player looks at a pressure situation as an opportunity to succeed, not an opportunity to fail. They sincerely want to be there. They walk the talk! They are not afraid or worried about the potential end results, and they don't want to be taken out of the game. The clutch player says, "It's just another at bat. Challenge the hitter, or hit the ball hard," instead of focusing on being the hero or scapegoat. They know there are no guarantees. Clutch situations are part of the game. Clutch players know that no one expects them to be successful 100 percent of the time. The only expectation is that they are ready, prepared, and focused 100 percent of the time.

A player who has a lot of success often has a lot of failure as well. Look at Babe Ruth. He struck out 1,330 times on his way to hitting 714 home runs. He struck out 15 percent of the time he was up. That's a lot of failure. But what is he known for? His successes—his home runs—were only 6 percent of his at bats. Yet, to this day, he is still known as the "Sultan of Swat." And then there's Ricky Henderson. One year he led the league in steals with 130 but was also caught forty-two times. He failed 32 percent of the time.

So if you want guarantees that you will be successful, go play against an eight-year-old girl's softball team. It's a safe bet that when you face a pressure situation, you just might be "clutch."

SIDE NOTE: For all you curious, diehard baseball fans, the following are all the players selected the best "Clutch" player by position:

First Base—Albert Pujols

Second Base—Chase Utley

Third Base—David Wright

Shortstop—Derrick Jeter

Catcher—Joe Mauer

Left Field—Carl Crawford

Center Field—
Carlos Beltran

Right Field—Jermaine Dye

Designated Hitter—
David Ortiz

Pitcher—Johan Santana

Closer—Mariano Rivera

COMPONENTS
OF AN AT BAT

As stated at the beginning of the book, talent alone does not create success. There's more to success than the physical part of the game. Let's consider an at bat. In my opinion there are two aspects of an at bat: the physical and the non-physical. And within the non-physical, there are two distinct categories: mental and emotional. So for argument's sake let's just say the components of an at bat are physical, mental, and emotional.

The physical category, simply put, is the mechanics of swinging. The mental category is general baseball knowledge—baseball IQ: knowing/understanding where the team is/you are in the game.

The third category is emotional—your mindset. Simply put:

• Your beliefs shape your attitude.

• Your attitude shapes your beliefs.

• Your beliefs shape your mindset.

The following is a chart that depicts the three categories with a few examples of their respective components:

Physical	Mental	Emotional
Good mechanics	Know the situation	Fear of failure
Rotate hips	Hitters count	"Gotta get a hit"
Flat hands	Seventh inning approach	Embarrassed—two errors

Everyone understands and accepts the physical part of the game and, depending on what level the player is at, understands the mental part because there is tangible evidence. You see end results—batting average, the base hit, the great throw from the outfield to get the out at home, the shortstop backing up gets the out, etc. Thus players and coaches spend countless hours in the batting cages and take hundreds of ground balls and devote time on the field working on game situations during practice so that at game time the players' movements are, as one person described it, "a harmonious involuntary action that requires no thought at all." Simply put, muscle/mental memory.

However, the problem is that little or no time is spent by the players, or in some cases the coaches, on the emotional component. There is little acceptance and/or understanding of the importance of controlling their emotions, because subconsciously or consciously, in their mind, there isn't any tangible evidence that a player's mindset—his emotions, his beliefs—can interfere with the physical and/or mental components of his performance. Let's face it, there's no way to measure how many times you were successful or failed because you were not in the right frame of mind.

But I disagree. I feel there is tangible evidence that your emotions do play a role in your on-field performance. I realize this is a baseball article, but I thought that a recent incident in a Rams versus Green Bay Packer football game represents a good example.

Here's what happened. Late in the game the Rams scored and went ahead by two points. So, of course, they had to kick off to Green Bay. When Green Bay took possession of the ball there would be 2:09 time left in the game; Green Bay would have one timeout and the two-minute warning. Thus the offense, with Aaron Rodgers, considered one of the best comeback quarterbacks, was in a great position to at least attempt a potentially game winning field goal.

Green Bay's kick-off returner, Ty Montgomery, was told by his coaches to field the kick off and simply take a knee. It was the safe play, and the smart one, because Rodgers and the offense would be guaranteed to get the ball at their twenty-five. However, when the kick came, Montgomery disobeyed the coaches. He fielded it a couple of yards in the end zone and brought it out. Not only did he bring it out, but he only made it to the twenty-yard line. He cost the team five valuable yards and, to add insult to injury, he fumbled and the Rams recovered it, ending any chances for Green Bay to win.

Now here's where his emotions came into play. After the game it was revealed that Montgomery threw a temper tantrum laced with profanity and threw his helmet. It seems he was upset about Green Bays' previous possession in which he was taken out. As stated by one of his teammates after the game, "They took him out for a play and he slammed his helmet and threw a fit. Then they told him to take a knee, and he ran it out anyway. You know what that was? That was him saying, 'I'm gonna do me.'"

Because of his anger—and anger is an emotion—he went rogue. This led to his mental error—bringing the kick out of the end zone when a touchback would've worked just fine, which in turn led to his physical mistake—he fumbled. His emotions got in the way of his performance. Those two mistakes are tangible. You can see the end result. You see the misjudgment. You see the fumble.

Not convinced? Then let's look at a non-sport situation. You're in a car, and the car in front of you is swaying all over the road. You decide to pass the swaying car, and as you go by you notice that the driver is talking on his cell phone. As a matter of fact he doesn't even notice you passing him because he is emotionally involved with his phone conversation and not the physical aspect, the process, of driving the car. His swaying is the tangible evidence that his performance is following his focus.

But let's get back to baseball. Consider the following two questions:

1. What is the batter's objective once he steps into the batter's box?

2. What is the batter's #1 job to be successful?

Every time I ask players the first question I get answers along the lines of "Get a base hit," "Get on base," or 'Have good mechanics." I guess they are good answers but the reality is that they represent an end result. They are not objectives. If you whittle this down to its simplest form a batter's objective is to MAKE CONTACT! A team's offensive philosophy should be to produce runs. The only reason why a batter steps into the batter's box is to make contact—put the ball in play—to give the team as many possible opportunities to produce runs. Can't win if you don't score.

Now for those of you who are skeptical of my MAKE CONTACT statement, let's hear from someone who is considered one of the best to ever play the game—Hank Aaron. In an article titled "Run Production Is Ultimate Metric," published in the 2/8/19 issue of the *Collegiate Baseball* newspaper, he states, "I went up to the plate to put the ball in play…I couldn't go up to the plate and strike out…I had to be able to put the ball in play…I had to give myself the opportunity to hit the ball…Who knows what might happen?"

And here's an article about the Boston Red Sox in the 11/5/18 issue of *Sports Illustrated*:

During spring training, "Hitting Coach Tim Hyers asked Manager Alex Cora about rotating players through instructional hitting drills. Hyers would crank up a pitching machine near 100 mph or fire the nastiest breaking balls. Batters were charged simply with trying to make contact. Foul balls were cheered." That's right— professional players were told to just make contact. The end result of this mandate was that the Red Sox were baseball's best two strike hitting team in 2018.

In the post season the Red Sox hit an absurd .364 with runners in scoring position. The other post season teams hit .197. Now you know why they took care of their arch rival NY Yankees three games to one in the American League Division Series, the "expected to win" Houston Astros three games to one in the American League Championship Series and finally the National League Champion Los Angeles Dodgers four games to one to become the 2018 World Series Champions.

Moving forward, in order to MAKE CONTACT you need to examine the second question: What is the batter's #1 job to be successful? When confronted with this question, the players' answers were basically the same as for the first question. But again when you whittle this down to its simplest form, in order for a player to make contact, he has to see the ball. And that's why his #1 job is to SEE THE BALL. In fact, see the ball WELL. After all, you can't hit what you can't see.

When you don't control your emotions, you misdirect your focus, which has a direct bearing on your performance, just like the Green Bay Packer player and the mentioned car driver. So it only stands to reason that a player's misdirected focus in the batter's box can affect performing his #1 job. If before and after every pitch, negative thoughts like *I can't hit this pitcher* (Fear) or *I'm in a slump* (Anger) or *Oh my god, I made two errors* (Disgust) or *If I don't get a hit, coach will take me out* (Embarrassment) or *What if I make an out* (Shame) are running through your head, then negative emotions have determined your mindset/focus. Your mind is not on the process of the seeing the ball—pitcher's release point, pitch speed, pitch location, hitter's pitch count, contact. Rather your focus is on your beliefs, your attitude—like worry, self-doubt, or confidence.

Again, talent alone does not create success. You need to recognize and be in control of your emotions. The following are some emotions you will encounter and where they fall—positive or negative.

NEGATIVE	POSITIVE
Fear	Pleasure
Doubt	Pride
Frustration	Happy
Anger	Thrilled
Embarrassment	Confident
Shame	Relaxed
Anxiety	Trust
Confusion	Belief

Alan Jaegar, author of mental training book *Focused, Staying Focused*, once stated, "A pretty swing doesn't necessarily lead to pretty results." You can have the greatest mechanics, but without positive emotions you will reduce your odds for success. This is why you hear coaches make statements like "Stop thinking" or "Imagine flushing your thoughts down a toilet" or "One pitch at a time." The only thing running through your head when you are up at the plate—your at bat—should be See the Ball—Well. Control that.

I don't remember what sports psychology book I read the following quote from, but it does sum up my point: "One of the biggest causes of poor and inconsistent performance is mental and emotional constipation."

CONTROL

Dr. Tom Hansen, a specialist in sports psychology, wrote an article titled, "Your Performance Follows Your Focus." His message was that **your success as a baseball player is determined by your ability to stay focused on the task** at hand—regardless of circumstances. The following true stories illustrate what he means by "your performance follows your focus."

One night I was driving down a small road that leads toward the development where I live. All of a sudden a cat darted out onto the road in front of me. I slammed on my brakes. Turns out I just missed a cat that was chasing a field mouse. After muttering a few salty words about the cat, I continued on my way. But I have to admit I was impressed with the cat and his pursuit. For that cat it was as if nothing else in the world existed except for that mouse. If I had not hit the brakes, I would have run him over. But he went after that mouse as if I didn't exist. Only after he had caught the mouse did he notice me and then run off into the woods.

Okay. I hear you. Here you are reading an article that you thought was going to be about baseball and instead it's about some stupid cat. So here's a baseball-related story.

For nine years I coached a Showcase Fall travel team comprised of better players with college aspirations. To assist them we provided a player profile of each player that we or the player could give to the college coaches. This profile included their running times. One of the running stats we recorded was the player's speed from home to first. We had each player go up to the plate, hit a pitched ball—like a game situation—then run to first so that we could time them—several times. Each year we did this, the results were the same. Most of the time the players hit the ball weakly and sometimes even fouled the pitch off. Now keep in mind that these were select players, good hitters, facing a batting practice pitch. But yet no home runs, no hard line drives.

So what's the common denominator in both stories? That the success they experienced was determined by their focus on what they wanted. Let's look at the cat. What was most important to the cat, at that time? Do you think she was concerned about her form or how she looked? Do you think she was worried about making a mistake? Do you think she was thinking about the last three field mice that got away or what the other cats would say about her?

Baseball players know how important their running stats are and how they are perceived by college coaches. So what is their focus on? Their mechanics? Hitting the ball or running as hard as possible so that they get a fast time to put down on their profile sheet to impress the coach at the college they want to attend? At this moment getting a good hit is not what they are striving for.

WHAT CAN YOU CONTROL?

The moral of the stories is that controlling your focus plays a role in determining your success. As a player you need to understand that your success—or failure—is determined by your ability to stay focused on the task at hand.

Review the following commonly listed factors that can affect the outcome of a game:

- an umpire's call

- the crowd

- the weather

- field conditions

- your teammates' performance

- you getting a hit

- getting a batter out (as a pitcher)

- your attitude

- your opponent's ability

- luck

- having fun

There is only one factor you can control. Now, you might be saying, "I can control getting a hit or, as a pitcher, getting a batter out." But think for a minute. Have you ever smashed a hard line drive only to see it go right to the center fielder for an out? Or thrown a great pitch but the batter hits a soft fly ball just over the second baseman's head for a base hit? Or the umpire calls it a ball? These are just some of many examples of doing everything right as a batter or pitcher but still "failing."

The only factor listed above that you can control is your attitude. Actually the only thing you can really control is how you REACT—YOUR RESPONSE—to the various factors that occur. Look back at the above list. Except for "your attitude," Dr. Hanson refers to everything else on the list as "concerns." And "concerns" are not within your control. Don't waste time or energy worrying about concerns. You need to focus your time and energy on the controllable.

IMAGES

Included in controlling your focus is regulating the images in your mind and what you are thinking. Everyone, throughout the day, will talk to themselves. It can be nonverbal (thoughts not spoken out loud) or visual, by putting images in our heads. And the nature of those thoughts and images—positive or negative—can impact our body's reaction to the task at hand.

Here are some quick examples of the role images play, how they affect your focus, and how they affect how you react or your attitude. Let's say you just left practice, it's late, and you're tired—it's just been a long day. You walk over to your car, where your girlfriend is waiting for you. You tell her how exhausted you are and after you get a bite to eat at McDonald's you just want to go home. During dinner your conversation is mostly small talk and all you can think about is taking a hot shower and going to bed. You are mentally already home, in bed. When you stop the car to drop her off, your girlfriend leans over, kisses you, and tells you what you mean to her. She then gives you a hug and places her head on your shoulder. What images are running through your head now? How tired are you?

What if I repeat the word *girl* over and over to you? What's the image that pops into your head? It's probably going to be your girlfriend or an attractive girl. One minute later I hand you a picture of a girl—a rather unattractive girl—and I keep repeating the word *girl* as you look at the picture. I then ask you to put the picture down, close your eyes, and visualize a girl. What image comes to mind? I then repeat the exercise, but this time the picture is of an attractive girl—gorgeous. Now I say the word *girl* and whose image comes to mind? Are they the same each time?

Why is it that when your girlfriend gives you a kiss and a hug, you are suddenly not that tired? Your attitude changed when your focus was changed. And why does your vision of a girl change back and forth when I ask you to think about a girl? Because the images—the pictures—have changed. They changed because you focused on what you want—a pretty girlfriend, a pleasant moment—and NOT what you don't want.

Now, before I go any further, for you skeptics out there, I have done this girl/picture exercise several times during my coaching career, and each time the results are the same.

Also notice that I said "change the image" and not "block out the image." It's too hard to block out an image or thought. For example, if you are thinking about a pink elephant and you don't want to, you will probably say to yourself, *Don't think of a pink elephant*. But the problem is the image of a pink elephant will pop up in your head. If you don't want to think of a pink elephant, you need to change the image—put a new image in your head—think black swan or red car.

And also notice that I did not say "stop thinking." I hear this statement from coaches a lot. But not thinking is not possible. Human beings are always thinking. Our brains are constantly taking in information. It's what separates us from fish! You want your mental energy focused on the task at hand. So just like changing the images running through your head, you need to change or gain control of what it is that you are thinking.

SELF-FULFILLING PROPHECY

It's a physiological fact that the body will do what the mind tells it to. Realistically when you run images and thoughts constantly through your head—positive or negative—you are predicting the outcome. Putting a thought or image in your head is just like a self-fulfilling prophecy.

A self-fulfilling prophecy is a statement that alters actions and therefore comes true. For example, a person thinking *I'm probably going to have a lousy day* will likely have a lousy day. What about the player who, after watching the pitcher warm up, tells himself, *I can't hit this guy!*

When you make negative outcome predictions, you open the door to unconsciously altering your actions or behavior, which actually helps make the prediction come true. For example, you visualize what happens and thus reinforce the self-prophecy. It becomes an expectation. So by the end of the day when a player does have a lousy day or strikes out or hits a weak ground ball, as he walks back to the dugout, he says to himself, "I knew it!"

I'm sure there are some who might question the validity of self-fulfilling prophecies, so let me tell you the Bill Buckner story.

In the bottom of the tenth inning of the sixth game of the 1986 World Series, Bill Buckner, playing first base for the Boston Red Sox, booted a ground ball hit by Mookie Wilson of the NY Mets, allowing the winning run to score. It capped an improbable comeback and became the most famous error in World Series history. By winning the game, the Mets tied the series and forced a seventh game.

Which the Mets won.

Because of that one play Buckner just might be considered the biggest scapegoat in sports history. But there's a creepy part to the story which is mentioned in the book *It Takes What It Takes* by Trevor Moawad. Nineteen days before the game, during an interview with a local TV sports reporter, Buckner said, "The dreams are that you're gonna have a great series and win. The nightmares are that you're gonna let the winning run score on a ground ball through your legs." This is exactly what happened.

We will never know if Buckner would have fielded the ball cleanly if he had never said what he said. But we do know that as stated in the book, "the fact that usually sure-gloved Buckner said it out loud means the thought of letting a ball go through his legs was on his mind." Did that thought cross his mind as Mookie Wilson's grounder approached? We will never know. But what we do know is that in 1985, one year prior to that fateful game, Bruckner set the Major League record for assists by a first baseman in a season with 184—a record that stood for twenty-five years. So why is it that a "sure-gloved" first baseman made one of the most famous errors ever?

A player who predicts outcomes is preparing himself and his muscles to play into the prediction. As Kenneth Baum, a sports performance consultant, states in his book, *The Mental Edge,* "If you come to the plate in the ninth inning of a crucial baseball game and you are thinking to yourself, 'Just don't strike out like you did last time!' your chances of swinging futilely for a third strike are almost guaranteed. In reaction to negative self-talk, as you anxiously stand at the plate, you might unconsciously change your stance, or your muscles may react differently to the pitched ball. These subtle adjustments could sabotage your athletic performance."

HAVING FUN

There is something else that you can control—albeit indirectly, because it depends on how you respond to your feelings about your performance—and that is having fun. You can't lose **sight of why you play baseball** in the first place.

Did you start playing as a kid so you could get a college scholarship or lead the team in hitting? No, **you played because you loved baseball**. You enjoyed it. When I ask high school players why they play baseball, they answer, "It's fun" or "I like the competition." The most common answer is "It's fun."

Players who are struggling with their performance have probably made the decision that the game is no longer fun. It's not fun because to them struggling really means failure. Failure is humiliating. Their perception then starts a vicious mental cycle:

- Failure is humiliating.

- Failure and humiliation lead to frustration.

- The boredom factor of the game—time between pitches/plays—allows too much time to think about the failures and the humiliation.

- Frustration leads to failures, which continues the humiliation.

And thus when players fall into this trap, the fun is taken out of the game.

Let's face it; everyone's favorite player is successful. In their interviews after the game, when the reporter asks, "How do you feel," their response is usually something like "Everything seems natural, easy" or "I'm relaxed and feel confident." Do they ever start off by mentioning their physical abilities? They do not. In fact the only time there is any mention of physical abilities is when they make a statement like "I'm seeing the ball well."

Subconsciously they may not know it and they might not say it, but essentially they are having fun and playing for the enjoyment—both of which are positive emotions. Thus the reason for their success. As former Major League player Dave Winfield, member of the 3,000 Hits Club, states, "Normally, you have fun after you do well, but I wanted to have fun before I did well and that helped. Sometimes you have to say to yourself that you're going to have fun and feel good before you go out there."

Players must not forget that baseball is a game of failures. So you need to have a willingness to risk failure, even if it means doing what is out of your comfort zone. You can't fall into the trap of thinking every game you play is about leading the team in some stat or getting to some level of play you want to get to in the future. Same end result. **Play with the love of the game,** the passion, the joy, and the fun that you had as a child. Don't focus on the circumstances that are making that difficult. **Play the game right now**. Don't be focused on what you did in the past or what might happen in the future—play in the present. **Play the pitch you're on right now**. Focus on why you *play*.

Whether you are fielding, pitching, or up at the plate, control your focus. Control the images in your head. Be sure they are positive. Reinforce what you want to do and not what you fear you might do. And run these thoughts over and over. As a pitcher, saying to yourself, "Low strike, low strike" is better than "I can't get behind on this guy." Or "sliders away" would be better than "don't hang the curve." Predict—self-prophesize—a positive outcome. And remind yourself why you play baseball.

DOES YOUR TEAM
HAVE A TENDENCY TO
SELF-DESTRUCT?

There was an article written by Jeff Janssen in the February 2010 issue of *Coach and Athletic Director Magazine* titled "Striving for Last Second Success." He was giving coaches tips on how to successfully manage players facing stressful situations. As I was reading the article it hit me that in reality, most of the tips he listed could be directed to players as well as coaches. Because as he stated, "As humans, stress and pressure cause us to do some strange and unusual things."

Consider what physically happens to the body during the stress of competition. It causes tight muscles, a loss of coordination, shallow breathing, rapid heart rate, and excessive sweating. But what does it do to the player mentally? As Janssen says in the article, it "scrambles your players' brains. Athletes under stress have a hard time tuning in to your coaching, processing what you ask them to do, and executing their roles and responsibilities. They have trouble focusing on the task at hand, making smart decisions, and often feel overwhelmed, confused, and harried. It's no wonder that the breakdowns that occur in crunch time are often the result of mental breakdowns."

With that said, the following are some of the suggested tips for coaches, but I have followed each one up with my thoughts on how they relate to the player.

Show the face your team needs to see.

COACH

One of the best lines from Duke Basketball coach Mike Krzyzewski's book *Leading with the Heart* is "A leader must show the face his team needs to see." As one of the top maestros of March Madness, Coach K reminds you to manage your own emotions under pressure if you expect your players to do the same. Regardless of how you actually feel internally, externally you must show your players confidence when they are doubtful, composure when they are panicked, and optimism when they are on the verge of giving up.

PLAYER

Show your opponent the face they need to see. Have you ever been at a ball game and heard your coach say, "That player looks confident" or "That player plays with confidence"? Ever wonder what he saw that made him make that statement? The answer is the player's body language. Body language is a form of communication. It is the window to your mind. It tells your opponent how you feel about yourself. It tells everyone where you are mentally.

The confident player has a presence about themselves. They stand out; they seem to be full of energy. They look calm and in control. They act like they belong. They act like they have been there before. They are always talking to their teammates, always giving them encouragement. They don't use rushed or awkward gestures. They walk up to the plate with an almost cocky attitude.

Now just as the confident player shows it through his body language, so does the player who is not confident. You've seen him. He's the one:

- Walking off the field with his head down.

- Arguing with his teammates over a mistake or an error on the field.

- Kicking dirt after he's not made a tough play.

- Shaking his head from side to side.

- Slumping his body, especially while he's sitting on the bench.

- Sitting by himself, staring, not talking to anyone.

Tom Hanson, famed sports psychologist and co-author of the book *Heads-up Baseball; Playing The Game One Pitch At A Time*, recently wrote an article about "White Line Fever," which is a reference toward pitchers who throw lights out in the bullpen but once they "cross the white lines" get hammered. He quotes Dennis Eckersley, who pitched in the Major Leagues in the late 1990s. "A pitcher might be scared to death in a game but you can't show it. You must project confidence that lets your teammates know (and your opponent) you are in control. If the body acts confidently, you will be confident. If you act confidence out, you begin to think it."

Now, in his time Dennis Eckersley was considered one of the best relief pitchers who ever played. He attributed his success to making sure he carried himself with confidence. So much so that, as a closer for the Oakland Athletics, he earned himself the reputation as "The Man." Even when he went into a game and didn't feel like "The Man" he would, as he would say, and I quote, "fake it. You do. The next thing you know it works. You can't let on that you're not throwing well. There's a body language; I really believe it. You've still got to act like you're the man. You can't fake a good fastball, I'm not saying that, but you have to give the impression that your stuff is on time."

It's been quite a while since Steve Garvey played any baseball. He played for my favorite team at the time, the Los Angeles Dodgers. He was a hard-hitting, home-run-hitting first baseman. Yet to this day I still remember the response he gave to a reporter during an after-game interview. Garvey had just hit the game-winning home run in the bottom of the ninth inning. The reporter brought up the fact that in his previous three at bats, he had struck out, looking rather foolish. The reporter mentioned he was surprised that Garvey didn't show any emotion, get upset, throw his helmet, or bang his fist on the water-cooler when he went back into the dugout, especially after his third strikeout. Garvey replied that he would never do that because "once you show the opposing pitcher that he beat you, he has."

While you probably never heard of Dennis Eckersley and Steve Garvey, they were primetime players in their day. But it doesn't matter if they are current or past players. The way they handled their body language is still relevant today. When you show signs that the other team/player has the upper hand, they are in control and not you. And not only are you bringing yourself and your team down, but you are also reinforcing your opponent's confidence. They now feel they have the advantage. "Once you show the opposing pitcher that he beat you, he has."

Now for those of you who think body language is nonsense and that no one pays attention to it, consider the following conclusions from an extensive study researchers at the University of California, LA, came to regarding the believability of communication:

- Tone of voice and facial expressions account for 38 percent

- Body language accounts for 55 percent

- Words only account for 7 percent

The study states that this is "another confirmation that regardless of the verbal message, if the body language conflicts, the person will believe the nonverbal"—the body language. By the way, facial expressions are a form of body language, so that 55 percent is actually higher.

Interestingly, based on a study conducted by researcher John Gottman, a psychology professor at the University of Washington, it was determined that eye rolling is the number one predictor of divorce. It seems it is construed as a sarcastic, nonverbal gesture. When someone rolls their eyes, the message being sent is that:

- They disagree with who is talking.

- They don't like how the person talking is saying something.

- They are frustrated or overwhelmed with what is being said.

- They don't respect the person talking.

Body language is part of your mental game. It's a window into your mind. It's a reflection of your emotions, but it also tells your competitor how you feel. You control it, so be aware of it.

Reframe pressure as a fun challenge.

COACH

The players of former North Carolina men's basketball coach Dean Smith were always amazed by how calm he was in late-game situations. Whenever Carolina was down or in several tight situations, his players remembered that Smith always conveyed that the team was right where they wanted to be. He would often remark in a pressure-packed situation, "Isn't this fun?" or "Wouldn't it be great to come back and win this one?" Take the pressure off your players and reframe the situation as a fun challenge.

PLAYER

Whenever we faced a tough situation late in the game, my assistant would say, "Boys, this is going to be a great game to win" or "We got them right where we want them." Didn't matter which one, it would always get a laugh. Whenever I ask a player why he plays, the most common answer is that it's fun. When faced with the pressure of the game, the stress, we sometimes forget why we play. In essence we lose control of our rational reasoning and let our emotions take over. We allow too much negative "end result" thinking to cloud our thoughts. *What if we lose? What if I make an error? What if I strike out?* These thoughts erode our confidence level. Doubt creeps in, and doubt means inhibition. I also feel that doubt creeps in about a player's personal value as well.

We are a media-led nation, and we live in a headline news society. ESPN's *Sports Center* is a good example of today's headline news formats. It's must-see TV. We determine our sports heroes' value on the amount of attention they get and the records they set and the mind-boggling contracts being signed today.

Young players in particular see the highlights and the attention given to what are perceived as "positive recognition events" such as records or statistics and getting your name in the paper. They unwittingly think this recognition helps their image. Obviously it's not for the big-time money like the pros, but at this stage of their life, just like for the pros, they feel it will help boost their image and how they measure up to their peers. In their mind it helps determine not only their value with their peers, friends, and family but also their own self-value. Failure is catastrophic! A negative end result, in their mind, has a negative effect on their image, their value.

And then there's the influence social media plays today. Just visit Facebook, Snapchat or Instagram. One of the most common mistakes that players, especially young players, make is that they place far too

69

much emphasis on personal image. They are now playing to be the star pitcher, the player with the most home runs, or a member of the State Championship team and not for what got them into the game of baseball in the first place. Because it's fun. Because of the competition.

Go with what they know.

COACH

Take the advice of the late, legendary Boston Celtics coach Red Auerbach on this one. Auerbach said, "With my teams, when we'd be down to the end of a game and we'd have a timeout, I wouldn't make my players nervous. I wouldn't pull out a clipboard and give them a new play. To me, that makes them nervous. Why can't you come down with twenty seconds to go and say, 'Hey, run the four play. Execute it right.'" Auerbach understood that players need to go with what they know in pressure-packed situations. Avoid the temptation of throwing something new at your players, because odds are it will only confuse them and not your opponents.

PLAYER

Don't try to be someone you are not. Let's say you are a singles hitter; that's what you are. It's the bottom of the seventh inning with two outs. You are up. A home run would be great but that's not you. You are a singles hitter, so focus on getting to first and not rounding the bases.

You have the weakest arm of any of the outfielders on the team. There hasn't been a time in any of the practices that you have thrown a ball that reached home plate. So don't think you can now, in the bottom of the seventh inning, with the tying run rounding third. Do what you know you can do—hit the relay man.

You're a fast ball pitcher. If you are lucky, you throw about every fifth curve ball for a strike. If the bases are loaded with two outs, this isn't the time to start the batter off with a curve ball. Don't attempt to suddenly become a curve ball pitcher.

You're the slowest runner on the team, so why would you decide to stretch a single into a double with the team down one run late in the game with no outs?

Don't try to be someone you are not. And do not measure your success based on the success of others. If the batter before you is a home run hitter and he hits a home run, good for him. If you are a singles hitter and get up and get a base hit, good for you. His success does not take away anything, any value, from your success. Your level of "feel good" should be the same as his. You need to keep your focus on yourself and what you can do and not what others do. Only do what you know you can do!

Focus your players on what you want them to do.

COACH

I can't count the number of times I've heard a coach unwittingly say, "Whatever you do, don't foul," "Don't fumble," "No wild pitches or passed balls," or "No service errors," etc. Focusing your players solely on the negative things you want them to avoid only plants the seed of doubt in their mind. It puts negative images in their head. Instead, talk more in terms of what you want your players to do—"We need to play smart defense," "Take care of the ball" or "Trust yourself." Focusing on the positive skills you want them to execute plants seeds of success in their minds.

PLAYER

Everyone talks to themselves. I call it self-communication. Whether it's nonverbal (not spoken out loud) or visual, we put images in our heads. And the nature of the thoughts—positive or negative— can impact our body's reaction to the task at hand. As Kenneth Baum, a sports performance consultant, states in his book *The Mental Edge*, "If you come to the plate in the ninth inning of a crucial baseball game and you are thinking to yourself, 'Just don't strike out like you did last time!' your chances of swinging futilely for a third strike are almost guaranteed. In reaction to negative self-talk, as you anxiously stand at the plate, you might unconsciously change your stance, or your muscles may react differently to the pitched ball. These subtle adjustments could sabotage your athletic performance."

A player who predicts outcomes, especially negative ones, is preparing himself and his muscles to play into the prediction. Putting a thought or image in your head is just like a self-fulfilling prophecy. A self-fulfilling prophecy is a statement or thought that alters actions and therefore comes true. For example, a person thinking, *I'm probably going to have a lousy day* might alter his actions so that such a prediction is fulfilled by his actions. Now keep in mind that the altering of actions is an unconscious gesture. We don't even realize we are doing it.

Remember the sports psychologist and his wife vacationing at the beach? The wife was taking too long to get ready, so the frustrated husband headed down to the beach to wait and discovered how peaceful it was. Rather than argue with his wife, he started his workout and relaxed and it changed the course of his day.

It's a great example of controlling your internal feelings. Focus on what you need to control your internal feelings. Coaches can encourage, reward, and cultivate, but nobody can teach you to have high energy or a good attitude. So when you are feeling angry, down, upset—negative—you need to take action so that you can change the course of your day. Just like the sports psychologist did.

I don't remember where I found the following quote but it sums up the message. "Days are made of moments—and each moment you have a choice on your focus and actions."

DRILLS - WORKING ON YOUR MENTAL GAME

Part of the success formula is being concerned with your mental game—taking a breath, having a pre-pitch routine, or having a "one pitch at a time" mentality. So how and when do you work on your mental game? Well, the answer as to *when* is easy: during practice.

At practice players work hard on their mechanics. They take hundreds of swings to develop muscle memory—automatic pilot—because they want to be prepared to face the inevitable pressure of performing in game situations.

So if you make the decision to concentrate on your mental game, then you need to work on it during practice, just as you do on the physical aspects and just as hard. If you spend little or no time working on your mental game—developing what I refer to as "mental memory"—you can't expect yourself to be totally prepared in game situations.

The amount of time you spend working on your mental game will determine the degree of success you will have when you transfer from practice to game situation. Subconsciously, you work on your physical game so that you can feel confident and relaxed. And for those same reasons you must work on your mind. If your mind is relaxed, clear, and confident, then you will put yourself in the best possible position to reach your potential success level.

The following are suggested drills you could incorporate in your practice time. They are the *how*. Quite frankly some seem too simplistic to be effective, but if you just go through the motions, they won't work. If you are not sincere in your approach, they won't work. If you don't use the same focus that you use when you work on the physical part of your game, they won't work. Your attitude and your honest effort will determine if you have any success. And you control that!

Every coach has his own way on how to conduct practice. In doing so he controls your movements at practice. So if you decide to do any of the suggested drills, you need to discuss this with the coach and get his approval. But nothing stops you when you are not at the team practice but working on your own.

Pitchers in the bullpen—work on pitch recognition

When the pitchers are working out in the bullpen, step into the batter's box (you are not swinging):

Have a plan—what drill are you doing today?

Track the ball all the way to the catcher's glove—literally turn your head back to the catcher.

OR

Call out the type of pitch—curve, fastball—the minute you recognize the pitch. This should be before the catcher receives the pitch.

OR

Call balls and strikes.

OR

Play the "lane game." Remember, there are three basic hitting zones—the inner (lane 1), the middle (lane 2), and the outer third (lane 3) of the plate. Decide before entering the batter's box that for, say, the first ten pitches, you will say out loud, "yes" or "green light" to only those pitches that are in the inner third part of the plate—lane 1. Repeat this process selecting a different lane.

At the "soft toss"/tee station—work on pitch locations.

Have a plan—what are you working on today?

Think mechanics.

Act like you are in the batter's box, with game-like focus. Don't allow anyone to talk to you except the coach.

Don't allow the "tosser" to rapidly toss the balls. Be in control—take one quality swing at a time and slow down.

Instruct the "tosser" where you want the ball—low and away first five, up and in second five, etc.—and don't swing if it's not tossed to the location that you are working on.

Move the tee height. Don't leave the tee height in the same position—work on up, in, out low pitches. Establish a schedule:

Monday—everything middle / outside—take one set over the plate—three sets of five swings—one set high—one set low—one set middle.

Tuesday—everything middle / inside—take one set over the plate—three sets of five swings—one set high—one set low—one set middle.

Alternate every other day.

In the batting cage, practice your game at bat approach.

When you are next in line to get into the cage, act like you are in the on deck circle. Don't allow anyone to talk to you. Think mechanics.

Practice "cleaning your head." Don't step into the batter's box until your mind is devoid of negative thoughts. Outside the box you can think of mechanics, pitch count, your homework assignment—anything—but in order to step inside the box, you must clean your head of all negative thoughts. This is a drill created by noted sports psychologist Alan Jaegar, who states, "You will find that most hitters will have a hard time making this transition—a sure sign that their mind is way more active or tense then they are aware." What he is saying is to clear or slow down your thoughts, check in, and be sure all thoughts are positive.

Practice stepping into the batter's box the same way you would in a game—lead foot outside the box and back foot in—AFTER EACH PITCH.

Work on your pre-pitch routine—each pitch—and include working on your breathing. Draw air into your stomach as your belly is gently pushed out; when full of air, relax and let the air flow out as your belly moves in.

Play the "pitch-hit" game, which helps focus and timing—go from soft focus to hard focus—move eyes from the pitcher's face to his release point.

NOTE: Instruct hitter not to be concerned with where the ball goes or how hard it is hit. This is a focus drill, so be concerned only on saying *pitch* and *hit* at the right time.

Hitter says "pitch" the moment the ball leaves the pitcher's hand.

OR

Hitter says "pitch" the moment the ball leaves the pitcher's hand and says "hit" as the ball hits the bat.

On the field—simulate a game at bat.

Put on your game face—it doesn't matter if it's a coach pitching or one of your pitchers on the mound. It's game time!

Perform all of these before you swing pre-pitch routines. Clear your head, do your pre-pitch routine, take a breath.

Have good body language. During a game, once you are in the batter's box waiting for the pitch, don't just stand there with your bat on your shoulder—you need some type of movement before the pitch. For example: take two half swings toward the pitcher (you are not going all the way around) and then get the bat in position.

After each pitch, look down at the third base coach. (I know he's not there but what would you do in a game?) You never want to miss a sign, so get in the habit of looking down every time—it is part of your at-bat routine.

After practice—you're home:

Evaluate your practice. Make an honest evaluation of how you were today. For instance: When you worked off the tee, did you let anyone interfere with what you were doing? In the batting cage, after every pitch—and I mean every pitch—did you do your pre-pitch routine? Did you clear your head before each pitch when you were hitting on the field? Or did the sight of the two swing and misses creep into your head? How did you react when you thought the coach didn't give you as many pitches as the other players in the batting cage? When the coach was going over the first and third defensive strategy, did you listen to what he said or continue to pout about the number of pitches you saw in the cage?

Now, if you decide practice or part of practice did not go well, ask yourself the following:

- What was I trying to do?

- What went wrong?

- What part of practice went wrong?

- What do I need to do to fix it?

If you decide that practice or part of practice did go well, tell yourself the following:

I had a good day at practice. Say it to yourself three or four times—*I did well today, I did well today, I did well today, I did do well today!*

Feel yourself being in a good mood—having fun and getting your work done.

If you had a bad day at practice but you responded well and didn't get frustrated—cleared your head—then tell yourself you had a good day because you responded well. Say it to yourself: *I responded well today!*

The next day at practice as you are putting on your cleats, remind yourself that you are working on your mental game and why—because you want to be confident, calm, and relaxed in game situations. You want to be able to handle distractions and be able to face the potential consequences. Because as a sports psychologist stated; "When the mind / body is in a relaxed state your natural instincts and reactions can take over without inhibitions. A relaxed mind allows you to see the ball better, longer and more specifically...and this equates to more patience and better plate discipline."

FAIL TO SUCCEED

Tom Brady made the following statement during an interview with radio personality Howard Stern: "There's a lot of things in my life where they didn't go exactly how I hoped they would go, but in the end, they went exactly the way they needed to go because I could never have experienced what I needed to experience to grow as a person if I hadn't experienced them that way."

Said another way; in order to be successful you have to fail. If you allow it, something positive will come from mistakes. Not convinced? The next time you turn on a light bulb imagine how many times Thomas Edison must have failed before he succeeded. Or did you think that on his first attempt or by the end of the first day he figured out how a light bulb works? In the process of inventing the light bulb in 1879, Thomas Edison tried and failed more than 1,000 times. Someone once asked him if he had ever become discouraged and considered giving up. Edison answered, "Those were the steps on the way. In each attempt, I was successful in finding a way not to create a light bulb. I was always eager to learn, even from my mistakes."

Ever hear of Kentucky Fried Chicken? Colonial Sanders did not reach his renowned status until he was over sixty years old. He held numerous jobs as a salesman, unsuccessfully, before he actually 'made it." When asked about all the jobs he had before he became famous, he stated that he never felt that he failed but rather, he learned what jobs he wasn't good at.

Then there's Abraham Lincoln. He faced a series of failures and obstacles before he became president and brought the Civil War to a successful conclusion:

He suffered the death of his sister when he was young.

He suffered from depression in his early thirties.

He suffered the death of his two young sons.

He failed as a businessman.

He was defeated for nominations as a candidate for Congress in 1843 and 1844.

He was defeated as a candidate for the Senate in 1855 and 1859.

He was defeated for nomination as a vice presidential candidate in 1856.

Yet Lincoln persevered and became one of the most important Presidents in US history.

And let's not forget Babe Ruth and Ty Cobb. Ruth set records for the most home runs but also set records for the most strikeouts. Cobb set records for most stolen bases and also for the most put outs on attempted steals. If you ask a 'baseball person' who owns the record for the most home runs or the most stolen bases, they know the answer. But if you ask them who owns the record for most strike outs or put outs on attempted steals, the last two people they would even consider are Ruth or Cobb.

All of the people mentioned are known for their successes not their failures. If they didn't learn from their mistakes, how is it that they were successful? They weren't afraid of any possible mistakes. They accepted 'failures' as part of the process to learning. They were not afraid of taking risks. Ty Cobb didn't give up trying to steal because he got thrown out the last time. Successful people accept that mistakes are part of the training to learn a skill or perform a task. They know that failure could lead them to success. SO YES! Even successful people fail. The key is they don't focus on the mistake or failure but rather look at the challenge to be successful.

PROBLEMS WITH FOCUSING ON MISTAKES

EMPHASIS OF THE VALUE OF WINNING

Players who focus on mistakes are probably placing too much emphasis on the value of the game. They view it as if their entire meaning on earth will be determined by how they perform or the results of the game. Don't misunderstand. The game is important. You should commit all your energy to perform to the best of your abilities. And, yes, if the team loses or if you make a mistake it's natural to be upset. But the fact is, in the overall scheme of things, your value as a person is not determined by the outcome of a baseball game. You are not a failure. Believe me; if you make a mistake your parents will still love you. Your friends will still like you. Your teachers will still talk to you. If your teammates thought you were 'cool' before the 'error', they won't think any less of you afterward. The mistake does not mean it's the end of the world. Don't take the fun out of the game. Remember why you play.

IMAGE

Players who focus on mistakes are probably too concerned about how they look. They get embarrassed or feel they looked stupid when they made the error or mistake. They usually feel foolish. Nobody wants to look dumb. After all, you want to be "one of the guys." You want to be part of the 'in' group at school. Only nerds or geeks look stupid. There's no way you'll do anything that risks jeopardizing the way your friends think about you. So when you think it's a risk you become passive and avoid or hesitate to make the play. You have lost confidence.

FAILING

No matter who you are, no matter how hard you try, you will not be perfect at all things all the time. Mistakes are inevitable. We all screw up at some time or another. And that's okay. We're human. Players who focus on mistakes put their confidence level in jeopardy. Instead of focusing on the mistake focus on what caused the mistake. **Focus on the correction.** Concentrate on what you need to do to 'make the play' if you get another chance. Ask yourself, "What could I do to prevent the same mistake from happening again?"

It's okay to accept responsibility for the mistake—but it's not okay to dwell on it. If it's in your nature to dwell on something, then dwell on the correction so that at the end of the game you can say with conviction, "Yes, I made a mistake, but I didn't let it bother me. It didn't affect my play. I stayed in the game. I didn't fail. I succeeded because I stayed focused on the correction and not the mistake." Dwell on that because you cannot allow an error or mistake to determine your confidence level.

CRITICISM

Players who focus on mistakes are probably too concerned about any potential criticism. They associate criticism with fault, so for them it's a negative. When the coach pulls a player aside and says something like "I want to give you some constructive criticism" the player listens but does not hear. He listens to the coach being critical but doesn't hear any of his instruction or suggestions on how to get better. His feelings are hurt, and he goes into denial and resists. But how else do you become aware of what you need to work on if you don't allow yourselves to consider the criticism?

Consider this—you go to an Italian restaurant and you order your favorite meal—spaghetti and meatballs. Your dinner comes and after one bite you realize that there is way too much garlic in the meatballs. You decide you can't eat them so you push them aside. The waiter notices, comes over, and asks if there's anything wrong. Not wanting to hurt the chef's feelings, you respond with "Everything's just fine." After all, you don't want to appear to be critical of the chef. But how will the chef know he has a problem if no one tells him?

Instead of looking at what you feel is criticism—a negative—accept it as constructive instruction—a positive. Consider it as a way to start the instruction process. Constructive criticism is a means to pass along corrective information, which can include a critique or an analysis. And yes, within that analysis there may be the discussion of a fault—something that you are doing or not doing; it's also passing along information that is designed to help you, not hurt or embarrass you. It's not an announcement that you have failed. As far as the chef goes he is learning that he needs to cut down on the garlic in his meatballs.

Some coaches, however, will be just plain critical and offer no suggested corrections. When you encounter one, stay in control. Don't immediately think of all the reasons why he's wrong, why you don't like him or feel he's hurt your feelings. Instead listen to what he feels is an issue. Then rather than just ignore him reflect on the issue, because if he's mentioning it, there's probably something there. Do some honest soul searching and ask yourself, *If it's true what could I do to correct it?* In other words, do some self-instruction.

It is human nature to interpret criticism as a negative. In your mind it's unfair and unjustified. It's an attack on your self-image. But it's not a sign that you have failed. Rationalize it as a message. If you fail to learn from the mistake, then it is a sign you have failed.

FIGHTING SLUMPS

The following are some indications of a player who is either in a slump or heading into one. Call it a cause and effect chart:

CAUSE	EFFECT
Feeling tense	Muscles tighten which affects how fluid swing will be
Feeling tense	Facial muscles tighten which controls eye movement which causes rapid eye movement thus makes it difficult to see / focus on the ball
Forget performance cues	Not concentrating on pitchers idiosyncrasies like his release point or always throws curve ball on 0 - 2 count
Paralysis by Analysis'	So fearful of striking out that you don't swing - no matter how good the pitch
lack of trust	Swing at pitches outside the strike zone
Hesitant	Too many checked swings
Off balance	Over swing - try to do too much
Pre determine pitches	Decide "I'm swinging at the first pitch or the next pitch. Never see if it's a good pitch or not
Feeling sad	Sit by yourself during the game
Fear getting up	Dread playing - wish game was over
Excuses	Blame the umpire

BREAKING THE SLUMP;
BE IN THE HERE AND NOW

In his book *Sports Slump Busting,* Alan Goldberg, a sports psychologist, states that "peak performance is a byproduct of your mind and body working together in perfect harmony. Instead of cooperating, your mind starts sabotaging your body." And when that happens, your focus of concentration is not where it needs to be: the "here and now."

To understand what he means, let's first look at what he means by the "NOW." Time is divided into three zones—the past, the present, and the future. So when you are up at the plate or in the on-deck circle consider what zone you are in mentally. The batter who plays in the past time zone is the one thinking about his last few at bats that did not go well or the error he made in the fourth inning or going 0 for 4 the last time he faced today's pitcher. This is the critical part because it can be the cause or the reason you are still in a slump. In an article he wrote for *Collegiate Magazine* Goldberg states, "Across all sports the one mental characteristic that consistently separates the best from the rest is the ability to quickly rebound from mistakes and setbacks and focus on the play of the moment." In other words, get into the present zone.

The batter who plays in the future time zone is thinking, *I gotta get a hit!* or whether the team is going to win or lose, or *If I strike out and we lose it's my fault.* There's also the usual sound of *What ifs!* What if I ground out again! or What if I hit into a double play! or What if I don't get a hit!

The problem is that these negative performance reminders and pre-performance predictions ignite the domino effect, which goes like this: Your performance affects your belief in your ability, which creates your attitude, which puts you into your mindset. Good performance lets you trust your ability, which makes you feel good, which puts you in a good mood. Negative performance causes you to not trust your ability and feel bad, which puts you in a bad mood. And the end result of a negative domino effect is that physically you tighten up and play tentatively.

Negative reminders and pre-performance predictions distract the player from concentrating on where he needs to be. They prevent him from being in the correct zone—which is the present zone. If you carry past or future focus into the batter's box you'll be in more trouble because you will be less attentive to performance cues like the pitcher's delivery, his pitch selection tendencies, or his release point. The batter who plays in the present zone is attentive to the physical details required to perform the task he is facing at THAT moment.

A great example of this statement is Nick Foles, then quarterback for the Philadelphia Eagles. To refresh your memory, in 2017, he was the backup to Carson Wentz. Halfway through the season Wentz got hurt and was replaced by Foles, who proceeded to direct the team not only to a winning season but also to winning the Super Bowl. He then followed that up in 2018 by again replacing Wentz in a relief role, again directing the team to a winning season and a victory over the Chicago Bears in their opening playoff game. Now you can only image the interviews and articles written about his amazing success. After the Bears game, as written in the 1/12/19 issue of *Sports Illustrated*, "When asked once more to explain how he keeps doing what should not reasonably be done, he said the same thing he's always said: 'Just staying in the moment.'"

As Dr. Goldberg states, "Most players in a slump flip-flop from past to future and back again as they get ready to perform. In order for you to bust a slump and maximize your playing potential your mind has to be in the NOW and nowhere else." You have to do what Nick Foles said, "Just stay in the moment." He could have easily said "I play in the present zone."

Let's now look at what Dr. Goldberg means by the HERE. "If you've just committed an error and you're thinking about what the coach is going to do with you or if you're at the plate and someone from the opposing team is razzing you and you feel yourself getting upset and angry or if you were just called out by the umpire on an obvious bad call and you're still thinking about going up to the umpire…you are in the wrong place mentally." Your mind cannot be on the bench or in the stands or in front of the umpire. When you do that you are somewhere else.

You can't focus on your present game if you are over THERE.

A good example of this is how Odell Beckman, who at the time was the NY Giants' wide receiver, reacted in a 2015 game against the Carolina Panthers and his confrontation with the Panthers' cornerback Josh Norman. It was so contentious that it was referred to as a rumble. That there were five combined penalties, three times Beckman was tagged for unnecessary roughness, and he was later suspended for one game is evidence enough.

Rather than give you a play-by-play description of their fights, the following are some of the comments written by various sports reporters specifically about Beckman's performance:

"Before the Giants first drive of the contest was complete, Beckham was already off his game. He dropped what should have been a 52-yard touchdown."

"Beckham had more penalties than catches in the first half. He was flagged three times in the contest. He had more fights than receptions through two and a half quarters."

"Beckham did not have a catch in the first half. Instead, he had two drops. He beat Norman badly deep on the second offensive play of the second half but…It was another incompletion that could have been a long touchdown."

"It began when they tangled on the second Giants offensive play of the contest. After the dropped touchdown, it continued. This was the first of many scrums between one of the league's best cornerbacks and receivers."

Now read what was written about the game itself. The so-called rumble "was exactly what the Carolina Panthers wanted…they took the Giants player out of the game mentally. The Panthers hit, poked, and prodded the Giants star receiver early in Sunday's game…and Beckham took the bait—hook, line, and sinker. He was busy battling Norman with after-play pushes and hits instead of catching passes and making the big plays that had become a weekly ritual throughout his first two-plus professional seasons."

Beckman was intimidated. By allowing the Panthers to 'get to him' he ended up over THERE. And because he was not HERE he was not focused on performance cues, which resulted in dropped passes. His mind and body were not working together in perfect harmony. He was not focused on his game. He was not playing in the HERE AND NOW. And oh by the way the Giants lost.

In the end, probably the simplest explanation I have found about focusing during performing is a phrase coined by Seattle Mariners coach Scott Servais: "Be Where Your Feet Are."

You can't control what happened yesterday.

It does no good to worry about tomorrow.

Focus on what you can control today.

SUGGESTIONS—OVERCOMING SLUMPS

Terry Orlick, PhD in the psychology of sports and physical activity, was conducting a study and interviewed some of the world's best athletes, coaches, and scouts to get their views on the ingredients necessary to "make it" to the highest level in their sport. In his book

In Pursuit of Excellence, he writes the following conclusion about his study: "Within each sport there was disagreement about the physical attributes…but total agreement on the psychological attributes. Commitment and self-control were seen as the keys to excellence."

What the coaches and scouts were saying is that having the greatest mechanics is not the only concern you should have. You need to be concerned about controlling your mindset. And you need to make the commitment to control your mindset.

In my opinion probably the biggest culprit behind slumps is allowing too much "noise" to run through your head. You are probably thinking too much. Notice that I did not say "stop thinking." Not thinking is not possible. Human beings are always thinking. Our brains are constantly taking in information. It's what separates us from fish! Too much thinking about mistakes, poor performances, the "I can'ts," predetermined results, etc.—all negatives—is possible. So with that in mind the following is a suggested process to help you quiet your mind. It may be a way to prevent or stop the noise so that you don't think yourself into a slump.

SUGGESTION 1:

Commit to be a believer. You have to believe that the mental part of the game does have an influence on your physical game. Commit to spend time during practice working on controlling your mindset. This is crucial.

SUGGESTION 2:

Recognize exactly what zone you are in. Make a conscious effort to check in to see where you are—every at bat, every time you are in the on-deck circle, after every pitch. Commit to be honestly aware. As sports psychologist Alan Goldberg stated in a *Collegiate Baseball* magazine article; "The heart of slump busting is a process of recognizing when your mind is in the wrong mental time frame".

Be honest with yourself when you check in. Your honesty will be critical. Take ownership of your thoughts. No excuses! If you lie to yourself, you are doomed for failure.

SUGGESTION 3:

Think outside the box. Compete in your own "one pitch at a time" game. The design of the game is to make each pitch an individual competition. The length of the competition is one pitch, not the at bat and not three strikes. Game one is over after the first pitch. Game two is over after the second pitch and so on. That's it. The intent of the game is to get you to think "THIS pitch is the only one that matters," not the last one or the next one. And when that pitch is over, THIS pitch is important, not the next one or the last one, etc. It should help you to get into the right time zone—the present zone.

Now, in order to play the game you must follow the rule. Notice I did not say "rules." That's because there is only one rule: you must develop and use a 'pre-pitch' routine, and that routine must include a breathing technique of some kind.

Before each pitch—game—go through your pre-game routine. After each pitch assess and declare the outcome of each pitch—win or loss. For example, a foul ball is a win. Umpire calling a pitch a ball—good eye—is a win. Swinging at a strike and missing but maintaining your balance—the swing felt good—is a win. Swing and miss is a loss. Then after you have determined win or loss, get ready for the next game—pitch. Get ready by going through your pre-pitch routine.

The purpose of competing in your own game is to find some positives out of an at bat, even those that have a negative end result. There's an old expression, "Find something positive out of a negative." The reasoning is that finding something that helps you feel good about yourself helps silence the noise—negative thoughts—running in your head. This in turn should help you to get into the right time zone—the present zone.

You can even take the game one step further. At the end of the at bat total up the number of wins and losses. If you have more wins than losses then declare yourself the winner.

Now before I move onto the next suggestion I'm sure most of you are thinking that what I'm suggesting doesn't seem plausible. Maybe it is and maybe it isn't. But what I do know is that there is a lot of downtime in baseball. For example, you have to wait two or three innings between at bats and you spend a lot of time out on defense. So instead of pouting on the bench and out on defense, you could take the time and rerun, pitch by pitch, that at bat to determine your wins.

Quite frankly it's a gimmick to help you control your emotions. It's a way to get you to feel good about yourself. When you feel good about yourself, you will feel proud, happy, relaxed, and, most importantly, confident. All positive emotions.

SUGGESTION 4:

Be self-instructional. In the 'think outside the box' suggestion I said to assess and declare. Why? Let's say you foul off the first pitch. If you tell yourself "I should have driven that one" or "I always hit that low pitch" then you are making judgment statements. Judging is usually negative self-criticism—beating oneself up. Judging creates the noise.

You may be saying, "But, Coach, shouldn't I be self-critical about my performance?" The answer is yes. But you want to do so in a positive manner. Instead of being self-critical you need to be self-instructional. Read the following excerpt from the February 13, 2012 issue of *Sports Illustrated* describing the at bat of St. Louis Cardinal player David Freese when he hit a game-tying home run in the bottom of the ninth inning of game 6 of the 2011 World Series.

"Freese had never faced Texas closer Neftali Feliz until the Cardinals were down to their last out in Game 6, down by two runs with two on. Feliz threw two sliders, one for a ball and one for a strike, before unleashing a 98-mph fastball that Freese, late with his swing, fouled off. The Rangers had St. Louis down to its last strike." Now here's where it gets good. After that 98-mph pitch, he says, "I didn't realize it was that hard. He flat-out blew it by me. *Get ready earlier.* That's the first thing I told myself: *It's probably coming again.*"

Notice he didn't say "I should have swung at that pitch" or "Wow, was that fast" or "I can't hit that." Rather, he said, "Get ready earlier—it's probably coming again." He objectively analyzed what happened and came up with a possible solution for the next pitch. He self-instructed. He was his own teacher. I guess you could call it positive self-criticism but I would prefer to call it 'self-instructionalism." Instruction is positive—it's quiet. Criticism is negative—it's loud.

Probably the best example of being self-instructional is the Kirk Gibson story. It occurred in the bottom of the ninth inning of Game 1 of the 1988 World Series—LA Dodgers versus the Oakland Athletics. Gibson hit what has been described as the most dramatic home run in baseball history. You probably have heard the story or have seen that iconic scene of Gibson hobbling around and pumping his fists as he rounds second base.

What made it so special was that he was hurt—so hurt that he did not start the game nor did he come out onto the field when they did the pre-game introductions. In fact when he was summoned by Manager Tommy Lasorda to pinch-hit, he wasn't even in the dugout—he was in the locker room!

Let me set the stage. Dennis Eckersley was on the mound for Oakland, and the Dodgers were down 4 to 3. With two outs and a runner on first, Kirk Gibson stepped into the batter's box. On each pitch he swung at, he almost fell down. It was painful to watch. But miraculously, he worked the count to 3-2. As he was standing in the batter's box waiting for the next pitch he called time and stepped out of the batter's box. A few seconds later he stepped back in and sent the next pitch over the right field fence.

It's quite a story—real drama. But there are some things you don't know. Like, why did he call timeout? Was it to relax, collect his thoughts? During a recent interview he was asked to discuss the dramatic story, and he mentioned that when he stepped out of the box, at that moment, he remembered something one of the team scouts had said during the pre-game scouting reports: "Whenever Dennis Eckersley gets a 3-2 count on the batter he likes to throw a back door slider." Gibson added, "I wasn't trying to hit a home run. I just wanted to make contact."

Gibson was successful because he wasn't spending time being critical of—judging—his feeble swings. He analyzed his situation and when he remembered the scout's comment, he instructed himself on what to do. It was as if he knew what pitch was coming! He just wanted to make contact!

SUGGESTION 5:

Use cue cards. A cue card is a card with brief notes or a picture that a speaker or actor has available so that they can readily remember what they want to say or do. A cue card can also be verbal—a word or statement that serves as a reminder. Probably the most famous verbal cue card I can think of is *See the ball, hit the ball*. Can't tell you how many times I've heard that statement from coaches. In fact it has been written that Pete Rose, the all-time MLB leader in hits, used this statement every time he set himself in the batter's box.

Using cue cards can quiet your mind and get rid of any negatives. One of the most common images is a toilet. In other words, if you realize you are thinking negative thoughts, imagine flushing those thoughts down the toilet. I would suggest a more modern image, like the recycle bin on the computer. So just like junk mail, send the clutter to your recycle bin.

Another way to quiet your mind is to use a cue card that has a positive image. It's a way to have positive self-talk. For example, consider using the image of a baseball or an eyeball. Or before every pitch repeat the word 'Ball' to yourself several times. After all, your #1 job once you step into the batter's box is to see the ball—and to see it well. So clear your head and focus on one thing.

In the book *Coaching Mental Excellence*, the authors state that the reason positive self-talk is important is: "The human brain communicates to the body through words and pictures. No voluntary action takes place without a preceding thought. Therefore, performance of any kind is preceded by self-talk." In other words, the body will do what the mind tells it. Compete with your eyes and not with your mind.

Whether it's visual or oral, the purpose of the cue card is to condition your brain to clear away outside influences or negative thoughts and to reinforce what you need to do. Positive thoughts are essential to positive performance, just as negative thoughts lead to negative performance.

SUGGESTION 6:

Go on a diet—not a physical diet but a mental one. Commit to the process. And don't make the classic dieters' mistake. Most people quit their diet after two or three weeks because they aren't satisfied with the few pounds they have lost. They feel the size of the sacrifices they have made are much greater than the size of the results. Keep at it. It's going to take time. Be persistent!

There's an old adage—Rome was not built in a day!—which means important things take time. Slumps or potential slumps are not eliminated in one or two attempts. Just because in one or two games you made it a point to check in and you had the same bad results does not mean this does not work. Improvement is a progression. You will have some ups and downs, so keep at it. It's going to take time.

While it's important that you check in during games, you have to practice the HERE AND NOW process at practice. It's the same as players developing their physical skills. In practice their goal is to develop muscle memory by constant repetition of such tasks as fielding ground balls, bunting, etc.—to the point that the technique of fielding the ball or bunting the ball just happens. So at practice your goal should be to develop *mental* memory, by constantly checking in while you are performing the various physical tasks. Ask yourself, "How do I honestly feel right now?" or "What am I thinking about right now?" or simply "What time zone am I in?" You do this in practice so that you reach a point where you are on automatic pilot, and at game time you just do it.

Now, I want to be clear—these suggestions are not a guarantee that you will get out of your slump. It's a process. And within the process two psychological components are necessary for it to work: commitment and self-control. You control the decision to use cue cards. You decide to take the time to check in to determine what time zone you are in. You decide to play my 'One Pitch at a Time' game. And you decide not only to make the commitment but also the degree of that commitment to the process. What was it that Terry Orlick, the PhD in sports psychology, discovered when he interviewed some of the world's best athletes, coaches, and scouts? "Within each sport there was disagreement about the physical attributes…but total agreement on the psychological attributes. Commitment and self-control were seen as the keys to excellence."

FIVE TOOLS

Whenever we are asked to describe a baseball player, we use statements like "Man, can he hit" or "He has a rocket for an arm" or "He runs like a deer." But in the baseball world the expression "five-tool player" is used to describe a player's ability. The tools being referred to are:

1. Speed

2. Arm Strength

3. Fielding Ability

4. Hitting for Average

5. Hitting for Power

These tools are considered important in evaluating a player and also setting a minimum bar or threshold. You could say they are a measuring stick of a player's attributes.

Notice that all *of the tools* are tangible. They are physical, real, and in most cases measurable. And because they are young, high school players will accept them as viable and will spend time working on them. They accept them as legitimate and will take ownership of them. But truth be told there actually is a sixth tool.

This sixth tool can be the critical factor in either utilizing the five tools well or more commonly in stifling them. The sixth tool is a player's mental makeup. But herein lies the problem. One's mental makeup is underrated and undervalued by most young players. They don't realize/accept/understand that there are attributes that require no physical talent but actually play a role in their physical success. But these attributes are intangible; mental makeup is not measurable, so it's hard for young players to believe it has any effect on their physical end results. Most young players overlook it and don't take ownership.

However, intangibles are the attributes an athlete possesses or the behavior he exhibits that require absolutely no physical talent but play an important role in a player's success. Measurable or not. Remember, players are not equal in their playing ability but they are equal in their ability to work on the mental part of their game.

The following are some intangible tools that have significance when describing a player.

ATTITUDE—CONFIDENCE

Attitude is a series of thoughts. As defined in the dictionary, it's "our state of mind as we approach our lives…the mental message (thoughts) will dictate the physical action…the body tends to do what it hears." If this is true, and I'm sure it is, your attitude—your state of mind—plays an important role in your approach toward the physical part of your game, because attitude controls confidence levels and in turn energy levels.

If you tell yourself—your attitude—that you can make the play or you can get the hit or you can make the throw—high confidence level—odds are good that your body will function fluidly and efficiently. This self-talk won't interfere with your muscle memory. But if you tell yourself—your attitude—that you can't make the play or you can't get the base hit or you might throw the ball away—low confidence level—odds are you will be tense, lose your fluidity, and be inefficient. This self-talk interferes with your muscle memory. Your attitude—an intangible—good or bad, affects how your body will perform physically—the tangible.

If you don't have internal control, you won't have external control. Hitting with power or average won't matter if your attitude is "I can't hit this guy." Having strong arm strength won't matter if you lack the confidence of throwing a strike in crucial situations. All the speed in the world won't matter if you have fearful instincts about stealing.

So let's look at practice. Think about the quality of your effort at practice. Is it high or low? How much improvement in your fielding and hitting abilities will you experience if your heart is not in it? How much reinforcement of your muscle memory will you accomplish if your energy level is low? What's the quality of your work ethic, the level of passion or desire to learn? Are you willing to try something different? Take a risk? My point is that if you can't control your attitude during practice, how do you expect to be in control at game time?

You need to be in control of your attitude at practice; if you don't, the odds are you will start a snowball effect that may eventually affect you in a game. A snowball effect refers to something small—a snowball—that builds upon itself and becomes larger and larger until it gets too big. Before you know it, too many practice mistakes initiates questioning yourself, which could lead to lack of confidence, which could bleed over to game time. Bottom line, because you don't control your attitude during practice, you can't or don't know how to handle game mistakes. And the strength of your tools diminishes.

STRONG WORK ETHIC

Someone with a strong work ethic works as hard as he can and keeps trying to improve. I can't tell you how many times I have seen players do well due to their 'god given talent' only to falter as they go up levels of play. Up to that point they have experienced success and have been told how great they are, so they become complacent and "settle" on their work ethic. What they don't realize is that the level they have reached isn't compatible to the level of play, which is why they may be faltering. They have peaked. They need to change the intensity of their work ethic. They need to drop the habit of doing the same thing over and over at practice and be willing to try doing some things that are clearly different from what they have been doing or what others are doing. They need to accept the fact that there's room for improvement in their intangibles as well as their tangibles. They need to take ownership of their inability to want to work harder on their game.

Let's face it; the coach should not have to motivate a player to be relentless to work hard. It's up to the player. If you are an athlete seeking to be a champion or just trying to improve your skill level you must be relentless with your work ethic. Here's an example:

As an infielder you realize your backhand is weak, so you decide to take extra ground balls working specifically on your backhand. Now, it's easy to say you want to, but it's hard to keep at it, because when you work on something you are not good at, you will experience a lot of failure. And failure brings on frustration and maybe even humiliation.

So how does the player react when frustration rears its head? He decides to take less ground balls or take a lackadaisical approach or stop altogether. Why? The reason is twofold. First, the player decides it's just too hard; he can't do it. It takes too much time. Second, in the player's mind, the constant failure is embarrassing. After all, his teammates are watching. So to avoid the embarrassment the player takes an "it's no big deal" attitude or comes up with an alibi. So when he misses that next ground ball he tells himself and anyone who is willing to listen that he wasn't really serious anyway or the ball took a bad hop. He's now going through the motions.

But this is where being relentless comes into play. Being relentless means you keep on trying to improve. You don't develop arm strength during the game. You don't develop muscle memory to improve your fielding abilities during the game. You don't 'fix' fielding issues during the game. You don't learn how to hit an outside pitch during a game. But you can at practice. You can if you concentrate. You can't if you take time off—just go through the motions—on some pitches, some ground balls, etc. Being relentless means being patient. Improvement in baseball skills often comes in spurts. It requires a lot of work. The problem is that we live in a microwave society. We have instant coffee and instant credit, but there is no such thing as instant development in baseball skills.

Being relentless means the player takes ownership of their inability to want to or work harder. He forces himself to concentrate more and constantly urges himself to try harder. Every day at practice he needs to act like it's game time—every ground ball, every swing, every pitch. You can't give up. You have to go into it knowing that you are going to fail—a lot. Remind yourself that by failing you learn. Take it one ground ball, one swing, one pitch at a time. Let's be honest—it doesn't take any physical talent to go all-out on every play in practice. Have the attitude that good enough is not good enough for you.

Being relentless means you are not concerned about being embarrassed or what others think. Your focus is on improving. Lamar Jackson, the quarterback for the Baltimore Ravens, epitomizes what I mean. During a post-game interview during the 2019 season he wore a T-shirt that said, "Nobody Cares; Work Harder." A reporter asked him if that was a statement about his mentality. He stated "Absolutely. That's every day. Nobody cares about what you're doing. You've got to work harder. If you want to be the best, you've got to work hard at being the best. If they're doubting you, work harder, it doesn't matter. It's their opinion. I'm just going to go." As far as I'm concerned the statement on his T-shirt could have been "I don't care what you think."

By not being relentless you will slow down the process of improving your physical game, like developing muscle memory or fixing fielding issues or learning how to hit an outside pitch. Essentially it slows down the process of elevating your physical abilities—the value of each of your five tools. By not being relentless you speed up the path to peaking.

PASSION—LOVE OF GAME

When an athlete is playing well everything is great and he seems to play effortlessly. He is a great teammate. But how does he react when he begins to falter as he goes up levels of play or goes into a slump or can't throw a strike? He may give in to the pressure and stress, and/or begin to point fingers away from himself and onto just about anything or anyone else (i.e., the coach, umpire, weather, etc.). This selfish attitude, and that's what it is, is where lack of passion or purpose comes into play.

Passion gives you purpose. It gives you energy. It gives the player 'juice' for playing the game. It helps you to focus on the task at hand. A player who has passion for the game plays with heart. He absolutely loves to play baseball. He plays for his pleasure, NOT OTHERS'. Passionate athletes don't make excuses for their failures and shortcomings. Instead, they use them as lessons, building blocks toward getting better. They stay mentally prepared.

A web page called Baseball Think posts various baseball-related articles from professional and college coaches and scouts. There was an article dated April 2009, "The 5 Tangibles Sought By a Major League Scout" in which the author, Phil Nicoletti, a scout for the Cleveland Indians, states, "When I attend a game I am not always looking for the potential prospect to shine ….you already know this guy has tools or you would not be looking at him. But, how does he handle failure? I personally want to see a player fail …I want to see how a guy carries himself after going 0-4 with 3 K's. Does he hang his head? Does his temper get the best of him? Does he take his failures at the plate with him to the field?" In other words the scout is saying what good is having the tools if you can't control your emotions, which prohibits you from getting the best out of the tools you have? He is looking for the sixth tool.

A player who has love for the game does what he does, plays the way he does, because he is not looking for any reward, recognition, or admiration. He realizes that team glory will bring individual recognition. He gives 100 percent when asked to do things he does not like to do—bunting, for example, or "wearing" a hard hit groundball off his chest. He puts himself well below the team and does whatever it takes to make his teammates better. Anything to help the team.

In an article about passion and purpose, Chris Stanovich, a licensed clinical counselor, states, "I believe we all have passion and purpose in our lives .... Unfortunately in sports, not every athlete has passion and purpose for playing their sport—while some do, many play because they are good at the sport, or because others in their life (like their parents) expect them to play. Playing sports without passion and purpose ...limits athletes from reaching their full athletic potential."

HIGH BASEBALL IQ

Baseball IQ is a determining factor when separating players with equal tools. While we know that not all players have the same 'skill' ability, all players do have equal ability to be a good student of the game. This equalizer could be to become a good or better student of the game. Have a better or higher baseball IQ than others.

One of the best examples of having a better or higher baseball IQ is Derek Jeter's "Flip Play" against the Oakland A's in game 3 of the 2001 American League Division Series. In the seventh inning with the Yankees leading 1-0 and Oakland's Jeremy Giambi on first base, Terrence Long hits a double down the right-field line. Yankee right fielder Shane Spencer retrieves the ball but when he throws home to get Giambi, who was trying to score, he misses both of his two cutoff men and the ball sails over their heads.

But out of nowhere Derek Jeter appears from his shortstop position and races toward the first-base line, positioning himself as the 'trail man." He grabs the errant throw and flips the ball to Yankee catcher Jose Posada, who tags Giambi out. Not only is it the game-saving play as the Yankees hang on to win 1-0, but they go on to win the next two games against Oakland and advance, face and beat the Seattle Mariners in five games to win the 2001 American League pennant.

To the casual baseball observer, Jeter was way out of his shortstop position. But to the baseball experts—good students of the game—he knew he was right where he was supposed to be—reading an errant throw from right field. Think about it—in a play that almost never happens, he instinctively knew what to do.

You need to be a good student of the game because the better you understand the game the more apt you are to make smart decisions on the field. Like Derek Jeter. A high IQ baseball player has good instincts. He knows what to do in the heat of the moment. Let's say you're the pitcher and the ball is hit to the first baseman. Do you automatically cover first? Or you are the third baseman and a ball is hit hard to your glove side; do you react instinctively and know where to throw if there's a runner on first base? The shortstop makes a great play behind second base using a glove flip behind his back. While most people think it's his athletic ability, that play is actually mostly instinct. It's a play made by someone who excels at being a student of the game.

Speaking of athletic ability let's look at one of the five tools—speed—where instincts plays an important part. Usually when you try out for a team the coaching staff wants to know how fast you are. So to measure your speed they have you run the 60-yard dash. Now running the 60-yard dash is a physical activity. It's a great way to measure you against the other players. It's tangible. But here's what it *doesn't* measure: your ability—your instincts—in tracking down a hard hit deep fly ball. It doesn't measure your general base running skills. It doesn't measure your base running intelligence. You can be the fastest player on the team but if you can't run the bases efficiently you are a liability on the bases.

The problem with speed is that it's tangible. Instinct is the intangible aspect of speed. Instinctively running the bases or tracking a baseball sometimes is more important than speed. I have coached a lot of players who didn't break any speed records in the 60-yard dash, but still graded high in base running skills. They weren't fast but had the uncanny ability to read the ball off the bat, take an extra base when they saw an opportunity, or steal a base because they were good at reading a pitcher's move.

Let's go back to my previous statement about players who do well only to falter as they go up levels of play. One reason why this happens is that as you go up levels the 'game speed' changes. It's faster. And the faster the game moves the faster your instincts must come into play.

CONCLUSION

The following is what Jeff Janssen, a top expert on sports leadership, had to say in a web seminar in front of college and high school baseball coaches. His topic was the makeup of players on a team and the level of their commitment, and he described each level:

LEVEL 1—THE RESISTANT PLAYER

Every coach has a vision of where they want their program to go. The Resistant player has his own vision, so he will resist whatever the coach is trying to do. It's all about the player and/or his parents— their vision, their values. It's what's best for them and not the team, so they question the coach's credibility. They are constantly shooting down his ideas.

LEVEL 2—THE RELUCTANT PLAYER

The Reluctant player is also one who has not bought into the coach's program. They question things in their mind and show it in their body language. You've seen them. Uninspired work effort, rolling of the eyes, slumped shoulders—always questioning things. "Why do we do that drill? Why that offensive? Why don't I play more?"

LEVEL 3—THE EXISTENT PLAYER

The existent player is just there. He takes up space. He has his jersey and gets his picture taken in the team picture. His head and heart are somewhere else. It takes nothing to be distracted or not pay attention.

LEVEL 4—THE COMPLIANT PLAYER

The Compliant player is the 'box checker." If you ask him to run two laps, he runs two laps. No more, no less. His attitude is "I did what you asked me to do." Complaint players do barely enough to get by, not get yelled at and not stick out like a sore thumb. And even though they do the bare minimum they expect praise for it. They are looking forward to their 'participation ribbon."

LEVEL 5—THE COMMITTED PLAYER

Their hearts are in it. They see the work they put in as an investment not a sacrifice. They see the bigger picture. They know they have to put in extra time. They know they need to train in off season because they see a possible positive payoff for themselves and for the team.

LEVEL 6—THE COMPELLED PLAYER

This player sets high standards for himself and encourages others to reach that standard. The Compelled player is invested. He doesn't have the patience or tolerance for resistant, reluctant, existent people because they are a threat to the team culture. There are too many people pulling in the wrong direction, and dead weight on the team means more work.

Coaches are looking for players who see things like work ethic as an investment, not a sacrifice. They know that talent alone does not create success. So if you want to improve the physical parts of your game, the tangibles, you have to accept the importance of the intangibles. There is a direct correlation between improving your work on the intangibles to the improvements in your physical performance—the tangibles. While it's nice to hear statements like "Man, can he hit" or "He has a rocket for an arm" or "He runs like a deer," you don't want to hear "He's dumb as a rock when it comes to baseball IQ" or "He's not a hard worker" or "Sometimes he just goes through the motions."

Realize that the competition for making the team or becoming a starter or for scholarship money is sharper than ever. Especially with the fast growing number of sport specialization instructors high school players are working with. Due to the high level of competition, you need a "point of difference." You have to be good or better at something that the others you are competing against don't have. The Resistant player and the Compelled player can be equals in talent but something like a sixth tool—embracing intangibles—probably will be the difference maker.

FOR WHAT IT'S WORTH

KEEP YOUR EYE ON THE BALL

"Keep your eye on the ball" may be good advice, but according to the book written by Robert Watts and Terry Bahill, engineers by vocation, it's impossible to do. *Keep Your Eye on The Ball—Curve Balls, Knuckle Balls, and Fallacies of Baseball* states that by applying physics, physiology, and other scientific principles, they have determined that the batter can track the ball until it is about five feet in front of the plate. After that, due to the fact that the ball is moving too fast, the batter's eyes are actually 'behind' the ball (the 'front' of the ball is headed towards the catcher). Essentially, the ball is past the optimum point that the batter can physiologically see a ball in front of him.

In the first third of the ball's flight, the batter gathers data and forms his mental model of the pitch. In the middle third, he computes (predicts) when and where the ball will cross the plate. Then he starts his swing. In the last third of the ball's flight, the batter observes errors in his mental model so that he can track the next pitch better or updates his mental model and perhaps checks his swing.

THE RISING FASTBALL

Many baseball players have described the rising fastball: this pitch starts normally, but right in front of home plate, the ball jumps up a half foot, making it hop over the bat. According to the laws of physics, such behavior is impossible. While physicists have confirmed that there is no such thing as a rising fastball they suggest that it's a perceptual illusion. The batter tracks the ball in the first third of the ball's flight. But he underestimates the pitch speed (mis-times the pitch – see Quicksand) thus incorrectly computes (predicts) the height of the ball when it crosses the plate (that point at which bat and ball make contact). At the start of his swing, the batter takes his eye off the ball to look at the predicted point that the bat and ball will make contact, but when the ball comes back into view it is higher than he thought it would be.

PERCEIVED VELOCITY

From conversations of players during an at bat, players sometimes sense that a pitch seems faster or slower than the speed registered on the radar gun. While that seems crazy, there is a theory that explains why that happens. Perry Hubbard, a researcher, conducted a 10 year study on the timing of hitters. To confirm his findings, he analyzed a 4 million pitch data base from Inside Edge, a company that tracks pitches and batter results in major league games. From that study he invented a concept called Effective Velocity. This Effective Velocity is described as the study of baseball pitch speeds and how location changes the reaction time of the hitter.

In the 10/1/06 issue of *Collegiate Baseball*, in an article entitled "Effective Velocity," Hubbard goes into detail on how the speed of a pitch is viewed by hitters. Depending on the pitch location, the hitter may feel that the speed of the ball can be as high as 4 more miles faster or slower than its actual speed.

Imagine dissecting home plate into 5 'lanes' a pitched ball travels through. The following chart indicates what Hubbard discovered is the perceived speed difference in each lane.

+4	+3	+2	+1	0
+3	+2	+1	0	-1
+2	+1	0	-1	-2
+1	0	-1	-2	-3
0	-1	-2	-3	-4

The left side of the chart is the left-handed batter facing the pitcher. Reverse the numbers for a right-handed batter. Now, suppose the batter is facing a 90 mile per hour fastball. For the left handed batter a 90 mile an hour fastball will appear to be going 94 mph if thrown high and inside. And that same 90 mph pitch can appear to be going 86 mph if thrown low and outside. For a right handed batter a 90 mph fastball will appear to be going 94 mph if thrown high and outside. And that same 90 mph pitch can appear to be going 86 mph if thrown low and inside, even though the actual speed of the ball is a constant 90 mph. The supposed change in speed is the hitter's perceived velocity and is why the batter mis-times the pitch.

ADD TWO MILES AN HOUR
TO YOUR FASTBALL

Tom Verducci, a sports writer for *Sports Illustrated*, wrote an article about spin rates using data from Trackman (a Danish radar tech company). While the main point of the article was 'spin rate', a side point was made about a pitcher's release point. What the Trackman data revealed was that for some pitchers, their fastball is perceived by batters to be faster than the actual measured velocity. This is sometimes referred to as "sneaky fast" or the fastball has a "late hop."

The Trackman data suggests that a major cause of this effect is the span on the pitcher's stride extension in releasing the ball. They concluded that if the pitcher can reduce the distance that the ball travels to home plate, then the flight time for the ball will be faster than expected. Thus a pitcher's momentum and stride can produce a release point closer to the batter. The data showed that pitchers whose extension is approximately one foot longer than average can add around 2 mph to their effective velocity.

Thus for these long extension pitchers, the ball seems to get to the batter faster than the visual appearance of the speed of the pitch. The necessary reaction time for the batter is less than expected. The result? The batter's timing is messed up. The article also went on to state that the release extension is related to strike outs and swing and miss rates as well.

FORM OVER SUBSTANCE

I once attended a workout conducted by a Colorado Rockies scout for a group of Pennsylvania high school players who were selected to play in an Olympic style showcase event called the Keystone Games Competition. Standing next to the scout and his assistant, watching each player take his turn hitting against live pitching, each of us would make comments about the batter. The assistant had a habit of pointing out to us how each batter emulated a particular pro player—the way they stood in the batter's box or the way they swung. At one point, as one player was halfway through his turn, the assistant stated, "Look, he stands just like Albert Pujols." At that point the scout quickly shot back, "Yeah, but he sure don't hit like Albert Pujols."

Of course we all laughed, but as I was driving home after the workout that whole sequence of events ran in my head. One thought that kept popping up in my head was the expression 'Form over Substance,"because that's what the scout was really saying. This expression basically means that looks seem to be more important than content; or the value of the content doesn't matter if it's visually appealing. You may have heard this expression as 'Style over Substance."

Kids are quick to emulate their favorite pro player. They work hard on getting their stance or swing or mannerisms to look exactly like the pro. Now I know why they do this. First, there is the "if it works for him it should work for me" mentality. Second, it's a quick fix. Again, we live in a "microwave society" where we expect everything right away. However, the problem is that what kids are seeing from their favorite player is the end result of his countless hours of hard work. It's the finished product. Read the following excerpts from an article which appeared in the local newspaper about then Philadelphia Phillies Chase Utley.

A young Chase Utley would take swings in a batting cage until he ran out of quarters. Then he'd earn a few bucks picking up balls or trash and take more hacks. The **strong work ethic** Utley possessed during his childhood in Southern California has only intensified now that he's in the major leagues. A two-time All-Star second baseman for the Philadelphia Phillies, Utley is never satisfied. He wants to keep improving, so he's always working to get better.

Need a minute to chat with Utley? "Better catch him on the run. He's polite and mild-mannered, but he's usually too busy to talk and doesn't care about self-promotion."

Utley arrives early at the ballpark and leaves late. He takes extra batting practice, hits off a tee, watches video, and makes sure he's ready for every at-bat. "I've never seen a guy as prepared as Chase," Phillies manager Charlie Manuel said. "He's always early, and he hits every day. He eats it and sleeps it."

The countless hours Utley spends working on his swing and studying pitchers have made him an elite player. Utley's sweet left-handed swing is close to perfect. It's short, compact and generates a lot of power. All that extra work in the cages and the rigorous off-season training program has certainly paid off.

Utley is a great example of the end result of players' countless hours of hard work. Today we live in an 'I—Me' era where players put so much emphasis on style and themselves that Utley is downright boring. He was admired for what would be called his **hard-nosed**

attitude. As mentioned in the article, "He would rather win a game than watch himself on a highlight reel. Whether he hits a routine grounder to first base or goes deep, Utley puts his head down and runs hard. There's no showboating, no flashy handshakes, no exaggerated celebration. 'That's not me,' Utley said. 'I don't think that's a good way to represent yourself.' Utley has substance."

THE QUESTION

Now that you have read about Utley, the question I need you to ask yourself and honestly answer is "Does this article describe me?" Take a look at the list of positive descriptive statements from the article about his work ethic:

- rigorous off-season training program

- always working to get better

- arrives early at the ballpark and leaves late

- takes extra batting practice

- makes sure he's ready for every at-bat

- countless hours

- studying pitchers

- hard-nosed attitude

From this list I want you to write the word 'yes' next to each statement that you feel accurately describes you. Again, be completely honest with yourself. But then go back to each of the ones you answered yes and write a brief comment that defends your answer.

COUNTLESS HOURS

Notice that a lot of the positives are time related. Take 'countless hours' as an example. Logically you could use your high school practices to defend your 'yes' answer. I'm sure you go to each and every one and you work hard. But be sure to consider individual time versus team time. What do I mean by that? Well, let's look at a typical practice. Have you ever sat down and really analyzed how much time you actually spend on your hitting? Your pitching? Just your individual time?

Due to time constraints and rules, the average amount of practice time a high school team spends is in the two and a half hour range. But keep in mind that about one half hour is spent on loosening up and throwing to warm up your arm. So realistically the true practice time is in the two hour range. The average number of players on a varsity team is in the 15 to 17 range. If one of the two hours is set aside for hitting, and if only the batting cage is being used, then that leaves about 4 minutes per player.

Okay, it's unlikely that only the batting cage is being used, so assume there are multiple stations—say three others. Each group at each station would consist of about four players. If one hour has been set aside for hitting, that means each group spends 15 minutes at each station. This equates to about 3 minutes per person per station. But let's not forget dead time—the time spent moving between stations, picking up the balls, deciding who's going first, fixing your gloves, getting ready, talking to each other, etc. I feel comfortable with my 12 minute estimate.

Now let's look at the quality of the time spent at each station. Honestly I don't know any player who doesn't stay focused, concentrate, and enjoy being in the batting cage or when taking live pitching on the field. Everybody likes live hitting. So that time spent is probably quality time. Every day!

But what about at the other stations? What's the quality of your individual time spent on soft toss, hitting off the tee, etc.? It may be good for the first week or two but what about by the end of the third week? Same intensity? Same quality? I doubt it. It's monotonous, boring work...just swinging continuously, hitting a ball into a net. And let's not forget that not too many high school programs have enough coaches on their staff to position one at each station, giving individual instruction and monitoring the station. At this point it becomes form over substance.

For the benefit of those players who insist every minute they spend at all of the stations, every day, is quality time, the total amount of individual time they get is about 15 minutes. So if you practice 6 days a week, your total individual time spent is around one hour and 12 minutes.

That's the hitting scenario. Let's take a quick look at pitching. Think about what you do in practice to prepare to pitch a complete game or the maximum pitches allowed by rule for one day. Right now the high school pitching rules allow for between 75 and 100 pitches. Now keep in mind that to experience success, those 75 to 100 pitches have to be competitive pitches. Simple logic says you can't expect a pitcher to stress his body on the day he is pitching by throwing 75 to 100 pitches without first preparing it to do so. And realistically, to prepare so that you can throw that many competitive pitches, you probably need to throw about 275 to 300 practice pitches a week. Maybe it's one third working on velocity, one third working on command and control, and one third on velocity with command. It's throwing the baseball hard 3 days a week and throwing at about 50-70 percent another 2-3 days a week. But how can you do that if you don't "have the time" to prepare to do it? Let's not forget that once the season starts, your individual time will diminish. So just like with hitting, if you analyzed the time spent on pitching, by the end of the week, how much was actually individual time?

You have limited amount of time at practice, so get the most out of that time.

ALWAYS WORKING TO GET BETTER

Let's say you answered yes to "always working to get better" as a positive attribute, and playing on a travel team is one of your reasons why. Players on a travel team find themselves spending most Fridays, Saturdays, and Sundays playing in various tournaments, and while playing these weekend games is not a bad thing—in fact these games offer you feedback on the things you are doing well and more importantly what needs work—but it involves hours of playing. Even with showcase baseball, we go back to the question of how much time is individual development time. When do you work on areas that need improvement?

Now, for those of you who don't think this is important, consider a recent interview between a coach from Youth Baseball Network in 2018 and head baseball coach Mike Martin of Florida State. When Martin was asked, "What is the one thing that…concerns you about the future of the game?" he answered, "I'd like to see more teaching going on in these summer programs and what I'm seeing in travel ball programs. There are too many guys that don't know the fundamentals, and that's something we just can't get away from."

By the way, for those of you who don't know, Mike Martin is a legend in college baseball. He is the all-time winningest coach in NCAA Division I college baseball and has coached for 40 years, retiring in 2019. The man knows what he is talking about. He knows you need to find time to constantly work on your fundamentals.

Playing extra games is a good thing. But along with the growth of travel and showcase teams is the perception players (and parents) attach to them. Unless something has changed since I retired, the makeup of these local travel teams can be dubious at best, and just because you play on a travel team, it does not mean you are a great player. Nor does it mean you are one of the best. Quite frankly all it means is that you are on a team that travels. (I'm not referring to teams like Team USA). Whether you think you are a superstar on the team or you really are, you still need to practice. For some players being on a travel team is form over substance.

Your God-given talent is only going to get you so far. Eventually you reach a level where everyone is on the same talent plane, and in order to reach your potential, set yourself apart from others, and achieve whatever your goal, you need to accept the reality of other variables—one of which is individual hard work—focused hard work.

RIGOROUS OFF SEASONING TRAINING

Let's say you answered yes to "rigorous off-season training" as one of your positive attributes. But when's the last time you evaluated your training program? What qualifies your training as rigorous? In a recent conversation with my 45-year-old son I happened to state that the high school basketball team at the school where I had coached lost by one point in the States Final. Their star player—a freshman—scored 45 out of the team's 72 total points. When I told him the player's name my son immediately said he knew him and that he wasn't surprised by the kid's success. At that point, curious, I asked him how he knew him.

My son goes to the YMCA at 6:00 every morning, and each morning he notices a young kid there working out. In fact he used the word "intensely" to describe the extent of this kid's workout. But here's the interesting part. My son also mentioned that there were always two or three other kids with him, but the other players sat around talking while the 'star' freshman did his reps. And that's why my son wasn't surprised by the kid's success.

You may have an off-season or in-season training program, but just because you show up with your buddies it certainly does not validate that it's a rigorous workout. Neither does the quantity of your reps. The validation comes from the intensity and the quality of the reps. Showing up does not mean you are training rigorously. It only means you can check off the "I worked out" box. Showing up could be form over substance.

The problem is that too many high school players' concepts of how much effort they should and do put into their personal development is not close to the reality of what they should and could do. As stated by Ken Mannie, Michigan State's Head Strength and Conditioning Coach, in an article for Scholastic Coach magazine, "A good portion of the players that do not make it (in college) did not prepare well enough to do so. They let everything ride on the fact that they were good players and ignored all the other variables."

My intent is to get you to evaluate your work ethic. Success is not going to come instantly but must be worked on constantly. Don't think you can master a skill in a short period of time without going through the time-consuming process that it takes to learn and master a complex sport skill. It's the process of a player's individual time. It's more than practice with your team or the once-a-week lesson from the local "guru." It's how often you devote time. It's the intensity and the quality of your time. Yes, it can be monotonous and boring, but if you view a strong work ethic as necessary for your improvement and you see incremental success, it will take on a whole new level of importance.

There's no magic bullet—one little detail that will put you over the top. It's the other variables. It's the old 80 percent/20 percent rule. You can achieve 80 percent of your potential by putting forth 20 percent of your effort. But the last 20 percent of your potential will require the other 80 percent of your effort. It's not for the faint of heart. You have to work your butt off for that last 20 percent because if you have higher aspirations then there is more you can do. You need to change—be different than everyone else. You cannot continually do the same thing, the same way. As stated in sport psychologist Terry Orlick's book, "There is no way to achieve a high level of excellence without a high level of personal commitment."

Moving on… Everyone spends a lot of time with their team. Everyone participating in sports, and in your case baseball, has aspirations to reach a specific goal. They have expectations. Your goal could be to make the State Playoffs or a college team, to be picked for an elite travel team, become a professional player, or simply be the best high school player.

While these dreams are worth pursuing, players often overlook the tremendous amount of time, preparation, sacrifice, and hard work required.

Let's go back to the question I asked you to pose to yourself: "Does this article describe me?" Perhaps I should have asked, "If Chase Utley emulated your current work ethic would he be as successful as he was?" You see, what you watch on TV is the end result of a tremendous amount of individual time, preparation, sacrifice, and hard work. Chase Utley was successful and made it to the pros because he worked on his skill development.

It's okay to emulate your favorite player, but beware of form over substance. Emulating any player's style—form—only means you look like him. But if you emulate work ethic—substance—it will put you on the path to possible success. In the Utley article it stated, "In an era when players put so much emphasis on style, Utley is downright boring." So, get boring. Start working on the last 20 percent. The more of that last 20 percent you can develop, the closer you will be towards reaching your potential, your expectations, and your dream. Because being good enough now may not be good enough in the future.

HOW BIG IS LITTLE

Players, especially young players, need to understand that the "little things" are not always so little. That there is a reason why coaches repetitively do drills. Those small details do matter in the scheme of things. To give yourself (and the team) a chance to be successful you need to do things that barely, if at all, get noticed. I realize that this is hard to understand. Everyone remembers the batter who gets the game-winning hit. After all, it will be one of ESPN's Top Ten Plays. But who remembers the game-saving diving catch by the third baseman in the fourth inning that kept them in the game? That play won't make ESPN's Top Ten Plays. You need to understand that by taking care of the little things big things can happen.

2015 COLLEGE WORLD SERIES

Every year, before the season even starts, the No. 1 goal for all 298 NCAA Division I baseball teams is to make it to the College World Series. But out of those 298 clubs, only a select few make it. In fact only eight make it.

In the bottom of the 10th inning of a tied, decisive game three at the Louisville Super Regional, Cal State Fullerton found itself on the verge of its season ending when the leadoff hitter for Louisville reached base. A sacrifice bunt was in order.

Everyone in the ballpark, as did everybody watching on television, knew it. And Cal State Fullerton's defense knew it, too—including second baseman Taylor Bryant. As Louisville's hitter laid down a textbook sacrifice bunt, Fullerton's catcher fielded the ball cleanly, and without a play at second, shuffled his feet toward first to take the "sure" out. When the ball left the catcher's hand, it was apparent that it was a bad throw. Sure enough—the throw sailed over the first baseman's head and was headed toward the right field corner. But the ball never made it that far.

Bryant was backing up the play, in position behind first base, exactly where he was supposed to be, when he was supposed to be there. Had he not been there, Louisville's runner from first would have likely scored easily, and the Cardinals would be on their way to the College World Series.

But Bryant was there. His simple backup of first base not only saved the game, but it saved Fullerton's season. Fittingly, the Titans later scored a run to win the game and earn the right to move on to the College World Series—largely because Bryant was backing up a base.

Who knows how many times Bryant had made that sprint to back up first base, only to watch his teammates throw and catch the ball without issue to get that "sure" out. Who knows how many times Bryant practiced backing up first base, only to realize his energy to be in position, just in case of a bad throw, was for naught.

THE DERIK JETER FLIP

My favorite story of how little things lead to big things is the Derek Jeter 'flip' play, which actually did make ESPN's Top Ten plays.

During the third game of the 2001 American League Division Series between the New York Yankees and Oakland Athletics Derek Jeter made what is still considered to this day as one of the best plays of all time in baseball history. In the seventh inning with the Yankees leading 1-0 and a runner on first base the Athletics batter hit a double down the right-field line. The Yankee right fielder retrieved the ball but when he threw home to get the runner who was on first trying to score, he missed both of his two cutoff men and the ball sailed over their heads. "There was no chance we could make an out at home," Yankee second baseman Alfonso Soriano remembers thinking.

But out of nowhere Derek Jeter appeared from his shortstop position, racing toward the first-base line, positioning himself as the 'trail man." He grabbed the errant throw and 'flipped' the ball to Jose Posada, his catcher, who tagged the runner out. It turns out that this was the game-saving play as the Yankees hung on to win 1-0. That play totally changed the momentum of the entire series for the Yankees who went on to win the American League pennant.

IN WITH A BANG—VILLANOVA WINS THE 2016 NCAA TOURNAMENT

Villanova played North Carolina in the 2016 Basketball NCAA Finals, which would go down as one of the better games in Tournament history. It was a back-and-forth game, but late in the second half Villanova did manage to go up by 10 points. However, with only 9 seconds left, they had let their lead shrink to 74-71 and North Carolina had the ball. On their possession, Marcus Paige, the North Carolina guard, connected on a three-pointer to tie the game, leaving just 4.7 seconds left on the clock.

Now if you watched the game, what you would have seen in those final 4.7 seconds is that Villanova called time out—the team huddled around the coach to discuss what play to run—then went out and successfully scored a three-pointer to win the game 77-74.

Seems simple enough. But there is a part of the success story that many don't know. As described in a *Sports Illustrated* article, when Villanova called time out with 4.7 seconds left, there was no panic in the huddle. "They already knew what the next play was." Every player knew they were going to run a play called 'Nova." It's a play they try to run whenever there is between four and seven seconds left on the clock and they need to go the length of the floor. As the article stated, "It's the endgame sequence they run three or four times a week in practice."

So they won a game on a play that they ran over and over at practice. Wait...there's more. Apparently, when they ran that play, there were four designated perimeter positions—the two corners and two 'slots' a few steps to the right and left top of the key—spots on the floor where the shooter needs to position himself. In fact in practice the team manager taped X's on the floor so that the 'shooter'—in this case Kris Jenkins—knew exactly where to go. The following are excerpts from the *Sports Illustrated* article describing what Jenkins does in practice. Jenkins has taken thousands of threes from those 'X's on the final play of the game. "He automatically drifts to a familiar place" and when he catches the pass he is one step behind the right slot.

The coach, Jay Wright, teaches a specific way he wants the shooter to 'catch and shoot." In fact *Sports Illustrated* used the word "indoctrinates" to describe how he gets his method across. It's a two-step approach as opposed to a jump-stop. The following is *Sports Illustrated's* description of Jenkins' shot on that final play: "Now watch Jenkins' feet: the way he flows from catch to shoot, without dribbling, it's habitual. His inside (left) foot lands first, then his outside (right) foot, slightly in front."

But that's not the end of the story. As unbelievable as it may seem, in 2009 Villanova won the game that got them into the 2009 Final Four with the 'Nova' play. That's right—the same play. During the post-game interview of that game, Scottie Reynolds, the Villanova player who sank that game-winning shot, was quoted saying, "It's something we do every day in practice."

2019 OREGON LITTLE LEAGUE BASEBALL TEAM

The 2019 Oregon Little League baseball team won the Northwest Regional in Southern California and thus earned the right to play in the Little League World Series in Williamsport, Pennsylvania. They scored two runs in the final inning of the championship game to dethrone defending champ Idaho in a 5-4 victory.

But how they scored those two runs is what made the game interesting. Trailing 4-3 in the bottom of the sixth inning, one out, nobody on, the Oregon batter hit a double. He then advanced to third when the next batter hit a comebacker to the Idaho pitcher, who made the play at first. Now there were two outs. One more out and Idaho would be on their way to Williamsport.

But here's what happened. After catching the ball from the pitcher the first baseman feinted a throw to third base. But the Oregon player got back so he threw the ball to the pitcher. The catcher then walked toward his dugout apparently to talk to his coach. But because no one called time out the play was still live. When the catcher walked toward his dugout the Oregon player on third realized that no one was covering home and ran home and tied up the game. Oregon then scored what turned out to be the winning run when the next batter hit a double and scored on a misplayed groundball by the Idaho infield.

Think about it. A twelve-year-old pays attention and basically wins the game for his team.

1992 NATIONAL LEAGUE PLAYOFF GAME

It's the seventh game of the National League playoffs—the game that decides who goes on to play in the World Series. In the bottom of the ninth, Pittsburgh and Atlanta are tied 2-2 and the bases are loaded. On second base is Atlanta Braves player Sid Bream. Up at the plate with a 2-1 count is Francisco Cabrera. He lines the next pitch into left field for a base hit. The runner at third scores to tie the game. Left fielder Barry Bonds fields the ball cleanly and throws home to get the runner (Sid Bream) who is trying to score from second. As quoted in the *Sports Illustrated* article, Bonds "throws the ball on a line six feet inside the third base line…Cather Mike La Valliere makes a sweep tag as Bream slides. It's too close to call …but the umpire" does and calls him SAFE! Braves win! Cabrera is the hero!

But wait—Sid Bream was probably one of the slowest players on the Braves team. So slow, he is described in the *Sports Illustrated* article about the game as "slower than bread mold." Is this the same Sid Bream who was playing on a bad ankle and beat the throw? Yes… because he knew a 'little thing." It's been said that he mentioned that with a 2-1 count, bottom of the ninth, game on the line—pressure— the pitcher's focus would be on throwing a strike to the batter and not on the runner at second. So he would not even notice that when Bream took his lead he took extra steps—more than usual. It turns out the extra steps made the difference. Now Cabrera was the hero, but 'slow poke' Sid had a lot to do with that!

I wonder how many times Cal State Fullerton's Taylor Bryant, or the Yankees Derik Jeter or Villanova's guard Kris Jenkins said to themselves, *These drills are boring* or *What a waste of time*. I wonder if Sid Bream asked himself, *How many more times do I have to listen to this?* when the coaching staff discussed this type of situation. Do you think he had a know-it-all attitude? Did he hear but not listen?

When you are at practice and starting to get bored with a drill or listening to the coach trying to get a specific point across (maybe a "'chalk talk") remember:

Caring about doing the right thing is the right thing to do.

Caring about little things means you are a team player.

Caring about the little things is showing love for the game.

Caring about the little things shows respect for the game.

Caring about the little things shows character.

Caring about the little things shows commitment.

So practice with a purpose, knowing that each small aspect of a drill means your actions on the field will be automatic or, as Kris Jensen's shooting mechanics—habitual. Practice with a purpose, knowing that each small aspect of a drill relates to the greater picture of individual and team goals. Pay attention because in the end learning and caring about the little things helps get you to big things—like winning! You should care "just in case."

MENTAL TOUGHNESS

I'm sure you have heard the expression mental toughness, but what does that mean when it comes to sports? Based on a definition in the *Journal of Applied Sport Psychology*, it's having the natural or developed psychological edge that enables you to: generally cope better than your opponents with the many demands (competition, training, lifestyle) that sports places on a performer, and specifically be more consistent and better than your opponents in remaining determined, focused, confident, and in control under pressure.

Let's look at some core distinctions of mental toughness.

- Winner's mindset—having the attitude that you will win or play at your maximum level consistently.

- Hyper focus—being able to perform at a peak level without getting distracted, having mental clarity, and being at ease. Being able to be in the zone—the present zone.

- Stress optimization—being able to manage stress and pressure in the moment without doubt, fear, or anxiety.

- Failing well—being able to extract the value and learn from the failure and funnel it into the next performance. This is the best time to have a bad memory.

- Maxing out limits—the ability to extract maximum physical effort in the experience of pain, mental and physical stress, and physical discomfort and to perform in spite of unpleasantness.

- Preparedness—planning for any performance and having a backup plan for any circumstance.

Mental toughness in baseball starts with your ability to prepare.

Are you doing everything you can to be prepared to play? Mental toughness is your ability to effectively prepare for upcoming games. Too many baseball players mistakenly set themselves up for failure because of their level of commitment and how they prepare. They work overtime on their strengths but limit their time on their weaknesses. And there is a reason why.

Whenever they attempt to do something they don't know how to do or have never done before or are just starting to learn, they struggle. And how long they struggle is determined by the level of the skill at which they are working. That's natural. Now, let's face it, it's easy to "want to"—I want to get better, I want to work on my backhand, etc.—but it's harder to keep at it. Especially if you are struggling. After all, who wants to fail—a lot?

Time becomes a factor. So because a player is struggling, they decide they're spending too much time and give up too soon. Not only do they start to minimize time but also their effort level toward perfecting the skill. But this is exactly the time to have mental toughness. It's only natural when experiencing failure to feel frustration, but this is the time to work on failing well. Failing well is accepting the fact that it takes time to correct or learn something new and become good at it. Failing well is understanding that to experience success you have to go through failure. Having the ability to take ownership of the mental part of preparation puts you on the road to mental toughness.

Consider what Tiger Woods revealed in a social media post one week prior to the 2019 British Open. Because it was being played in Ireland, he knew there was a five-hour time change, so he decided to get up at one o'clock every morning that week to simulate being in Ireland at 6 a.m.—thus eliminating any effect the time change would have on him physically.

He wrote, "If you want to get better, if you want to win, if you want to accomplish your goals," you need to do something out of the norm. Most people would not even consider getting up so early. To them it's the 'flea on the elephant' in preparation. But Woods knows he needs to take ownership of his preparation so that he can be sure he has done everything to reach his goals. Even something that some people would think is insignificant. This is an example of being mentally tough.

Mental toughness in baseball starts with your ability to handle failure.

If you can't handle working on self-improvement in practice you certainly don't have the ability to quickly bounce back from game day errors, miscues, lousy calls and strikeouts. If you have trouble letting go of your failures and tend to carry them around with you, then chances are good that you'll consistently play below your potential. Instead of making excuses accept the mistake.

Everyone makes mistakes, so be aware and analyze what went wrong. And more importantly don't judge yourself—this is no time for thoughts like *I stink, I can't do this, I'm not good, I'm bad,* etc. Pay attention to the facts—what happened. Tom Hanson, sports psychologist, feels you have to have a mindset of "non-judgmental awareness." This means keeping "good" and "bad" at a distance." He feels that judgment generates emotions that obstruct learning. Being non-judgmental keeps you focused on the facts.

An example of what Hanson is saying is revealed in a postgame interview with New Orleans quarterback Drew Brees after he broke the career touchdown passes record with 541 and the record for best completion percentage in a single game. He was 29 out of 30, which is 96.7 percent. Think about that—he missed one time. During the interview he was asked about his mindset. He stated, "You always think about the one you miss. If I just set my darn feet and throw it to the running back." He didn't make that infamous statement, "My bad." He didn't dwell on some negative thought. Instead he paid attention to the facts—he didn't set his feet. That's why he completed 29 out of 30 throws. He stuck to the facts. So if you want to understand what a winner's mindset is you need to look no further than this postgame interview.

By the way, the "My bad!" statement is not a true acceptance of fault. Infielder bobbles the ground ball, picks it up, and throws it away—runner scores. Player looks at his teammates and says "My bad!" That's not an analysis. That's an attempt at getting instant atonement. Players who are quick to say "My bad" are:

- Looking for a "quick fix" forgiveness.

- Saying, "It's okay now."

- Saving face—"I'm still a good guy."

- Saying, "Don't criticize me."

- Trying to lessen the severity of the mistake.

An honest analysis of the error would be "I bobbled the ball because I panicked or I rushed my throw. I need to stay calm and focus on the mechanics of picking up the ball." Instead of looking for atonement or excuses, think honestly about what did go wrong so that you can prevent it from happening again.

How would you feel if while flying in an airplane that seems to be out of control you hear the pilot say, "My bad." Or you're on the operating table and you hear the surgeon say, "My bad." I think you would agree that it would be unacceptable. So why is it acceptable when the shortstop says it after his error?

There was an incident in a first round 2019 NCAA Basketball Tournament game that just might validate this thinking. Michigan State, the second seed, was playing Bradley, the 15 seed. So everyone assumed Michigan would win handily. But it wasn't all smooth sailing against the underdog. In fact early in the second half, coach Tom Izzo was so upset at the way the team was playing, in particular with freshman forward Aaron Henry, that he stormed onto the court during a timeout and started shouting at Henry. And the 'chewing out' continued in the team huddle.

Michigan State did eventually win, but after the game there were a lot of discussions about the visibly heated chewing out. We will never know what Aaron Henry said to coach Izzo during the incident. After the game, in an interview with ESPN, Izzo explained he was upset with Henry for not getting back on defense.

He was quoted as saying, "What's wrong with challenging a kid that makes some mistakes? Aaron Henry did some things that you can't do as a starter on a top 5 team .... They were effort-related. I did get after him." Again, we will never know what Aaron Henry said to coach Izzo, but to finish Izzo's quote: "The 'my-bads' are out the window." I'm guessing that up to the point of being chewed out, Henry was not grasping the importance of playing defense and that Izzo was not accepting Henry's 'my bad' as an explanation for his bad defense.

Mental toughness in baseball starts with your ability to handle pressure.

The cornerstone of peak athletic performance on the ball field is your ability to focus on what's important and block out everything else. Do you know how to stay cool in the clutch? Can you effectively manage the stress of the competition? Can you block out the razzing crowd, your rowdy opponents, and the scouts in the stands? Without the ability to relax you can't play good ball.

In order to handle pressure you need to be aware that the pressure is affecting you. You have to be aware of what and how you are feeling. It's up to you to recognize that you are distracted by the pressure. Accept it but respond to it. So the questions become "If I feel the pressure how do I combat it? How do I refocus?"

One answer is *cue cards*. Remember Suggestion #5 in the Fighting Slumps article (see page 95). Suggestion #5 called for cue cards—mental images and thoughts—to help you focus. But they can also improve your ability to handle pressure: Instead of focusing on the situation, use a cue card to put an image in your head or say something to yourself that is specific to your performance. For example, as a pitcher, before you throw your fastball, say to yourself, "Pound it, pound it" over and over. When throwing your changeup remind yourself, "Fastball body" over and over." As you step into the batter's box, put an image of a baseball or an eyeball in your head (see the ball, hit the ball). The purpose of the 'cue card' is to clear your head of all outside influences or negative, non-productive thoughts and refocus your brain. It allows you to block out other non-productive thoughts and to compete with your body—not fight with your mind.

Come up with your own cue cards. It doesn't matter whether they're verbal or visual or a combination of both. Whatever you choose, apply them when you are in the bullpen or in the batting cage at practice.

Mental toughness in baseball starts with your ability to handle doubt.

When it comes to handling self-doubt and negative self-talk, are you your own worst enemy? The cornerstone of peak performance is your ability to focus on what's important. And what's important is being aware and recognizing when you are running negative thoughts through your head. When this happens go back to your cue cards. Everyone needs a traffic light cue card showing the red light. The minute you are aware of your non-productive thinking, visualize the traffic light. See the red light and say to yourself STOP!

There's one common thread here, and that's self-awareness. In order to be successful at handling preparation, pressure, failure, doubts, etc. you need to be self-aware. It's up to you to pay attention to your emotions and thoughts and to have non-judgmental awareness. If you want to learn how to be mentally tough, stay away from "good" and "bad" and learn from your mistakes.

NOT FEELING WELL? YOU MAY HAVE WHITE LINE FEVER

There is an ailment that has many pitching coaches scratching their heads. It's called 'White Line Fever,' a condition that afflicts many young pitchers. They usually catch it when they enter a game. The player is relaxed, confident and aggressive in the bullpen and throws strikes. But when he enters the game, it's as if someone else has taken over his body. He completely changes his execution; his mechanics and timing are all messed up and totally disrupt his performance.

Why does that happen? Let's face it—same catcher, same ball, same weather, same teammates…what changes? What is so different about pitching on the sidelines than in a game? On the surface it's pretty obvious. In the bullpen there's nothing at stake. There's no umpire. There's no judgment. In a player's mind their performance doesn't count. They feel they don't have to get it completely right and thus tend to be *far more relaxed.* And because they are relaxed they tend to not think very much during their performance. Instead their focus of concentration is on all of the right things—the process.

However, all of this changes once players enter the game. Once they cross the white lines they suddenly realize that there are consequences. Now it counts. There's an umpire. And with an umpire each pitch will be judged. There's something at stake. The player thinks, *What if I make a mistake! I can't let the team down! What will coach / my father say?* They attach far too much importance on the outcome of their performance—they over think—and consequently they experience much too much physical and mental tension: Their focus, their concentration, is on the end results, the outcome of the competition, and other issues like pleasing others. Subconsciously they have concerns about their worth and in turn lose control of their confidence, so they change their approach—their process of pitching.

Signs players may be losing confidence include the following:

- They go from pitching to throwing. They decide they must throw the ball 1,000 miles an hour. They try too hard. And when that happens their mechanics break down.

- They decide they need to be perfect. They start aiming the ball and lose accuracy.

- They focus on pitching with perfect mechanics instead of competing. They become mechanical in their approach. As Tom Hanson states in his book *Heads Up Baseball 2.0*, the goal is to pitch with good mechanics without being mechanical.

- They express hope with each pitch. *Hope this is a strike. Hope the batter doesn't hit it.* They are not committed to the pitch. When you are hoping you don't believe you can do it.

The answer to why this happens is simple. It's pressure.

Pressure is defined as a perceived expectation of the need to perform well under challenging situations. It goes without saying that with any competition, naturally, there is pressure of some kind. I have read many articles about athletes and pressure and there is always one recurring theme: Pressure makes athletes tense, afraid, and worried.

While every player has their own thoughts on pressure, it's their mental response—how they handle it—that has an effect on their physical response. Some players see pressure situations as an opportunity to succeed while others see them as an opportunity to fail. And those players, when they cross the white lines, fear the consequences of a possible negative outcome. When that happens they question their confidence.

Let's look again at the definition of pressure. The two key words are 'perceived' and 'expectations." In a competitive environment, an athlete's attitude toward the value of the contest can change the degree of pressure he puts on himself, so it's the athlete who ultimately determines the size, scope, and extent of the pressure on him as opposed to the real value. And how the athlete manages his perceived value of the contest can have an effect on the outcome of his performance.

What are the consequences of a negative outcome? What is it players fear?

- They don't want to disappoint their parents or let down others.

- They want to avoid the pain or embarrassment after a mistake or bad game.

- They are concerned about protecting their reputation, their image.

- They want to avoid criticism from parents, peers, or teammates.

- They want to avoid judgment of their performance.

- They want to protect their pride.

- They have a strong desire to feel approval from others.

Notice they all indicate concern about their self-esteem. They feel that a negative outcome not only disappoints the people involved in their life but also has an effect on their value as a player (or person).

Simply put—a negative result means "I'm bad." For what it's worth, Steve Springer, author of *Quality At Bats*, has 35 years in professional baseball as a player, agent, and scout. He says: "Baseball is the biggest self-esteem destroying sport in the world."

As sports psychologist Tom Hanson states in an article he wrote for *Collegiate Baseball Magazine*, "Pitchers who don't perform at a high level during games feel their self-esteem is on the line and more than likely tense up rather than feeling that everything will be alright no matter what happens." He goes on to say that the player doesn't trust his ability, which leads to a loss of confidence, which leads to a fear of failure. Thus for those players who see "crossing the white lines" as an opportunity to fail end up playing tentatively and cautiously.

Obviously a player needs to maintain the very same focus, the same level of concentration in games that he maintains in practice. He needs to learn how to relax under pressure. He needs to learn how to stay focused on the *process* of his performance and not on the *outcome*. Focusing on outcome generates nervousness and over thinking. And when that happens thoughts like *I don't want to be the reason for the team losing!* or *I can't let my team down!* or *I can't let my coach (or father) down!* play over and over in their head. They have lost control of their concentration.

So what are some things a player can do to maintain his concentration? Hanson suggests:

- Have a pre-pitch routine.

- Breathe properly between pitches.

- Know how to carry yourself on the mound.

- Trust your body to perform.

It's been my experience that players are more willing to accept and try the first two than the last two because the first two are tangible. They are physical—you feel them—they are clear-cut—they are real.

It's just like when a coach suggests a change to your hitting mechanics. You see it—you accept it—you commit to it—no questioning about the merits.

The problem with the last two is that they have a mental aspect to them. They are vague, abstract. You can't see them. You can't wrap your arms around them. You question the merits of doing them. And because they are intangible it takes more of an effort to try them, accept them, and commit to them.

BREATHING AND A PRE-PITCH ROUTINE

If you want to control your performance you need to control yourself: your nerves, your thinking. One way to do that is to create a pre-pitch routine, which is a set series of steps to take prior to every pitch. It's a process. And that process should include not only taking a deep breath but a commitment to the breath.

Now, everyone's pre-pitch routine can be different. There are no set steps or number of steps. But to give you a sense of what a pre-pitch routine might be, see the following example:

- After throwing the ball take one step toward the catcher.

- After catching the ball walk to the back of the mound—two steps from the rubber.

- Touch the brim of your cap, close your eyes, and take a breath.

- As you step onto the rubber remind yourself of the game situation.

- As you take the sign from the catcher tell yourself something positive—i.e., "knee high strike."

The intent of the pre-pitch routine is to give the player a way to play the game one pitch at a time. To stay focused on the present time and not the past or the future. The intent is to keep the player thinking about the process of pitching right now, at this moment, and not the outcome of the last pitch (ball into the dirt—past time) or the possible outcome of the next pitch (Oh my God! What if I throw the ball in the dirt—again!—future time).

While using a pre-pitch routine helps you stay in the present moment and focus on the process of pitching, it also serves another purpose. It distracts you. Whoa! Distract you from what? Well, if between every pitch, no matter the outcome of the pitch, you follow your pre-pitch routine you won't have time to think about whatever your fears are. It's a way to block out expectation thoughts. It's a way to block out any past and future thoughts. It does so because between pitches there's not enough time to do both.

And to help make sure your pre-pitch routine is narrowing your focus to the present, you should talk to yourself. As you perform each of your steps, say them 'out loud'—to yourself. I'm not suggesting you actually say them out loud so that everyone can hear you, but rather say them 'out loud' to yourself so that you 'hear' them.

- After throwing the ball say to yourself, *One step to catcher.*

- After catching the ball tell yourself, *Go to the back of the mound.*

- When you get to the back of the mound, tell yourself to *face home plate.*

- Before stepping onto the mound, tell yourself, *Fix my hat; now close my eyes, now take a breath.*

- After you finish taking your breath, check in—ask yourself, *How do I feel?*

- After you check in, step onto the rubber and remind yourself of the game situation.

- As you take the sign from the catcher tell yourself something positive—i.e., *knee high strike.*

Every pre-pitch routine needs to include taking a breath. It helps both physically and mentally. Taking a breath:

- Helps release tension in your muscles. When something bad happens it leads to nervous and/or negative thinking, which leads to tense muscles and less fluidity. (Physical)

- Brings oxygen to your brain, which helps clear your thinking. (Physical)

- Enables you to "check in" with yourself to see if you are in control. If you can't get yourself to take a deep breath it may be because your mind is going too fast. (Mental)

- Helps you get control—slow the game down. The game seems to speed up when you aren't in control. (Mental)

- Energizes you when you are feeling sluggish. A sign of sluggishness is suddenly finding yourself yawning. (Physical)

- Helps you control your mindset. (Mental)

Now, I realize that there are many who will downplay the importance of a pre-pitch routine. It's been my experience that the most difficult instructional component within the framework of coaching is to convince players of the importance of the integral parts of their mental game. You see, everyone buys into the physical part. It's tangible. You see the strike outs. But can you prove it was only because of mechanics? Can you disprove that because you were mentally in control, you were in control of your mechanics? Is there a way to measure how the mental part plays on the physical part? That's the problem. There is no way of measuring. How many of your strike outs were a direct correlation of your pre-pitch routine—BEFORE EACH PITCH? There's no way to measure it, and that's why it's hard to for players to buy into it.

KNOW HOW TO CARRY YOURSELF

There is an old expression, "Body language speaks volumes." Body language is a nonverbal form of communication in which physical behavior is used to express or convey information. Body language is the window to your mind. Body language shows your thoughts and how you really feel. Body language is vital in athletics.

Gymnasts are asked to execute incredible displays of athleticism, but notice what all of them do when they finish their sets. They keep a cheery attitude—they smile—even after a bad performance. Even though it's the last thing they want to do. But they do so to gain control of their emotions. Smiling is a sign of positive body language.

Your body language tells your mind your confidence level. Confident athletes have a presence. Notice their display of positive emotion, how they act, after a successful play. It can be intimidating. A great example is the Boston Red Sox relief pitcher Craig Kimbrel. Have you seen him in his set position? Crouched over—arms extended out—staring down at the batter? Looking menacing! Talk about body language. How about the body language of a player who feels defeated or did not make the play—especially a critical game-changing play? They roll their shoulders, hang their heads, and look pained or sad. As someone once mentioned, players who look defeated are similar to a balloon deflating, as the air, adrenaline, and excitement leave their body. It wilts in sadness and frustration.

Developing the ability to control you in the heat of battle is an essential component of playing the game. When you are in control, all other aspects of playing well, such as making good decisions and using your best mechanics, become easier. Nerves of steel are an integral part of baseball, especially in high-stress situations with everything on the line.

As anyone involved in sports knows, confidence is critical for a player's success. Sports psychologist Tom Hanson feels that the player needs to project an air of confidence—have a sense of mission and purpose. "A pitcher might be scared to death in a game. But you can't show it. You must project confidence that lets your teammates know you are in control. If the body acts confidently, you will be confident. If you act confidence out, you begin to think it." And as H. A. Dorfman states in his book *The Mental ABC's of Pitching*, a pitcher needs to "establish the habit of acting who you want to be rather than the person you don't want to be. Winner or loser?"

TRUST YOURSELF

Terry Orlick, who has a PhD in sports psychology, states in his book *In Pursuit of Excellence*, you need to remind yourself that "you are not asking yourself to do anything unreasonable—only to perform as you can perform." What he is saying is that game situations should not control your trust level in yourself. When you are performing don't ask yourself to do something you can't do. Rather trust your preparation. Trust your instinct. If you threw well in the bullpen then you can trust you can do it in a game.

For example, if your average fastball is 85 MPH, then that is what you can throw. You can trust that. Commit to it. You know that when you perform you have the capacity to do that. When you don't trust you start to hope. Hoping to throw faster doesn't work because when you hope you are not committed. Deep down inside you know that's not you. At that moment you are asking yourself to do something unreasonable.

When you don't trust yourself you really are doubting yourself. And when there is doubt there is a tendency to hold back. For example, a pitcher who is afraid he is going to throw another ball slows down his arm speed and tends to guide the ball instead of throwing the ball. I'm sure you have heard the expression "He's aiming the ball." The result usually is a slow, hit-able ball. And as sports psychologist Alan Goldberg states in *Sports Slump Busting*, "Peak performance requires athletes to go all out at all times."

In the section on belief and trust, I used walking across a plank as an example of trusting your body. It goes like this: If I laid down a two-by-ten-foot plank on the ground and asked people to walk across it, everyone would probably do it because it's a no-brainer—no thinking—no doubts. They trust they can do it. But take that same board and raise it ten feet off the ground. Most people will slow down and hesitate to go across because they're thinking *I might fall off* or *If I fall, I might get hurt.* They have doubts. They are allowing the height of the plank to affect their belief system…their trust level. They aren't being asked to do something they can't do. They did it when the plank was laid on the ground.

Another example: I used to drive from Philadelphia to Pittsburgh. Because Pittsburgh is located on the other side of mountains, you have to drive through tunnels to get there. I was always amazed by how many cars that zoomed past me only to dramatically slow down as they approached and went through the tunnel. Then after going through the tunnel they would speed back up again. The width of the lanes were no different inside the tunnel than outside. I believe people slow down because all of sudden they don't trust themselves. *What if I hit the sides?* They see potential danger. And when that happens they are subconsciously questioning their ability to drive through the tunnel. They are allowing the tunnel walls to affect their belief system. The tunnel is not preventing them from doing something they were already doing. I'm pretty sure they didn't think *What if I drive off the side of the road* when they were not in the tunnels because they had already flown past me.

Think about when you go out a door. As you approach the door you gaze down—make eye contact with the door handle. But when you reach the door you don't keep your gaze on the handle; you lift your eyes up and open the door. You trust that you don't have to stare at the handle and that you will instinctively grab the door handle and that you won't walk into the door.

In a recent issue of *Sports Illustrated* there is a picture of Red Sox players in their locker room at Fenway Park. I noticed the following quote made by Carl Yastrzemski (commonly referred to as 'The Yaz') embossed on the wall: "I think about baseball when I wake up in the morning. I think about it all day and I dream about it at night. The only time I don't think about it is when I'm playing." What a great way to say trust yourself.

Lastly, one of the best quotes that sums up trusting your body to perform comes from the all-time great Ted Williams. "The master carpenter doesn't need to see the nail to hit it square every time."

I want to be clear—trusting yourself does not guarantee anything. It's a suggested process to help you get well. To get rid of your "White Line Fever." Terry Orlick conducted a study in which he interviewed some of the world's best athletes, coaches and scouts to get their views on the ingredients necessary to make it to the highest level in their sport. In his book *In Pursuit of Excellence,* he concludes: "Within each sport there was disagreement about the physical attributes ....but total agreement on the psychological (mental) attributes. Commitment and self-control were seen as the keys to excellence."

So for this to work you must be totally committed to focusing on trusting your body. You have to work at it. Be patient and persistent. Rome wasn't built in a day, which means important things take time, so 'White line fever" will not be solved or eliminated after one or two attempts. Just because you tried a pre-pitch routine once or twice, had what you thought was good body language and felt you had trust but still had bad results doesn't mean it doesn't work. It takes time. There are ups and downs. Improvement is a progression.

Wanting and willing are two different things. You control the 'willing." It starts at practice when you are doing your bullpen work or pitching in a scrimmage game. You must take the same approach as players developing their physical skills. In practice their goal is to develop muscle memory through constant repetition of tasks like fielding ground balls, bunting, etc. to the point where fielding the ball or bunting just happens. So at practice commit to constant repetition of your pre-pitch routine. Develop your mental memory. Reinforce it at home. Before falling asleep, while lying in bed, visualize your pre-pitch routine. Reinforce in your mind what it is you want to do. Your goal is to reach automatic pilot so that at game time, you just do it. You want to be as confident as that master carpenter Ted Williams mentioned.

ONE PITCH AT A TIME

While the expression "play the game one pitch at a time" may be familiar, the meaning may not be. What message is your coach sending when he says this? Do you know what he wants you to do? In most cases, players do not because coaches don't teach, know how, or spend time practicing playing the game one pitch at a time. They associate the statement with the physical aspect of playing the game rather than the mental aspect.

The message within the statement is to quiet your mind. Get control of your thoughts. Develop the right mindset. As Terry Orlick mentions in *In Pursuit of Excellence*, in order to have success you need to have control over your mind, your emotions, and your thought process. The problem is that it's easy to say but hard to do. Especially for baseball players.

Baseball is a sport that inherently has too much downtime between plays and pitches. It's a slow game. But most sports are fast paced—constant action—one play after another. If you miss a shot, or miss a tackle, get ready because here comes the next play. But not so in baseball. Think how long a batter must wait between his at bats. In baseball it's quite possible that throughout the game you might be involved in one defensive play and in some cases a ball might never come your way.

Too much downtime opens the door to too much thinking. Realize that almost all baseball training is focused on the 2 or 3 seconds of action—the ball is moving. But what are you doing during the crucial 15 to 20 seconds between pitches? Players are responsible for their thinking and they decide what they want to run through their heads between pitches, plays and at bats. But therein lays the problem. While some players decide to focus and do things to quiet their mind, too many clutter their head with noise. This noise comes in many forms, one of which is worrying—worrying about failing at the task at hand (I gotta get a hit!) or what players, coaches, or parents expect or think of you. Noise comes in the form of repetition, as in repeating statements like "I can't hit this guy." It can be visualization—reruns like in an old movie, visualizing over and over in your head your last strike out or the error you made.

I have read many books about the mental part of the game, and the one common suggestion to play the game one pitch at a time is to create, practice and commit to an at bat routine. It's a way to quiet your mind. It's the only moment in which you have the power to control the three parts of an At Bat: pre-pitch, during the pitch, and after the pitch.

The following is an example of an At Bat routine. You can create your own, one that you feel works for you. Then commit to it—on every pitch.

PRE-PITCH—Get ready.

- Just before stepping into the batter's box take a breath.

- Then put your back foot in and keep your front foot out of the batter's box.

- Look at the label on the bat and say to yourself—*I'm in control.*

- Now put your front foot into the batter's box and take two half swings (don't swing all the way around—think swing and stop when the bat is pointing at the pitcher)—think, *Big swing, big swing.*

- Now go into quiet mind mode—remind yourself of the pitch to anticipate probable pitch—use your cue card—visualize a baseball or say to yourself, *Ball, ball, ball.*

DURING THE PITCH - Perform

- Trust yourself—be confident.

- Your swing is on automatic pilot.

- Go, go, go to no NOT no, no, no to go.

- Swing at your pitch / strikes / the pitch—strike—dictated by the situation.

AFTER THE PITCH - Evaluate

- Take a 'lessons learned' approach.

- Quickly process what went right and what went wrong.

- Based on pitch count/pitcher's habits/result of that pitch, what do you need to do to respond?

The intent of a routine is to give direction to your thoughts and actions. But I think the most important intent is to put your mind on automatic pilot. It's the same as training to develop your swing—to develop muscle memory—but this is mind memory training. Once you approach your at bat, the only thing you are focusing on are the steps that make up your routine. Doing so blocks out or flushes all other thoughts and/or negative emotions.

Now, let's go back and look at the reasons behind some of the steps.

BEFORE EACH PITCH – Get Ready

- Take a breath—feel the breath. Take some of the tension out of your muscles and slow things down to control anxiety and nervousness.

- Look at the label on the bat and say to yourself—*I'm in control.* Check in with yourself—what zone are you in—past, present, or future? If you determine you are not in the present zone, it's time to call time out and step out of the box and start the process over.

- "Big swing, big swing" is a way to get loose, flex your muscles—a way to reinforce your swing muscle memory. It shows the pitcher your confident body language—you look like a hitter. Remind yourself to be aggressive.

- Cue cards are reminders that your only job up at the plate is to see the ball—pick up the ball at release point.

DURING EACH PITCH - Perform

- Trust yourself—commit to yourself.
- Your swing is on automatic pilot.
- "Go, go, go to no go NOT no, no, no to go"—controlled aggression. In your mind you are swinging until the location of the pitch tells you otherwise.

- Swing at your pitch. Look for the pitch that is dictated by pitch count or based on after-pitch evaluation. Depending on the pitch count, swing only at your pitch. Pitch counts dictate location and type of pitches thrown. Pitchers have pitch selection tendencies based on pitch counts (for example, on 0-2 does he always throw a down and away curve ball?).

AFTER EACH PITCH – Evaluate

- Take a lessons learned approach. What are the facts? What really happened?

- Analyze—be self-instructional and informative. For example, fouled off a tough pitch. Umpire called a pitch a ball—good eye. Swung at a strike—missed—but maintained balance. Swung at a pitch outside the strike zone—watch for curve next pitch.

Don't judge results. If you are telling yourself, *I should have driven that one* or *I always hit that low pitch, I can't hit his fast ball,* then you are beating yourself up. Judging is negative self-criticism. You are being hard on yourself.

Read the following except from an article about Mike Trout and his at bat routine. "I walk slowly to the plate and go through my routine with the bat and batting gloves and take that good, deep breath. A big thing for me is finishing that breath before I get back in the box. Once I finish that breath I'm ready to get back into the box. If I get beat on a pitch …I'll get out of the box, take a few deep breaths, finish them and tell myself something helpful like *See the ball up.* I'll review the last pitch to see what I did wrong. Once I get back in the box everything is in the past and I'm on to the next pitch. I look at it this way: He's got to beat me three times and I've only got to beat him once."

So Trout's at bat routine is as follows:

- Pre-pitch routine—"I walk slowly to the plate and go through my routine with the bat and batting gloves and take that good, deep breath."

- Breathing routine—finishing that breath means he feels the breath—he does not just go through the motions.

- Cue cards—"I tell myself something helpful like *See the ball up.*"

- Analyze—"I review the last pitch to see what I did wrong" means 'lesson learned,' not judgment.

If having an At Bat routine works for Mike Trout, then it might work for you.

AFTER THE AT BAT – ON THE BENCH

I prefaced this article by stating that baseball is a sport that inherently has too much downtime between plays and pitches. If you let it, that can be a bad thing. But downtime also gives you the chance to do a complete and thorough analysis of your at bat. Up at the plate you have seconds but on the bench you have minutes. On the bench is the time to analyze and NOT judge.

On the bench is when you should ask yourself; "What REALLY happened"? "I grounded out" is NOT the answer. That's the end result of the physical act of hitting the ball not an analysis. But 'I swung at a bad pitch" or "Pitcher threw a high fastball with 2 strikes" or "Late on the pitch" are. However if you want to know what REALLY happened you need to include an analysis of your mind set.

What was your mind set after the umpire called the way outside pitch a ball? With the runner in scoring position was 'I gotta get a hit' running through your head? Did you tell yourself you can't hit left hand pitchers? Were you still beating yourself up because of the error you made that let a run score? My point is that in order to know what REALLY happened you need to include 'checking in' on where your head was during the at bat. In order to make corrections you need to know what to fix? Is it physical or mentally or both? So don't waste bench time judging. If you do you are losing time to evaluate.

So what is the difference between judgment and evaluation? Evaluations are positive. Judgments are negative. Evaluation helps you determine what you want. Judgment can create confusion. Evaluation is expansive in nature. Judgments are constrictive. Evaluation gives you freedom of choice. Judgments limit your behavior. Evaluation merely states what is—in a neutral, objective manner. Judgment indicates an opinioned, subjective value. Evaluation can be seen as a mental or a scientific approach, while judgments are emotional in nature.

I once read that you lose control of your confidence when you judge yourself solely on your results, and I don't think I need to do much convincing on the importance of playing confidently. So evaluate, don't judge.

OTHERS

When faced with a pressure situation, some players see it as an opportunity to fail. They fear they might not perform to the expectations of "others." They fear the probable negative statements that will be made if the outcome of their performance is not positive. They have become conditioned to feel pain from the negative observations and statements that surely will be made by others.

Think about commercials and what advertisers are attempting to do. Companies pay tremendous amounts of money to create ads to promote products. The intent of an ad is to condition you to buy something. And to condition you, advertisers know that the controlling forces in our lives are pain and pleasure. Some people are motivated to take action—buy—if they feel it means avoiding pain, and some people are motivated to take action—buy—if they feel they will gain pleasure. Thus advertisers are trying to condition you to think a certain way the minute you see their ad, see their brand icon, or hear their jingle.

Let's look at Michelin tires. A past animated Michelin tire TV commercial showed a dad giving his daughter keys to what you can assume is her first car. Then the Michelin man throws new tires onto the car while the voiceover states, "You can't always protect her—make sure your tires will." As Dad is handing her the keys his daughter hugs him while mini windshield wipers on Dad's glasses wipe away his tears of joy. Good going, Dad—you are a winner! The intent of the ad is to get you to associate buying Michelin tires with insuring the safety of your child. Imagine the anguish if your child was involved in an accident. So buy the tires to avoid the pain of something dreadful happening and gain pleasure knowing that your child/family will be safe because of the tires. When you see the name Michelin you think safety. You are being conditioned.

You may be thinking *C'mon—what's one ad!* Well, Michelin (and other advertisers) is good at this process. They know you can't run one ad to get that message across to the consumer. So they run several more. Not the same one—new ones—but with the same message.

They followed up the original one. It went like this: While a voice can be heard expounding the quality of their tires, the ad shows a baby sitting in the middle of a tire which is slowly going round and round. The baby is wearing a fireman's hat and holding a hose. The voice continues to explain how well Michelin tires are made, but as the voice keeps going additional babies are added to the scene. These babies are also sitting in the middle of a tire, but each one is wearing a different hat and holding different objects associated with highly recognizable professions.

Same message. Same goal. Buy Michelin tires and you will avoid the pain of something dreadful happening to your future lawyer, teacher, or fireman, and by buying Michelin tires you gain pleasure knowing that they will be safe while driving. Good going, Dad—you are a winner!

Another favorite of mine is a recent Orkin TV ad. The scene is a new mom in the nursery room rocking her baby to sleep. Mom is staring lovingly at her baby. No words are said but the following message appears on the TV screen: "The Mitchells don't share their nursery with 200 cockroach hatchings. Home is where the bugs aren't." Orkin wants you to forget about the poisonous chemicals that are probably used in making whatever it is that is sprayed around the house. And there is a reason why they mention cockroaches, the bug that everyone associates as being filthy. So Mom and Dad, imagine walking into your baby's room and seeing a cockroach—A COCKROACH!—crawling across the baby's crib. Hire Orkin to avoid the pain of that ever happening and gain pleasure knowing that your child is safe from disease-spreading bugs. You are being conditioned to associate Orkin with cleanliness.

So who are these "others" and how are some athletes conditioned by them? Well, they are your parents, your friends, your teammates, society in general, and anyone else who you allow to determine what level of performance you must reach—all of whom consciously or unconsciously place too much emphasis or attention on athletic success as a measure of who is good, who is the best, who is a winner! Conversely, I contend that too much emphasis and attention are placed on athletes' failures as a measure of who is bad, who is the worst, who is a loser.

With social media and the Internet, we now live under a magnifying glass. Not only does information go viral right away, but for some reason, it has a permanency to it. So while the good is magnified on Facebook, Twitter, Instagram, Snapchat, and the like, so is the bad. Social media, particularly Twitter, can get crazy during and immediately after games. Win or lose, some fans have strong reactions to what they just watched. When things are going well and their team is winning, these fans are on top of the world. But when the team loses, it's time to bench players and fire everyone.

In the middle of the 2020 basketball season, Michigan State lost two games in a row for the first time that season. Apparently it got ugly. MSU head coach Tom Izzo was angry, but not so much at his team. He took aim at the Michigan State fan base. With a few fiery statements, Izzo blasted Spartan fans who had been abusing his players on Twitter. Via ESPN he stated, "I'm sick of it …Michigan State people out there that are abusing players on frickin' Twitter. I'm sick of dealing with what I gotta deal with on that …some of the stuff my guys have put in front of me …we're 16-7 not 5-20." Imagine—a winning season, but because it's not the level that the fans think it should be, the players are getting abused on social media. Apparently if you use Twitter you become a basketball expert!

Social media is obsessed with failures—think cyber bullying. Now not only are there too many ways to communicate mistakes but there are too many ways to communicate opinions. Opinions of others. Every day we learn of some devastating mistake an athlete has made that caused the team to lose or at the very least, changed the outcome of the game. Maybe we see or hear about it on ESPN. Maybe we watched the game and listened to the "expert" commentators give their opinions about the blunder. We listen to our friends' opinions of what happened at the school lunch table. We are bombarded with so-called expert advice.

So with this bombardment of communication, what's being emphasized? That someone did not perform—they failed. Or, as Gary Ward, former Oklahoma State head coach, states in an article in the October 2020 issue of *Collegiate Baseball*, "Blame, shame, judgment, and embarrassment are just a click away." Thus athletes think, *Imagine being that guy! Thank God that's not me!* I think we can all agree that failure has a negative connotation, and that some athletes subconsciously make that association. If they do, they can take it one step further and decide that if they fail they must be a loser. And who wants to be considered a loser?

How does this relate to an athlete's response to pressure? Well, if one of the controlling forces in our lives is pain, then, just like the goal of TV commercials, the bombardment of negative attention has that same conditioning effect on some athletes. They associate pressure as an opportunity to experience pain. When they compete, tension creeps in because they fear the ramifications of failing. Especially if it makes it into social media. *I don't want to be that guy! What if we lose? What if I don't get a hit? Oh my god! We have to win!*

For some players, social media, along with the everyday social pressures and parents, has become a source of anxiety. Others raise the level of importance, which in turn raises the level of pressure the player feels when he competes. So because an athlete wants to please others he becomes obsessed with thoughts like *I want to show them just how good I am. I'm going to make them proud of me. I hope I don't embarrass myself. I have to get a hit!* These are thoughts by someone who is trying to impress others. These are thoughts made by someone who is not competing for himself. These are thoughts of someone who doesn't realize that he doesn't have to prove himself to anyone. Players need to realize that baseball is what you do, not who you are.

In an interview after winning the 2015 ACC player of the year award, Deshaun Watson was asked about him possibly winning the Heisman trophy. He stated "The Heisman is not going to define me or who I am."

Players who are more concerned about their image have forgotten why they play the game. They imagine what will be said about them if they don't perform well, so for them the possibility of failing is a threat to their value as a person within their social community. "What will my parent, my friends, everyone think of me?"—a statement made by someone trying to avoid pain.

What these players don't realize is that they actually perpetuate their problem, because their fear of others affects their performance level. They suffer from "fear of chance." They believe that taking a chance is a bad risk—an opportunity to fail, not an opportunity to succeed. So they never take risks. They play tentatively and cautiously. They become indecisive in whether they should respond physically.

They play it safe. And because of their hesitancy, if and when they do react, it usually does not go well. Thus they perpetuate the problem.

Look at the following chart of types of chances and players' fears about them:

CHANCE	FEAR
Pitcher will not attempt to pick the runner off first base	I might throw the ball away
Pitcher never attempts a second throw against the same runner	I got lucky the first time—I might throw it away the second time
Pitcher throws the ball away on a pick off—never throws over again—in the game	I threw it away the last time—will probably throw it away again
Runner shortens lead at first after getting steal sign from coach	I might get thrown out
Runner gets thrown out trying to steal—never tries again	I got thrown out the last time—will probably get caught again
High fly ball, two players try to get under it—they look back and forth at each other—no one gets it	I might miss it— "You get it" NO "You get it"
Coach gives bunt sign	What if it goes foul

Let me tell you what happened to a varsity high school baseball team I recently helped coach. Because it was my first year there, I was unfamiliar with the players and thus did not know what to expect. Well, what I encountered was a group of players who practiced hard and were focused and willing to learn.

So when the season started, we all had high expectations. But at about one-third of the way into the season we had not won a single game. In fact every game was ugly. After another loss, the next day at practice, I noticed that the players' energy level, their focus level, was off. In fact they just went through the motions. After the practice I mentioned my observations to the head coach, who agreed and then proceeded to tell me that the reason for their attitude was that they were being harassed in school. Apparently after the first few losses some of their classmates, in particular the football players, had something to say. Add to that, the girls softball team, a team that had a history of always losing, had a winning record. Even the girls were winning!

Now, here's my take on how the team reached the *just go through the motions* point. As the losses mounted, we can assume that so did the comments. And they were probably more negative than positive. I made it a point to mention that the football team was behind a majority of the comments. They had a successful season and even made playoffs, so how do you think the football players felt about themselves? How do you think they portrayed themselves to their classmates, their peers, their friends? Winners or losers? Better than the baseball players? It is safe to say that the baseball players were probably reminded that even the girls were better than they were? I'm sure "y'all suck" was mentioned a few times.

So every day, in the hallways, during class, I'm sure even at the lunch table, someone had something to say. Think of the tweets. It became a bombardment of negative comments—so much so that it was brought to the attention of the head coach. And if it reached that point, then I'm sure the players felt it was harassment.

How did this situation arise? The baseball team allowed others to have too much influence over them. They elevated the pressure of others' opinions and comments over the actual pressure of playing the game. Remember what I said about advertisers. They know that the controlling forces in our lives are pain and pleasure. Because the players felt they were victims of harassment, they reached the point where they were conditioned to associate playing baseball with pain.

When a team loses often, it's normal for the players to get into a "we have to win" mindset. But for this team it wasn't just to gain pleasure in winning; their "have to win" mindset intensified because they wanted to avoid the pain of harassment. So when players feel they need to perform well, it increases the level of the pressure, which affects the outcome of their performance. They internally beat themselves up, and the first thing that happens is that they start to press. But when you press, you play tense, and playing tense usually leads to poor play. The poor play really comes from the fact that at this point the players don't feel good about themselves. Doubt dominates their mind. They have lost their confidence. They can't do anything right.

Eventually they lose their passion for the game. When you enjoy playing the game, you are having fun. When it's fun you place less pressure on yourself to perform. And when it's fun you have confidence. You are comfortable competing, which allows your talent to flow. But because of others, the high school team forgot why they played baseball. Because of others, they were getting attention, but unfortunately it was negative attention. Ultimately what happened was others stole the fun out of playing. They took away any enjoyment of participating. The players felt they were not going to gain pleasure by playing.

So by the time we reached that day at practice, the players were mentally beat and could only go through the motions. They had allowed others to take away the two reasons why players participate in any sport—to have fun and to compete. They had become conditioned to associate playing as an opportunity to lose—again—and an opportunity to be harassed.

Now, realistically, not all players are affected by the opinions of others, and I'm sure many of you feel that this doesn't apply to you. But I think subconsciously some players simply won't admit it. They refuse to accept that they are influenced by others. The definition of subconscious is "the part of the mind of which one is not fully aware but which influences one's actions and feelings." It's easier to say "I just had a bad day" than to stop and think—dig deep—to confirm what your thoughts really were to determine if they were elsewhere. And that's why away from practice, after the game, at home resting, you have to force yourself to stop everything; take some time to think deep and try to remember really what is/was running through your mind. If you don't, then you will never really know if others have an effect on you. If you don't, you are subconsciously avoiding being honest with yourself.

Let's go back to the Bill Buckner story and the aftermath of his one mistake.

In the bottom of the tenth inning of the sixth game of the 1986 World Series, Bill Buckner, playing first base for the Boston Red Sox, booted a ground ball hit by Mookie Wilson of the NY Mets. This allowed the winning run to score and capped an improbable comeback. It became the most famous error in World Series history, because by winning the game, the Mets tied the series and forced a seventh game. Which they won! Boston losing the World Series was blamed on Bill Buckner. Boston fans spoke unbelievably harsh about him. Sports writers across the county weren't kind either.

While it took a while for the criticism to stop, the association of losing/failure continued. Whenever a player made an error, sports announcers would refer to the play as "the player Bill Bucknered." In an article I read about the incident, the author referred to it as being iconic, which is defined as "widely known and acknowledged for distinctive excellence," but for some reason this author chose to use the word to insinuate that it acknowledged a distinctive failure. In the spring of 1996, Bill Buckner was named the hitting coach for a Major League team. When his appointment was announced, an article that appeared in my local newspaper contained the following quote by the team's manager when he was questioned by the local sportswriter as to why hire Bill Buckner and not someone else: "We hired him to teach hitting, not fielding." Think about it. That was ten years later.

But wait—there's more! In September 2016, I was watching a baseball game, and of course between innings there are commercials. Guess who the main characters were in one of the TV ads? Mookie Wilson and Bill Buckner, who became forever linked to that fateful play. They were part of an ad for the MLB Network. The advertisers wanted the viewers to associate Bill Buckner with the iconic mistake. Their message? If something like THAT happens this year, as a baseball fan, you don't want to miss it. So be sure to watch MLB Network.

Thirty years later, when Mookie Wilson was interviewed about the TV ad, he stated, "In all honesty I thought it was something that a week later would be forgotten …I underestimated the power of sports in people's minds and what it means in people's lives."

Here's the shame of it all. Bill Buckner was portrayed as a failure—synonymous with losing. Everyone focused on the end result and not the facts—what really happened. Let's review the game.

After the Sox scored two runs and took the lead in the top of the tenth, instead of bringing in a defensive replacement, Boston manager John McNamara chose to keep Buckner in the game for what should have been the final three outs. This not only would have been a sound baseball move, but it was something he had already done in games one, two and five because he knew that Buckner could not move very well. Buckner had a history of ankle issues. In fact Buckner twice had ankle surgery. Failure #1.

The Mets came back to tie the game when the Red Sox pitcher, Calvin Schiraldi, gave up three straight two-out singles. Failure #2. Schiraldi was replaced with relief pitcher Bob Stanley, who proceeded to throw a wild pitch. Run scores—tie game. Failure #3.

So there were three failures prior to that infamous ground ball. Failures NOT made by Bill Buckner. But regardless, *others* decided who to blame. They chose Bill Buckner and he became the iconic scapegoat.

That's what happened in the game. Now let's look at Bill Buckner the player. A quick summary of how well he performed as a player shows that he accumulated over 2,700 hits in his twenty-year career. He has a .289 career batting average. He has won a batting title and was an all-star with the Cubs. Here's my favorite stat. In 1985, one year prior to that fateful game, he set the Major League record for assists by a first baseman in a season with 184. Which is a record that stood for 25 years.

Now that you know the facts, would you consider him a winner or a loser? Unfortunately, because of where the emphasis was placed, we have been conditioned to associate him with losing. Who wants to be that guy! With the social media of today, ramifications of failing are immediate. Maybe now you know why some athletes become conditioned to see pressure situations as an opportunity to fail. To be a loser.

PRESSURE

Pressure is defined as a perceived expectation of the need to perform well under challenging situations. It goes without saying that with any competition, naturally, there is pressure of some kind, so it should come as no surprise that whenever an athlete puts his talents on display and holds them up for public scrutiny, it's natural to feel some nervousness. But pressure is something you create for yourself, not the situation you are in when competing.

I have read many articles about athletes and pressure, and there is always one recurring theme: Pressure makes athletes tense, afraid, nervous, and worried. Every player has their own thoughts toward pressure, and their mental response—how they handle it—has an effect on their physical response and in turn the outcome of their performance. Sports psychologist Dr. Patrick Cohn states, "Worrying about results, game conditions, and the opposing team can increase the sense of pressure experienced by ball players." He refers to them as the 'triggers for worry." Just like a gun—pull the trigger and the gun goes off and the bullet heads to the target—if a player focuses on the wrong things—worries—he will trigger the feeling of pressure when faced with certain situations.

CHOICE

Some players see pressure situations as an opportunity to succeed and some players see them as an opportunity to fail. The perception of those who feel it's an opportunity to fail view pressure as a threat. And when faced with pressure situations, because they feel threatened, they increase their sense of the pressure. Once a player feels the pressure is too excessive he has allowed the pressure to get to him.

Let's look at what happens when players feel the pressure is too excessive and how it affects their performance negatively:

- They freeze up in games.

- They over think their next action.

- They play tentatively, cautiously.

- They are afraid to make mistakes.

- They get anxious or worried about the outcome.

Excessive pressure can cause you to lose focus on what really matters, which is focusing on the process or what you need to do in the present to play optimally. Focusing on what makes you feel pressure tends to turn performance into a perceived life-or-death proposition.

But you have a choice as to how you perceive pressure. You are responsible for your thoughts. You control your belief system, your mindset. You can choose to focus on how good you will feel when you are successful or you can choose how bad you will feel if you fail. No one makes you associate mistakes with being a loser, so you and only you control how you will handle an error, and you and only you control how you will handle pressure.

When facing pressure situations, you have two choices as to what to focus on. Let's assume you are a pitcher facing bases loaded, 2 outs, and last inning. You have two choices. You can focus on what sports psychologist Dr. Patrick Cohn called "triggers for worry":

- The last pitch missed
- Walking the batter
- The importance of the situation
- How teammates or coaches will respond if a run scores
- Poor conditions, such as the wind
- The pitch being hit back to him
- Worrying about losing his spot on the team

Or you can choose to focus on the things you can control like:

- The process of throwing the ball
- Your routine for the pitch
- Selecting the right pitch to throw
- Visualizing the pitch
- Setting up
- Focusing on the target

So how do you handle pressure? Your nerves? Do you accept the pressure and the nervousness that comes with it or do you fight it? Do you recognize that nervousness is simply the desire to do well? Do you know that some level of nervousness is common in all performers? What does pressure do to you MENTALLY? Are you in control of your nerves? Have you ever taken an honest evaluation of your attitude toward pressure when placed in a competitive situation?

I'm asking these questions because it's the athlete who ultimately determines the size, scope, and extent of the pressure. If you can't control your nerves, your perception of the 'value of the contest' or the 'value of the situation' will increase the level of nervousness. And how you manage your perception will have an effect on the outcome of your physical performance.

Self-Control ->>>> Body Control ->>>>> Skill Control.

In the 7/16/18 *Sports Illustrated*, there was an article by Tom Verducci about Mike Trout, who plays for the Angels. The subtitle tells you: "Baseball's best player is having a season for the ages (Again!), But as the Angels struggle (Again!)." In the article Verducci states, "His excellence goes wasted by his franchise and maddeningly unappreciated by fans." One of the Angels' coaches, Dino Ebel, mentions a conversation he had with Mike Trout when he was a rookie. He was so inspired by Trout's sunny outlook that he went to him and said, "You come to the ballpark every day and you smile. You love being out there. You go 1 for 19 and everybody thinks, *What's wrong with Mike Trout?*—and you are the same guy. You never change."

That conversation was seven years ago. "A thousand games later, it hasn't changed a bit," Ebel says. "It's even getting better. I've never seen this guy come in, look at somebody and be down. He says hi to everybody, smiles at everybody. Every single day. A bad mood? Even on a bad day—we lose, he's 0 for 4—and he's the same guy. I've never seen this guy not being Mike Trout."

Based on the subtitle it would be understandable if Trout was upset or had a chip on his shoulder, but as you can see it is not the case. Trout chooses not to let what could be considered a negative to control him. Thus the reason why, as of right now, he is "baseball's best player." He chooses to control his nerves and has self-control, which enables him to have body control so that he can optimize his skill.

Self Control ->>>> Body Control ->>>> Skill Control

CHALLENGE

Accept pressure as a challenge. It's an opportunity for success. Look up the word "challenge" in the dictionary: "an invitation to competition." Whenever, as a coach, I have asked players why they play baseball, two of the most common answers are "It's fun" and "I like the competition." So if you play baseball because you like the competition then you must learn to enjoy the pressure that you know comes with competition. Accept pressure situations as your personal invitation to compete because it's fun. Otherwise, why are you playing?

Brian Cain is considered one of the foremost sports authorities on mental performance. He has an idiom concerning accepting pressure as a challenge called 'The Life of the Palm Tree." It goes like this: Palm trees will bend but will not break. They will roll with the wind and adversity, staying flexible under pressure in their strategy to survive the storm. The palm tree knows that it must adapt to the challenge and that when the challenge has passed it can pop right back up and continue to grow. Unlike the oak tree that is rigid, inflexible and has to get its way or it will buckle under pressure, the palm tree is flexible, chooses a path that works for the situation and then pops right back up ready to fight another round.

To go back to the *Sports Illustrated* article, Mike Trout is asked "What's the best part of hitting?" His response is "You have control of what you are doing. You're in the box. It's your box. I love hitting. You put in all that time and practice ….it's so much fun. I enjoy it so much." When the author, Tom Verducci, hears this he questions him. "The pitcher is the one in control …. You can only react to what he does." Trout responds, "I flip it. Because you know your zone …..you have to go in that box and own it. Think positive and it's yours." Now that sounds like someone who has embraced the competition, the challenge, and is having fun doing it.

Ironically, while I was writing this section, I received an email from Dr. Patrick Cohn, founder and owner of Peak Performance Sports, which specializes in sports psychology. He is a mental training expert in how beliefs, attitudes, and mindsets influence performance. In his email he listed a couple of key strategies athletics can take to help with their performance. One of them caught my eye immediately. He stated: "Remind yourself that baseball is a game and it's the reason you started playing in the first place. Baseball is not a life-or-death matter; it is a game of exciting challenges. He maintains that if you view the game as a challenge, you are more likely to be confident and maintain enthusiasm for the game."

NEXT DAY

Have a 'Next Day' approach. Start over! Brian Cain, a consultant in the mental game of baseball, states that if you truly want to win, you must focus on WIN: What's Important Now. And what's important is today. "Winning is the byproduct of being where you need to be when you need to be there. Be in the present moment ...for this marathon known as the game of baseball."

As we all know it's easy to come play every day when things are going well. But the challenge is when they are not. So look forward to the next day. Truth be told, the best part about the previous day's game or practice is that it's over. If you did poorly you can't change it, so forget about it because today is an opportunity to do better. A day to work on what you need to fix. If yesterday was an impressive win, then today represents a chance to do it all over again. Good or bad, whatever happened yesterday should not affect the way you go about your business today.

Remember, it's wrong to think that your performance determines who the best or worst is. That moment of glory does not make you a champion for life. It does not determine or change who you are. It merely establishes who did the best on that day. And conversely, that 'mistake' moment does not make you a failure. It merely establishes who was off his game on that day.

Realize that sometimes your best just might not be good enough. A good example of this is what happened to Yankees pitcher Mariano Rivera in the seventh game of the 2001 World Series against the Arizona Diamondbacks. Keep in mind that if you are playing a seventh game, this is it—win and you are the champs. As anyone who follows baseball knows, locking down a championship often falls on the shoulders of a closer, not a starter. Like umpires, closers performances are rarely remembered unless they stumble. Mariano Rivera, who at that time had saved more games than any other closer, experienced one of the most memorable World Series moments.

Rivera gave up a single to Arizona's Luis Gonzalez that scored the winning run and thus the World Series for Arizona. The single capped a thrilling come-from-behind ninth inning for Arizona. But here's what most fans forget. With the bases loaded in the ninth inning, the Yankees decided to play their infield in for a possible play at the plate. They were trying to prevent the winning run to score. But Gonzalez's single was really a 'blooper'—a 'bleeder'—just over short-stop Derek Jeter's outstretched glove. If the Yankees played at normal depth, Gonzalez's so-called single would have easily been caught and the game would have gone into extra innings.

Think about it. Mariano Rivera threw a great pitch—the right pitch—which in most cases would have gotten Gonzalez out. Instead he experienced what turned out to be one of the most memorable World Series moments. When asked about the game and that moment by a reporter, he states, "We gave everything, I gave everything, the whole team gave everything, and we fell short. Sometimes your best is not enough."

So no matter what happens—good or bad—move on!

WHO CARES

Develop a selfish, "who cares?" mindset. Now, don't misunderstand. Do care about winning and losing. Do care about your team and teammates. But don't care or worry about others' expectations or opinions. They are theirs, not yours. You can't control theirs but you can control yours. Let's reference a few successful sports figures to illustrate what I mean.

In the October 3, 2016 issue of *Sports illustrated* there was an article about David Ortiz of the Boston Red Sox—a look back on his career.

Back in 2003, a report came out with a list of players who were said to have tested positive for steroids. Ortiz's name was on that list. Obviously he denied that he took steroids, and Major League Baseball agreed that not all on the list were considered positive. Major League Baseball also admitted that they didn't even know what the substance was associated to the players. As a side note, Ortiz has never failed a drug test. But with all that said, people—others—believe what they want to believe, so whenever there is a discussion about Ortiz's greatness or if he will make it to the Baseball Hall of Fame, the naysayers bring up the steroid stain.

During the course of the interview Ortiz was asked what he could do to convince people otherwise. The following is his answer: "I don't think 1 can do anything. A noise comes out, and so you think I'm going to sit down and believe what somebody I don't know comes off saying. You know, the reality is that it's a noise…" While he does not say the words 'I don't care', his attitude does. To him it's noise—no big deal—"I don't care what others say!" And because he has this attitude, the "noise" does not disrupt his performance.

The opening paragraph of the *Sports Illustrated* article sums up his performance. "The man known as Big Papi is the all-time leader among designated hitters in hits, home runs and runs batted in; one of the game's greatest post season clutch hitters, and one of the most beloved players in Red Sox history. Babe Ruth, Mickey Mantle, Reggie Jackson, and Ortiz are the only players to have hit at least 500 home runs and won three or more World Series Titles."

Then there is Justin Thomas, who in 2018 was considered the PGA Tour's best golfer. In a *Sports Illustrated* article about him, the author mentions that during the interview there was a discussion about his clubs, which were built exactly to his specifications. "Thomas doesn't know even what kind of shafts he has in his irons. Asked how much the shafts weigh, he looks at the driver and says, 'This one is 60 grams. It says it.' Turns out it's actually 68 grams. Thomas goes on to say, 'It drives Tiger Woods absolutely insane that I don't know anything about my clubs.'"

I would imagine Tiger Woods is not the only PGA tour member who feels this way. But Thomas stated, "I don't care. I get fitted ... I use them and I play well with them. So what's the big deal?" He doesn't care what others think about the importance of knowing shaft weights. This is important because golf is largely a game of mental discipline, and Justin Thomas understands that caring about others' opinion might affect his game.

Let's not forgot one of the greatest quarterbacks who ever played—Tom Brady. An article in *ESPN the Magazine* just prior to the 2017 Super Bowl focused on his legacy and stated that Tom Brady "has little to say about anything outside of the required postgame comments."

In the article Brady spoke openly about his favorite book, *The Four Agreements* by Don Miguel Ruiz, and how its four tenets provided him with a road map for much of his thirties. These four tenets have given him direction in his life as a professional football player:

• Be impeccable with your word.

- Don't take anything personally.

- Don't make assumptions.

- Always do your best.

Brady stated; "It's kind of a mantra for my life. A lot of times, it's not about you. It's about how others feel about themselves and not necessarily about me personally." This sounds like someone who has a "Who cares' mindset. I don't have to list any of Brady's stats to confirm how good he was. His performance has not been disrupted.

Speaking of mantra, how about Tim Tebow's? He left the NFL and after more than a decade after he last played in high school, he decided to try playing baseball. So because of an invitation from the NY Mets in the spring of 2017, he attempted to start a new career. You can only imagine what was written and said about him and his chances.

Upon his arrival he was fully aware that no one was expecting him to succeed. He is quoted as saying, "I'm not going to worry about what everyone's written or what everybody's thinking. I think, for me, I just want to be able to continue the process, enjoy the process, enjoy every day, get to know my teammates and have some fun out there."

While he did realize how big of a challenge he had in front of him, he stated, "I think part of the challenge in it being so hard is part of why it's so much fun and why it's something that I'm enjoying and loving. It's a hard game, it's not easy …but I enjoy the process very much." Just a side note, as of the day I'm writing this, he has been promoted and is currently playing Triple A professional baseball.

And then there is Lamar Jackson, the quarterback for the Baltimore Ravens. During a postgame interview during the 2019 season, he wore a T-shirt that had the quote "Nobody Cares; Work Harder." A reporter asked him if that was a statement about his mentality. He stated "Absolutely. That's every day. Nobody cares about what you're doing. You've got to work harder. If you want to be the best, you've got to work hard at being the best. If they are doubting you, work harder, it doesn't matter. It's their opinion. I'm just going to go."

As far as others, you need to remind yourself of the old expression "If it was easy everybody would be doing it." So don't care what others think or say because they can't or won't do what you do. Because it's hard! Maybe, just maybe, others don't attempt to do what you do because they are fearful of the possible ramifications if they fail. They aren't accepting or facing a challenge, but you are. So when you hear "y'all suck" be sure to say to yourself "Who cares." You are with your friends; you're competing and having fun.

If you think about it, baseball is not inherently stressful. If it was, most people would not play. So if you are finding yourself doing well in practice but struggling in the game, I suggest you think about how you are handling the pressure of competition or what others might think or say. Don't assume everything is okay mentally. And when you do analyze how you're handling the pressure, you absolutely have to make it honest (be impeccable). Don't take it personally. Do take responsibility for your mindset. Remember, nobody controls your heart, your soul, or your mind except you. Do accept the challenge to correct your mindset. And do try your best to make corrections to your mindset. Your mental response to pressure will have a direct bearing on your physical response.

PULLING THE ROPE

Ever wonder what is it that makes a team—in any sport—a champion? A noted sports psychologist was asked this very question. When he gave his answer he needed a reference point, so he chose the 2011 World Series Champions, the St. Louis Cardinals. He stated that they became champions because they had team energy; they felt unstoppable. Everyone contributed. It was a "lesson in teamwork. They had THE FORCE."

So what the heck is 'THE FORCE'? The first thing that comes to mind is the individual player's physical performance. It's tangible; you can see it. However, there is more to THE FORCE than physicality. If you want the team to become champions, you need to include a mental component for a complete teamwork attitude.

To have complete teamwork attitude—THE FORCE—you need mental and emotional fortitude. Mental fortitude is described as the ability to focus on and execute solutions when in the face of adversity. Emotional fortitude is the ability to mentally and emotionally weather setbacks, disappointments, failures and frustrations.

Rather than use physiology jargon, let's look at a couple of true examples.

During the 2012 Olympics, two days prior to the gymnastics women's team event, Jordyn Wieber, the USA team's best gymnast and reigning world champion, had a less than stellar performance. So much so that she placed fourth and in turn did not even qualify to participate in the finals. All of the 'expert' commentators, the coaches, the fans, everyone picked her as the sure thing! Not only was she expected to make the finals but she was also picked to win it all.

I'm sure you can imagine how often and what the media said about her failing. Think about how devastated she felt. Imagine the loss of millions of dollars in endorsements. This was probably the most crushing moment of her gymnast life.

Now here's the intrigue. For team events, only 5 performers from the team are selected to participate. Well, it turns out that not only had Jordyn already been selected to be part of the team event, but she was the very first gymnast to perform in the USA's rotation for the opening round. How would she respond after such a huge personal disappointment? How would she respond after all of the articles and sport reporter's pontification about her failure? She nailed her landing, and not only did she not falter in any of the other events, but the American team went on to win the Gold medal and became World Champions.

The following is a quote from an article that appeared in the August 1, 2012 issue of *USA Today*. "An indication of her mindset might have come from a tweet earlier Tuesday: TEAM FINALS TODAY!! Really feeling the USA spirit and we are ready to go!!!!" And how about what she said during her interview after the Team event was over: "Today was pretty good redemption. I was pretty disappointed. I knew I had to mentally turn it around for the team."

Then there is the story about Hunter Pence, who at the time was the right fielder for the San Francisco Giants. To say he struggled in the 2012 Playoffs would be an understatement. This is how bad it was: Going into Game 2 of the World Series he had only 9 hits in 51 at bats and his on base percentage was a dismal .189. More than 81 percent of the time Pence stepped to the plate in the playoffs and through Game 1 of the World Series, the result was a Giant's out. You would think it couldn't get worse but it did. He struck out 14 times in 13 games and hit into two double plays. So imagine how he felt. But the following are some quotes/statements that were made about him or from him during his physical performance struggles:

"Throughout the playoffs Pence has exhorted his teammates to play for one another, stressing that the team's collective belief is stronger than any player's ego. Pence led the emotional charge, delivering raucous speeches that became a staple of the run through the Cincinnati Reds, Cardinals and Tigers. San Francisco's Closer Brian Wilson said, 'I saw Hunter Pence being that leader that everyone on the team looks to because he's …. Always in good spirits.'"

When a reporter told Pence what his brother thought was the reason for his struggles, his response was "He did not know what he was talking about. I've been having a blast. They pitched me good." Pence added, "There have been tough times, but I feel like I've had a pretty fortunate life ….with good friends and a supportive family around me. To be a part of the major leagues, I feel really spoiled. The main thing is to play for each other, to give everything we have."

Things started to change for him in Game 2. Pence ignited the key seventh-inning rally by the Giants, scoring the first run of the game and then later driving in the second run with a sacrifice fly in a 2-0 Giants victory. Want to guess who won the World Series that year?

Wieber and Pence's mental and emotional fortitude was instrumental in the team having THE FORCE. They both know that when you are not physically performing there are other ways to help the team. They chose to not let their personal failings affect the team's performance. Instead of putting their heads down and feeling sorry for themselves, they chose to remain positive. They did not have an 'it's all about me' attitude. They took a complete teamwork attitude.

Complete teamwork attitude is like playing tug of war, with your whole team on one side of the rope. Ideally, all individuals, together, pull straight back—straight in the direction of the goal—the team goal. However, while on the surface it appears that all the players are pulling straight back, others—individuals—are pulling to the side, to a direction they want to go.

Perhaps they pull in the 'I—Me' direction, where they are interested in only their stats—their personal performance—wanting to look good. Or they pull in the 'whine' direction—"Boo Hoo", "Poor me," "I'm in a slump," "I'm no good." No matter which direction they pull, they are selfish. And selfish thoughts are detrimental to team unity. Players who put their own failings or success above the good of the team, players with these self-promotion thought patterns, are pulling the tug of war rope in a direction other than a straight line path—the path to the team goal.

So what helps make a team a champion? Great tug of war players! Everybody contributes. Players who pull the rope in the right direction—like Wieber and Pence—understand that contributions come in different shapes. They know that the shape of their contribution will be by performing well mentally. Their contribution is to choose to accept responsibility for their thinking. Just like you can choose how to react when you strike out 14 times in 13 games or you don't qualify for the individual finals.

Wieber and Pence made the right choice as to what to think about. They chose not to whine. They chose not to pout. They chose to take it in stride—to move on. They chose to pull the rope in the right direction. The only thing they could control that could help the team was how they responded to their adversity.

So let's go back to my question. What helps make a team a champion? It's everyone on the team taking responsibility for their own thinking. As individuals, we have choices. No one forces thoughts into our head. You, as an individual, choose what to think about and you, and only you, choose how to act. You have to take ownership of your thoughts. Or as a quote from the book *Heads-Up Baseball* states, "Taking responsibility for your thinking means choosing what to think and how to act rather than blindly reacting to the events around you."

In 2010, *Sports Illustrated* selected Derek Jeter as their Sportsman of the Year. And of course they ran an article about him. During the interview he was asked what he thought were obstacles to winning. While he named five, the following three convince me that he understands complete team attitude. He knows what direction to pull the rope.

Self-promoters. "I never liked people who talked about themselves all the time, gloat," he says. "If you're accomplished and have done things, people will talk about it for you. I don't think you have to point it out. I'm not judging anybody. That's just the way I am."

Measuring success by individual statistics. "In this day and age, not just in baseball but in sports in general, all people care about is stats, stats, stats," he says. "You've got fantasy this, and fantasy that, where you pay attention to stats. But there are ways to win games that you don't get a stat for."

Negativity. Jeter wants nothing to do with negative questions from reporters or negative talk from teammates. He once went 0 for 32 and refused to admit he was in a slump. "We weren't allowed to use the word can't—"I can't do this, can't do that", Jeter says of his childhood. "My mom would say, 'What? No.' She's always positive. I don't like people always talking about negative, negative, negative, because once you get caught in that mindset, it's hard to get out."

Understand that an individual can set the stage for the team. Imagine Team USA's psyche if Jordyn Wieber had performed poorly on her opening routine. What would his team's demeanor be if Pence's actions led to him being the proverbial 'cancer on the team'?

Champions emerge when talent, leadership and sometimes good fortune—I call it fairy dust—are combined with everyone pulling in a straight line path to the team goal. Champions emerge when each individual player on the team understands that how they respond to their poor performance—whether it's real or perceived—can affect the team's performance. How individuals respond can determine if a team gets that thing called THE FORCE.

Now of course, everyone pulling in the same direction doesn't guarantee success. But it does give you your best chance. Remember, reaching team goals is usually more rewarding than individual accomplishments. So the next time your team wins but you go 0 for 5 with 2 strike outs, what direction will you pull the rope? Which tug of war guy are you? Are you the guy pulling in a straight line path toward the team goal or are you the guy pulling to the side? What's your contribution? Is it positive or negative? No wait! Change that question—is it positive or selfish?

QUICKSAND

We have all watched an adventure movie where one of the characters falls into quicksand. They always do the same thing—panic and begin flailing their arms and legs. And in a matter of minutes they sink away, because flailing their arms and legs is the worst thing they can do. The only thing they are successful in doing is forcing themselves farther down.

Truth is, it's not as hard as you may think to escape from quicksand. The correct thing to do is to make slow movements to bring you to the surface. Then just lie back and eventually you will float to a safe level. While quicksand remains a danger in adventure movies, there's very little to be afraid of in real life. As long as you keep a cool head in the situation and stay calm, the worst result will be a shoe full of wet sand.

What does this have to do with baseball?

There are two common denominators between the person in quicksand and a hitter who thinks he's not hitting: fear and panic. And they occur in that order.

While the person in quicksand fears he is going to drown, the hitter who thinks he's not hitting fears he is failing. And when that happens—in both cases—panic occurs. Panic brings about thrashing and flailing. However, there is a difference between the two. The telltale signs of panic from the person in quicksand are obvious. You see the physical action of his arms and legs.

But with the hitter, it's not obvious because you can't see the signs of panic. His thrashing and flailing are going on in his head! That's right! In his head! It's a mental action—technically (I'll explain the technical part later).

For a hitter this is the worst thing he can do. His thrashing and flailing come in the form of:

- Thinking too much

- Blaming mechanics

- Losing patience

As time goes on, the telltale signs eventually do show up physically. Signs like swinging at pitches way out of the strike zone or taking too many pitches, especially with 2 strikes. Another very common sign is the sudden obsession with spending MORE time in the batting cage.

These players never consider what might be the best and easiest thing to do. What was the advice if you fall into quicksand? The best thing to do is to make slow movements. Well, guess what—that's exactly what hitters need to do when they are not happy with their hitting or even when they decide to make a change in their mechanics. Take it in slow movements—Small steps—one thing at a time.

Instead of stepping back and thinking, analyzing their at bats, some players immediately run to their batting coach, thinking they are doing something physically wrong. But the reality is they don't understand why they aren't hitting the ball well. They have fallen into quicksand. They may be right in thinking that something is physically wrong, but it might not be their swing. Could it be something other than mechanics? Maybe!

I feel the number one reason for poor performance at the plate is mis-timing the pitch. And some players may mis-time the pitch because they are not physically seeing the ball well. As Tony Abbatine, a sports consultant wrote in an article for *Collegiate Baseball Newspaper* (3/9/18), "The mechanics of hitting are worthless once the game starts. But a player's ability to be on time and be able to recognize speed and location is what makes them hitters."

Warren Sphan, a famous Hall of Fame pitcher, once said, "Hitting is timing. Pitching is upsetting timing." Then there is what Geoff Zahn, ex Major League pitcher, now baseball clinician, wrote for an article in the 7/12/19 issue of *Collegiate Baseball*: "Pitchers today must make the hitters change the timing of their swing through the zone. While it is true that there are more pitchers throwing harder today than ever, they are easier to hit because they haven't developed enough speed differential to make the hitter change his timing."

A bad swing with good timing is better than a great swing with bad timing. So what would be some good reasons for mis-timing a pitch?

- a pitcher's command—pitch location
- not tracking or seeing the ball well—pitch recognition
- competition
- thinking too much—'paralysis by analysis'

PITCH LOCATION – MIS-TIMING THE PITCH

It goes without saying that hitting a round baseball with a round bat is difficult. Even more so when you leave the batting cage and get into a game. Obviously the pressure is different and the degree of difficulty increases dramatically in a game because the pitcher's goal is not to 'groove' a pitch right over the plate. A good pitcher tries to keep you off balance by changing speeds and locations. Or as I read in an article in *Sports Illustrated* analyzing the 2006 American League Playoffs, "The goal of both pitching staffs is the same: Get the hitters out of their comfort zone."

Let's go back to Perry Hubbard's study on the timing of hitters. As stated in the article "Effective Velocity," in the 10/1/06 issue of *Collegiate Baseball*, how a pitch is viewed by hitters depends on the pitch location. A ball may look up to 4 more miles faster or slower than its actual speed.

See chart on page 111 in the For What It's Worth article.

It's no wonder players sometimes mis-time a pitch. As we know, swing early and you will pull the pitch; swing late and you push the ball to the opposite field. And in order to hit the ball 'up the middle' you need to be perfectly on time. It sounds easy enough but just like a good batting average is .300 or actually failing 7 out of 10 times, the same is true with hitters being on time. Hubbard's study discovered that hitters were not perfectly on time very often. In fact it was less than 10 percent of the time, which equates to 1 for 10 or a .100 average.

The best example of a pitcher who was a master at making hitters mis-time pitches is Greg Maddux, considered one of baseball's all-time best pitchers. After playing for 17 years he had won 355 games, four Cy Young Awards and was elected into the Hall of Fame in 2014. When he entered the major leagues he threw consistently in the low 90's. However in his later years his fastball dropped off and averaged mid 80's. In an interview for *Sports Illustrated* he was asked why in his later years he was still as successful as in his early years. "I have to pitch better now than 10 years ago. I have to locate better because my stuff is not as good."

When you compare his career stats to other pitchers, his strike out totals are just average. But he had above average pitch command.

Because he could locate the ball where he wanted hitters had a hard time making good solid contact. A great example is a game he won on July 2, 1997 against the NY Yankees. He pitched nine innings with no walks, three hits—84 pitches. That's right—84 pitches. Think about that—an average of 9 pitches an inning! That's having command!

Milwaukee Brewers outfielder Geoff Jenkins described the end result of Maddux's 'locate better' attitude the best when he said, "He still keeps the ball down in the zone. I try to be aggressive against him and attack early in the count because the deeper you get in the count against him the more he seems to mess with you and out think you. It just seems like he hits his spots and all of a sudden it's the end of the night and you have a comfortable 0-fer."

Before the game starts, you watch a pitcher warm up and decide he doesn't throw that hard—you should hit him—but by the end of the game, you're walking away scratching your head, questioning yourself why you didn't get a hit. You swung through pitches and may have even put the ball in play, but when the game was over you had nothing to show for your efforts. You just faced a pitcher who had command of his pitches. He had you mis-timing your swing and you were taken out of your comfort zone.

NOT TRACKING OR SEEING THE BALL WELL – MIS-TIMING THE PITCH

I'm sure you have heard coaches say, "See the ball off your bat." This is good advice but not for the reason you might think. As stated in an article published in the October 1, 2004 issue of *Collegiate Baseball* entitled "Vision Training," "When a professional batter watches a pitcher throw a ball, he eventually loses sight of it 6-8 feet before the ball reaches home plate. Thus, when he swings …he is simply estimating where he thinks the ball will be when it crosses the plate 4/10ths of a second after the pitcher releases it." This 6-8 feet before home plate is referred to as the hitter's 'blind zone."

You don't physically see the ball go off the bat. But "see the ball off your bat" is still good advice, as the coach is trying to get you to track the ball—from the pitcher's release point to your "blind zone."

Ask yourself, "What do I look at when I'm in the batter's box waiting for the pitcher to throw the ball?" Got you thinking didn't I! Few players know what they should do with their eyes when they are up at the plate, but if I ask about mechanics, most players, without hesitation, will have something to say. That's because players spend a tremendous amount of time on mechanics and no time on visual skills. Understand that hitting is actually a visual skill, and you need to work on it because you can't hit what you can't see. You can have the best mechanics in the world, but if you don't see the ball, recognize the pitch, you aren't going to hit it. Having a picturesque swing is useless if you continually swing at bad pitches.

There are two philosophies about what your eyes should be doing when you are in the batter's box. One is to pick out a spot on the pitcher's hat or face and use a 'soft' focus as he is getting the signs from the catcher and beginning his windup. Just before the pitcher's hand reaches his release point—the point at which he releases the ball—your eyes shift to a 'hard focus." You then track the ball from the release point.

To help you understand this concept of 'soft' and 'hard' focus, imagine you are looking through a cone toward the pitcher. When the smaller hole of the cone is placed in front of your eyes and the larger hole of the cone is aimed directly at the pitcher's head or chest, this is soft focus. Now reverse the cone—place the larger hole of the cone to your eyes and aim the smaller hole at the pitcher's release point. This is hard focus. You then track the ball down the tunnel of the cone.

The concern some have with this process is that the hitter might over focus or stare. And when you stare or are fixated on an object, it diminishes clearness, which is why the second philosophy is referred to as 'scan and hunt." Proponents of this method feel that it's critical to keep your eyes active, by first starting at a location—maybe a sign on the fence in the outfield or the pitcher's feet—then moving them—maybe to the pitcher's body or head—and then moving to the release point. Keep them moving until you decide to shift to the release point.

Proponents of 'scan and hunt' feel it prevents staring or fixation of the hitter's eyes. They feel scanning prevents bugging out of the eyes and/or freezing like a deer in headlights, referring to a deer's tendency to freeze in front of an oncoming car. The deer is caught in a state of paralyzing bewilderment or fear, which restricts eye movement.

Either way, each method is a way to help you see the ball better. But no matter which method you choose to use, be sure to get your eyes to the release point at the right time. The right time is when the pitcher is about to release the ball. If you shift your focus too soon your eyes will focus on an object beyond the pitcher. When the ball does appear your eyes must re-adjust or catch up, which takes time that you don't have. If you shift your focus to the release point too late, the ball has already traveled several feet—your eyes have to catch up—thus shortening the time you have to see the ball. The shorter the time you have to see the ball, the smaller the ball appears, making the pitch seem faster than it actually is. Think of it as having your eyes behind the ball.

Your goal should be to have your eyes *ahead* of the ball. You should be tracking the ball to where it's going and not where it's been.

Dr. Peter Fadde, a professor and the director of the Learning Systems Design and Technology graduate program at Southern Illinois University, wrote an article titled 'Pitch Recognition Is A Skill That Gives You An Edge' for the 6/14/19 issue of *Collegiate Baseball*. In the article he mentions that sports science research has identified the flight of a baseball into three zones. Zone 1 is the first third of the ball's flight, in which the batter decides whether to 'fire' his swing. Zone 2 is the middle flight, where the hitter reads speed and angle. "Hitters process this information unconsciously to adjust their swing for when and where they expect the ball to reach the hitting zone." So in Zone 3, the last part of the ball flight, the hitter must jump their eyes ahead to where they expect the ball to be, because in most cases the hitter doesn't actually see the bat hit the ball.

Bottom line, whether you're too soon or too late, it doesn't matter. You have mis-timed the pitch.

One thing is for sure: The distance between home plate and the mound is 60 feet 6 inches. But when the pitcher strides, he releases the ball out in front of his body—about 4 feet in front of the rubber. Then there is the 6 to 8 feet of the hitter's 'blind zone' in front of the plate. If you subtract these figures from the total distance between home plate and the pitcher's mound, it leaves the hitter only 48 feet to see the ball, track it, and make a decision to swing or not swing.

Tom Verducci, a sports writer for *Sports Illustrated*, wrote an article about spin rates using data from Trackman (a Danish radar tech company), with a side point about a pitcher's release point. Trackman determined that the span on the pitcher's release extension has an effect on strike outs and swing and miss rates. For some pitchers, the fastball is perceived by batters to be faster than the actual measured velocity. If a pitcher increases his stride length, by reducing the distance that the ball travels to home plate, the net effect is that the flight time for the ball will be faster than expected. In fact pitchers whose extension was approximately one foot longer than average could add around 2 mph to their effective velocity. In effect the ball seems to get to the batter faster than the visual appearance of the speed of the pitch, and the necessary reaction time for the batter is less than expected. Sounds like a way to mess up the batter's timing to me.

So imagine mis-timing shifting your focus. How many feet has the ball traveled before your eyes catch up—get ahead of the ball? Three feet? Four feet? Five feet? There's really no sure answer because it will probably be a little different each time. But whatever the distance is, you must subtract it from the 48 feet. That now leaves the hitter less than 48 feet to see the ball, track it and make a decision to swing or not swing. Mis-timing your focus probably means you will mis-time your swing.

COMPETITION— MIS-TIMING THE PITCH

Let's go back to the Showcase Fall travel team I coached—better players with college aspirations. Each player was provided with a player profile that they could give to the college coaches. This profile also included their battings stats from their high school and American Legion season. Again, keep in mind that the team was made up of highly successful high school players, so they all had impressive batting averages, both high school and American Legion. About halfway through the season, I would create a chart, listing each player and comparing their high school and American Legion batting average to their fall batting average. The results were the same every year. Fall batting averages were always at least 100 points below those from high school and the American Legion.

As we explained to the players, due to the nature of our program, every pitcher they faced was someone's ace. And by the way, due to the format of the showcases the team participated in, in each game they probably would see three different pitchers—but three aces. So unlike their high school and Legion season, they never saw a "weak" pitcher. And on the defensive side, because the team they played against was also an elite team, the balls hit in the gap or in the hole were caught or the throw was made. Thus, the batting averages were lower because of the competition.

While no pitcher is un-hittable, you have to be realistic about the talent level that you are facing. There is a reason why that 'big name' pitcher got his reputation. If you feel you had an off day against a pitcher who is not the 'big name' pitcher, keep in mind that every player, no matter what their talent level, has his day—gets into a zone. Maybe this was the day he pitched the game of his life. And even if he is an average pitcher, you are human. You are not perfect. Periodically you and your teammates are going to have a bad day. Go check the scorebook—I bet you weren't the only one who had a bad day.

Respect the effort of the pitcher. Tip your hat to him; he threw some good pitches. He got the better of you that time. The reality is, no matter how good you are, there are times when the pitcher will be right and you will be wrong. Sometimes it has nothing to do with mechanics but a lot to do with timing. Remember, better pitchers know that "hitting is timing. Pitching is upsetting timing."

THINKING TOO MUCH — MIS-TIMING THE PITCH

The following is a description of a Major League player in the 2006 September 25th issue of *Sports Illustrated*. "The richest and most talented player in baseball was in trouble. He could not hit an average fastball, could not swat home runs in practice with any regularity, could not field a ground ball or throw from third base with an uncluttered mind and cooperative feet, could not step up to the plate without being booed and could not find full support in his own club house."

That's how Tom Verducci, author of the article, described Alex Rodriguez and his season up to late August 2006. To give you an example of how up and down his season was, in the month of May

Rodriguez was selected the American League Player of the Month, batting .330 with eight home runs and 28 RBIs. But from June 1st to August 30th—in 80 games—he hit .257 with 81 strikeouts while committing 13 errors.

So what was happening to Alex? Well, it wasn't, as the article stated, lack of effort. "If anything the 31-year-old Rodriguez works too hard." His then teammate Johnny Damon had this to say: "His swing is so mechanical. He's too good to be swinging like that. Just let it flow. See the ball and react." Another teammate, Jason Giambi, said, "He's guessing and doing a bad job of it." His manager, Joe Torre, felt he was predetermining what he was going to do when he went up to the plate.

Verducci described it. "Trying to catch up to fastballs, he started guessing and began his swing early, lunging at the ball with his hips drifting forward, creating a flaw that robbed him of even more power. Then as he carried the anxiety into the field his usual reliable glove began to fail him."

In essence what everyone was saying is that all the telltale signs of Rodriguez over thinking were there. Based on their description, you could say that because of thinking too much his thoughts were going in the wrong direction. His thoughts needed to be going in the right direction—focused on his at bat—and not focused on errors, bad umpire calls, poor pitching, or the score, or the pressure to win the game. Rodriguez averaged a strikeout per game in August because he was over thinking. He was mis-timing pitches.

So let's look at some of the signs that show a hitter is thinking too much:

- mechanical swings – focused on swing and not the process of the at bat

- taking a 'grooved' pitch for a third called strike—putting it into the umpire's hands

- 'paralysis by analysis'—taking pitches—fear of failure

- not willing to go deep in the count or swinging at first pitches—lacking trust

- guessing—swinging at pitches nowhere near the strike zone—lacking trust

- predetermining that he is going to swing—swings at anything

So how does a player get to this point? In my opinion, the player consciously or subconsciously decides that his hitting is off. There's something wrong. He has decided that his hitting is not up to his standard or the standard he believes is expected of him. That expected standard could be what he thinks the coach, his teammates, or his parents are looking for. This is the start of over thinking.

And it can start with something as simple as an 0 for 5 day. The player comes to the conclusion that because of his bad day, there must be something wrong with his hitting. He over thinks it. So the next practice he has to work harder—take more than the usual number of pitches in the batting cage. And with every swing there is judgment. At the next game, every at bat now has a sense of urgency. He has to perform! So a perception gives birth to a fear of failure. Thus the player tries too hard, becomes too aggressive, has less control.

When a player starts over thinking he starts questioning his ability. He loses trust—his faith in his ability. Just like the Alex Rodriguez example, the player doesn't trust himself to stay back and wait for the pitch, so he does what Rodriguez did: "began his swing early, lunging at the ball with his hips drifting forward, creating a flaw" in his mechanics. Or, in other words, because he lacked trust in his abilities his mechanics broke down.

Mechanical swings are a sure sign of over thinking. There is a breakdown in the player's muscle memory. Muscle memory is fashioned over time through repetition of a given motor skill and the ability through brain activity to remember it. Muscle memory starts with the visual cue. As the brain processes the information about the desired activity and motion such as hitting a baseball, one then commits to that motion thought as correct.

When it comes to swinging and hitting a baseball, the eyes see the ball—the visual cue—and the brain tells the muscles to swing exactly like they remember. The brain commits to that motion thought as correct.

But instead of your brain sending a message like 'see the ball, hit the ball,' it is reminding the muscles about all of the mechanical adjustments to your swing that you have been working on in practice. Ever have a videotape made of your swing? When the coach goes over the tape what does he do? He plays it in slow motion so that he can show you and discuss step by step each aspect of your swing.

The body will do what the mind—your brain—tells it to do. So if your brain is not telling your body to *see the ball, hit the ball*, then you short circuit or disrupt the message from your brain to your muscles. And if you go up to the plate thinking about the mechanics of your swing, you are doing what your coach did with the tape. Putting your muscle memory—your swing—in slow motion. It's no longer automatic, smooth, and fluid. Instead, just like the videotape—one frame at a time—it becomes mechanical.

Another sign that a player lacks trust is if he usually has patience at the plate but suddenly becomes a first pitch swinger. Players do this because deep down inside they don't want to face the dreaded 0-2 count. It's at this count that they have even less faith in their abilities. Anyone who has played this game knows that 0-2 and 1-2 are big time pitchers' counts and that the odds for success are against the hitter. These pitch counts instill fear into the hitter. Especially the fear of striking out.

While I'm sure no player will admit it, after many years of coaching high school baseball I'm convinced that there are players who feel this way. Why? The answer is simple. Their mentality is that while a ground out is a failure, striking out has a higher degree of failure. There is more embarrassment or humiliation with a strike out. Making contact has some measure of success but there is absolutely none in a strike out. So to be sure that the odds are on their side, to minimize their failure, they swing at the first pitch. Thus their focus is on not failing as opposed to seeing the ball, recognizing pitch type, pitch location, etc.

It's almost as if they don't care if they ground out or fly out (fail) because they have good reason as to why they failed. "I swung at a bad pitch," 'The umpire stinks,' and 'I needed to go up there hacking because he probably would have called it a strike anyway." Players feel less embarrassment or humiliation (especially in a pressure situation) because they believe they have a good reason why they failed. They can sell that excuse to their teammates, coaches, parents, etc.

There are several pitfalls to lack of trust. One is that it eliminates any clear thinking. When you lose faith in your thought process, it keeps you from making good decisions and interferes with pitch recognition. For example, you decide in the batter's box that you are going to swing at the first pitch. The problem is that the body does what the mind tells it to do. So when the ball is pitched, the mind is telling the body to swing, not see the ball and/or recognize the pitch. You are not reacting to the pitch but rather to the decision to swing at the first pitch. Thus you end up swinging at pitches out of or nowhere near the strike zone.

Lack of trust brings on a physiological element as well. Add this sense of urgency to the pressure of the games and you get tension. And when the body senses tension, it's a physiological fact that the muscles will tighten. Two things happen when your muscles tighten. First, you lose the ability to have a fluid swing. And second, because your eye movements are controlled by muscles, the efficiency of your eye movements goes down. They don't work as well. It hinders your ability to see the ball well.

Another pitfall is that it creates doubt. Consider this statement made by a sport psychologist: "When one's instinctive or intuitive athleticism is compromised by the analytical thought process, the athlete is no longer able to flow freely on autopilot." He is saying that if something like doubt or questioning enters the player's thought process, it has an effect on his physical action because one result of doubt is that it leads to hesitation and indecision. The reason you hesitate is because not only do you doubt your physical abilities but you also doubt your pitch recognition ability. So you start guessing and hesitate on each pitch. Your hesitation causes indecision to swing or not swing and when to swing. So because of your reaction time you miss time the pitch or miss guess. And a sure sign of mis-guessing is the player swings at pitches nowhere near the strike zone or takes called strikes on 'right down the middle' pitches.

Another problem with thinking too much is that you forget or don't focus on what your #1 job is as a hitter when you go up to the plate. When you think too much your thoughts have no direction. You are not focused on the task at hand. You are probably focused on any negatives or the circumstances of the game—like errors, bad umpire calls, poor pitching, or the score.

CONCLUSION

Tony Abbatine stated, "The mechanics of hitting are worthless once the game starts. But a player's ability to be on time and be able to recognize speed and location is what makes them hitters." Before you decide your hitting problem is mechanics, you should analyze your at bats. You need to be rational and not emotional about your at bats. Be rational about the effort. It's okay to be emotional about the end result of the play but be logical about the end result of the swing. For example, a line drive hit right at the fielder is an out. But that same ball hit two feet either way is a hit. The difference is the outcome. One is good and one is not.

This is where emotions come into play. It's natural to feel bad about the out. And you should because it has an effect on the game. But no matter the results, base hit or out, the swing mechanics, the effort was the same. You saw the ball well. It felt good. You knew once the ball went off your bat that you got good wood on it. Logic should tell you that the end result of the swing, whether the ball was caught or not, was good. Logic should tell you that a hard hit ball means your timing was good.

Be rational about your competition. Be aware of your thoughts. Don't panic. Are you really seeing the ball well? How's your pitch recognition? Don't assume it's your mechanics. What was the conclusion of the Hubbard study? Hitters are not perfectly on time very often. In fact it is less than 10 percent of the time, which equates to 1 for 10 or a .100 average.

I'll illustrate with a quick true story. It was opening day game—2014—and one of our players who had been up three times—just walked—did not get a hit in his first two at bats. I was coaching first base. When he reached first base he asked me, "What am I doing wrong?" While I did not answer him, hindsight tells me I should have warned him of the quicksand he was about to fall into.

RELAX

It's easy for your coach, your father, and everyone else to tell you to relax when you are up at the plate or on the mound, but let's face it, it's hard to do. Especially when it's a high-stress situation. It's hard because you're not sure how to relax. The people who are telling you to relax never give you any advice on how to calm yourself down! I've read several books written by sports psychologists, so I have some idea of what they suggest. But that's dealing with sports. So to come up with some suggestions besides what's in the sports books, I decided to do some research to see what psychotherapists suggest for anyone having anxiety in dealing with daily life experiences. The following is a culmination of that research and how it relates to sports.

ADMIT TO IT

Before you face a high-stress situation ask yourself, "Honestly, how do I feel?" Checking in on your mindset makes you realize where you are mentally. If you feel anxious or nervous, admit it. Take ownership of it. Trust me—you are not alone in feeling this way. It's okay—it's normal. Especially if you feel it's a high-stress situation. So by taking ownership you trigger the process of taking control of yourself. And when you are in control, all other aspects of playing well, such as making good decisions and using your best mechanics, become easier.

When you are in control you play the game one pitch at a time. When you are in control you are not worried about what might happen on that next pitch. So in order to start the calming-down process, you first need to recognize the anxiety. And the level of the anxiety.

BREATHE

If after checking in you don't like the way you feel—breathe! According to psychotherapist Scott Dehorty, "Breathing is the number one and most effective technique for reducing anger and anxiety quickly." This is why you need to include a breathing regimen in your pre-pitch routine. Ken Ravizza, one of the top sport psychology consultants in the country, feels that developing the ability to control yourself in the heat of battle is an essential component of playing the game. "One of the easiest, yet most powerful skills to help gain and keep self-control is a deep breath," said Ravizza. "Excess tension is a major obstacle to great performance. The breath can help free you of the tension and allow you to play your best baseball."

Taking the time to take a breath serves a number of purposes. The following are some found in the sports psychology book *Heads-Up Baseball: Playing the Game One Pitch at a Time*, co-authored by Tom Hanson and Ken Ravizza,

Taking a breath:

- Puts your focus on the present moment—what is going on right now and not what might happen.

- Enables you to check in with yourself to see if you are in control. If you can't get yourself to take a deep breath, it may be because your mind is going too fast.

- Helps you get control. The game seems to speed up when you aren't in control. A deep breath helps you slow it down. It helps you to relax.

- Helps release negatives like mistakes you have made out in the field. When something bad happens it usually leads to cluttered thinking, replaying the mistakes in your head, which leads to tense muscles. Remember, you can't control what happens to you, but you can choose how you respond to it.

- Energizes you when you are feeling sluggish.

- Helps establish a sense of rhythm in your pitching, hitting, or fielding. Good players choose to use a breath to help get into a tempo before each pitch.

Ravizza likes this so much because "your breath is the mental game's most versatile aid for a player because it can be used almost any time for almost any purpose." Dave Snow, former head baseball coach at Long Beach State University and former assistant coach with the U.S. Olympic baseball team, states, "If an athlete has the presence of mind to take a conscious breath, it is a good indication he is under control."

DROP YOUR SHOULDERS

When you take your breath, drop your shoulders as you exhale. If you are anxious your body is probably tense, so to help reduce or eliminate some of the body tension when you exhale during your pre-pitch breathing routine,, bring your shoulder blades together and then down.

PAY ATTENTION

When you exhale and drop your shoulders, pay attention to your body. Don't just go through the motions. I was watching my granddaughter's softball coach remind his players to breathe several times during the course of a game. Good advice except the players would quickly take a breath and quickly get ready. Your goal is not to mentally check off the 'took a breath' box or because your coach told you to do it. Your goal is to slow things down, so rushing in taking a breath is a waste of time. Slow down—take your time—feel your body—feel how you feel. You may discover that you need to take an additional breath.

SHIFT YOUR FOCUS

Shift your focus. Anxious thoughts can overwhelm you. You become overwhelmed because you start over thinking the situation, which actually makes you more anxious. Because as psychotherapist Scott Dehorty states, "We don't do our best thinking when anxious … we engage in survival thinking." In the baseball world, thoughts such as, *Bases are loaded, I gotta get a hit* or *If I don't throw a strike, I will walk in the tying run* are examples of survival thinking. So shift your focus to your pre-pitch breathing regimen or remind yourself of that change in your mechanics you have been working on—"hands back", etc.

Or shift your focus to your cue cards (see page 95 in the Fighting Slumps article)—something you feel comfortable with that can quiet your mind. Whether it's visual or oral, the cue card conditions your brain to clear away outside influences and negative thoughts and to bring on only thoughts of the process of hitting or pitching the ball. It's a way to get you to relax and not over think the next pitch, the next at bat end results. Cue cards allow you to compete with your body and not fight with your mind.

BE RATIONAL

When we become hyper focused on something we open the door to becoming irrational. In the end if you do everything you can and the end result was not what you or everyone (others) were hoping for, all that it was is disappointing. Some players, when facing stressful situations, put themselves into a 'what-if' cycle. Their subconscious leads them to irrational thoughts that don't necessarily make sense, like their value as a person or what others may think about them or the consequences if they fail.

Rationally, no matter the situation, it's not life threatening. You play because you like the competition and it's fun. No matter the end result—good or bad—rationally, your father still loves you, your best friend will remain your best friend, and your classmates will still talk to you. In fact, when you find yourself in the 'what-if' cycle, remind yourself that even if you are successful, rationally, the level of your father's love is not going to change, your best friend will not be more of a best friend, and the amount of time your classmates want to spend with you will not increase.

Rationally, no one plans to fail. No matter how good you are, how hard you work, you cannot escape the fact that you will experience setbacks. You can do everything right and still lose. And failures never come at a good time. So resign yourself to the fact that there will be disappointments. This is the reality of competition. And don't beat yourself up. It isn't going to change anything or make it better. In fact it might make it worse.

Let's look at two stories I found in the 9/9/19 issue of *Sports Illustrated*. First there's the one about Chris Davis, the Baltimore Orioles first baseman. Going into the 2019 season, he was one of the most feared sluggers in baseball. But sometime during the season, he was mired in one of the worst seasons in MLB history. How bad was it? He was in a 0 for 54 slump and had a .172 batting average.

Interestingly a nine-year-old baseball fan saw an article about him and decided to send Davis a letter. The letter read in part: "The way you play baseball has nothing to do with how good of a person you are ….Don't give up." The day after reading the letter Davis went 3 for 5 with 4 RBIs.

Then there's the story that a former high school teacher tells about Indianapolis Colt Quarterback Andrew Luck. Luck was the quarterback for his high school team in Houston, Texas. Now, football in Texas, no matter what level, is revered, maybe more so than religion. One day after a gut-wrenching loss Luck entered the teachers' room and sat down. The teacher, knowing the level of relevance put on football, figured that this particular loss might linger, so he asked Luck, "Tough weekend?" To which Luck replies, "No, it was a good one. We lost and it's just a reminder of things we can work on and pull together." Luck's perspective about football relative to the rest of the Texas was different. It was rational.

So if and when you find yourself in a 'what if' cycle, it's time for a reality check. Remember—what you do on a baseball field does not define you as a person. Just because something could happen doesn't guarantee that it will happen. Just because something negative happened in the past doesn't mean it has to happen today. I'm sure the situation you are facing is important, but it's only important at that moment. It is not a defining moment. You don't fail on purpose. There is a next day—you can start all over with no consequences. After all, rationally, it's just a baseball game.

ROLE PLAYERS—
THE STARTERS

Many times after a team wins the championship game, no matter what sport, when the players are asked their opinions about the team's success, they mention 'team unity' and acceptance of their roles. There is a direct correlation that successful teams have cohesion or what is commonly referred to as 'team chemistry."

If it's important to know that team cohesion is important to a team's success, it's also important to understand what causes conflict. In *Coaching Mental Excellence*, a book written by three sports psychologists, it states, "The variable most affecting team cohesion is the ability of group members to conform to assigned roles… The success of highly interactive teams is often dependent upon the ability of team members to understand, accept, and excel in their assigned roles."

So with that said, two problems a coach has in developing his team's chemistry is to first get his players to understand and accept their roles. And, second, get his star players to understand the importance of that role. Now let's face it, deep down inside, all players would like to be the hero—the star player. And in order for that to happen, a player would like to play a glamour position. One that he feels gets a lot of attention. What are some of the 'glamour positions? In football it's the quarterback or wide receiver. In baseball it's the pitcher or the 'clean-up' batter. In basketball it's the shooting guard. Aren't those the players who get all the attention?

As far as team chemistry goes, these players need to realize that if they don't have support from the non-starters or the role players, even if they play a glamour position, they won't experience the success that's possible from playing that position. Usually the only time players (along with fans, fathers, teammates, and even some coaches) truly understand the importance of a role is when the role player makes a mistake.

For example, how many times have you seen a football game decided by a field goal? So many times that it's taken for granted. The kicker is the hero. It's his name in the paper. Fans watch the replay on TV and hear about this 'heroic' event from the sportscasters on ESPN and all the sports editions of every news station across the country. The 'winning moment' is shown on the front page of every sports page in every newspaper. The field goal kicker gets all the credit. No mention of the holder.

But think about it. The holder's job—his only role—is to hold the ball. In order to do that he has to catch the ball while being on one knee, and place the ball, laces facing out and at just the right angle, consistently—every time. What about the center who hikes the ball? If he doesn't do his job, the holder can't catch the ball and plant it properly so that the kicker, the 'glamour' player, can successfully perform his duties. So the only time fans, fathers, teammates, and others realize the value of a role player is when he makes a mistake. How successful would the field goal kicker be if the holder didn't do his job? Consider this, the hero just might be the goat if the role player is someone who doesn't accept his role, is not focused, and thus doesn't place the ball just right—every time.

STARTER'S ROLE

Even if you aren't a team player and are only interested in your results, I have to believe you want to be on a winning team. And if you want to be on a winning team it only makes sense that everyone who plays in the game that day must play to their full abilities. Thus, in order to be sure that everyone has success, the non-starters need to feel that they have the support and trust of the starters.

At any given time throughout the season, the time will come when a non-starter will be called upon to perform, and to perform well. Maybe even in a critical game situation. So as a starter, how well do you treat the non-starters? How comfortable do you make them feel at practice? Do you treat them like an equal? How confident will the non-starter feel if the only thought going through his mind is the possible negative reception he's going to receive from his teammates if he fails? Can you expect him to be successful if he is fearful of possible critical remarks? If he doesn't feel your support, your trust, your belief that he has an important role on the team—guess what!—he probably won't be successful!

There is nothing in the world that people want and need more than the feeling that they're important. That's why your role as a starter (or team captain) is to make sure you are supportive of all your teammates, including non-starters, all the time. In practice make sure they get just as many pitches to hit as you do. Take as many ground balls or fly balls. Don't rush them. Give them equal time. Talk to them. Not just at practice but during pre-game warm-ups, during the game and after the game. A non-starter needs to feel he is part of the team. He needs to feel that he is important to the team. He needs to feel he is being supported by his teammates. He needs to feel he deserves to be there.

Even if, in your mind, he's not a member of your group, he needs to feel that while he's on the team, he *is* a member of your group. He needs to feel you are his friend. Talk to him; let him be part of the conversation, whether it's on the field or at school. Make the gesture to show him you are friends. Smart starters who want to win are good teammates to non-starters. Players who want to win make sure there is good team chemistry.

The following is a true story told by a successful company CEO during his motivation speech at a sales convention. It's a great example of the role you can play in your teammate's lives.

One day, when I was a freshman in high school, I saw a kid from my class walking home from school. His name was Kyle. It looked like he was carrying all of his books. I thought to myself, *Why would anyone bring all of his books home on a Friday? He must be a nerd.*

I had quite a weekend planned (parties and a baseball game with my friends), so I shrugged and went on. As I was walking, I saw a bunch of kids running toward him. They ran up to him and started picking on him. They said some pretty harsh things to him. When they were done, they pushed him down, knocking all his books out of his arms. His glasses went flying. He looked up and I saw this terrible sadness in his eyes. My heart went out to him, so I jogged over to him and noticed he had tears in his eyes. As I handed him his glasses, I said, "Those guys are jerks. They really need to get a life."

He looked at me and said, "Hey, thanks!" There was a big smile on his face. It was one of those smiles that showed real gratitude. I helped him pick up his books, and he asked me where I lived. As it turned out, he lived near me, so I asked him why I had never seen him before. He said he had gone to a private school before now. We talked all the way home.

Now I would never have hung out with a private school kid. But Kyle turned out to be a pretty cool kid. I asked him if he wanted to play a little baseball with my friends. He said yes. We hung around together all weekend and the more I got to know Kyle the more I liked him. And my friends thought the same.

Monday morning came and there was Kyle with the huge stack of books again. I stopped him and said, "Boy, you are going to build some serious muscles with this pile of books everyday!" He just laughed and handed me half the books.

Over the next four years, Kyle and I became best friends. When we were seniors, we began to think about college. Kyle decided on Georgetown and I was going to Duke. I knew we would always be friends, that the distance away would never be a problem. He was going to be a doctor and I was going for business on a baseball scholarship.

Kyle was valedictorian of our class. I teased him once in a while about being a nerd. He had prepared a speech for graduation. On graduation day Kyle looked great. He was one of those guys who really found himself during high school. He filled out and looked good in glasses. He had more dates than I had and all the girls liked him. Sometimes I was jealous.

Today was one of those days. I could see that he was nervous about his speech. So I went up to him, smacked him on the back, and said, "Hey, big guy, you'll do great!" He looked at me with one of those looks (the really grateful one) and smiled. "Thanks," he said.

As he started his speech he cleared his throat and began. "Graduation is a time to thank those who helped you make it through those tough years. Your parents, your teachers, maybe a coach.... but mostly your friends. I'm here to tell all of you that being a friend to someone is the best gift you can give them. I'm going to tell you a story."

I just looked at my friend with disbelief as he told the story of the first day we met. He had planned to kill himself over the weekend. He talked of how he had cleaned out his locker that Friday so his mom wouldn't have to do it later. He was carrying all his stuff home. He looked hard at me and gave me a little smile. "Thankfully, I was saved. My friend saved me from doing the unspeakable."

I heard the gasp go through the crowd as this handsome, popular boy told all of us about his weakest moment. I saw his mom and dad looking at me and smiling that same grateful smile. Not until then did I realize its depth.

The point of the speech was that it doesn't matter how good of a player you are, but it does matter how good you are as a teammate. It does matter how good of a person you are. So don't underestimate the power of your actions. With one small gesture you can change a person's perspective on his value, his role. Be a good teammate. Make a gesture. Be a friend.

SCRAPES AND BRUISES

To be successful in sports you have to fail. It's just like when you learned how to ride a bike. Even though your initial response was fear of falling—getting hurt—you were so determined to ride the bike that you knew you had to risk falling. Your determination got you to focus on riding the bike and not on getting hurt. Each time you fell during the initial learning process, while at that time I'm sure you did not realize it—by falling, you eventually figured out that it was what you needed to do to stay on the bike—and not get hurt.

Now that you are older I'm sure you will agree that the more you fell the more you learned. Falling taught you how to stay on. I'm sure you realize that back then, unconsciously, your falling was part of the process in learning how to ride the bike. Unconsciously you decided experiencing some scrapes and bruises was worth learning how to ride the bike. Your fear was getting hurt, not failing. And you didn't associate falling with failing. Falling was getting hurt.

Back then you were young, no expectations, no pressure, just the desire to learn how to ride that bike. But as you got older, especially if you played in sports, some of you were affected by what is commonly called 'fear of failure." With all of the social media today I can understand why a player could have fear of failure. It seems today everyone's favorite pastime is taking credit or placing blame. Now that you are grown up you realize that when it comes to sports, we live in the world of expectations, pressure, consequences, statistics, etc. Everyone is seeking social approval, so if you make a mistake you could think it's a failure and you could think you will be blamed.

Notice that I stated *you think*. You see, for many athletes, their sport, in our case baseball, is the single most intense thing in their lives. And when athletes are playing there is an audience and with an audience there are expectations and thus it becomes stressful because of the potential for failure. They believe that the stakes are high and so is the price if a mistake is made. Thus their instinctive reaction is that this stress is seen as a threat—a real threat, as opposed to an imagined threat. A real threat to what is near and dear to them. Their instinctive reaction—the stress of possible failure—leads them to fear failure.

But at this stage in your life, in order to be the best shortstop, pitcher, hitter, etc., you need to have the same desire that you had when you wanted to learn how to ride the bike. You have to have that same level of unconscientious determination. You need to understand that failure is positive feedback and a necessary component to success. Striking out or making an error is falling, not failing. Just like when you learned how to ride the bike, it's part of the learning process.

Back then you weren't thinking about how stressful it was to ride a bike. No—each time you fell off the bike, your desire, your determination got you back on the bike. Each time you fell, besides a scrape or bruise, you were taught a lesson. Each time you actually were getting positive feedback. For example, when you first started to learn how to ride, when you decided to stop, you probably kept falling down with the bike. This continued until you realized that when you braked to stop the bike, to maintain control, you needed to put your foot down to maintain your balance.

So in order to be the best shortstop, pitcher, hitter, etc., you need to control your thought process. In "Failure Is A Necessary

Component of Great Success" written by sports psychologist Brian Cain for *Collegiate Baseball* (10/5/12), he lists certain principles you need to keep in mind to help you to overcome or prevent fear of failure. The following is a summary of each one.

FAILURE POSITIVE FEEDBACK

"Without failure, you are without progress." Winning all of the time means you are not challenging yourself. "Success can mask weakness." Failure is a positive because it means you are competing at the right level. A very good example of this message behind the 'Failure Positive Feedback' principle is the answer that Kristi Yamaguchi, an Olympic Skating Gold medalist, gave when she was interviewed for an article in the 1/19/14 issue of *Parade Magazine*. She was asked what she had learned from competing. Her answer was: "Before success, you're going to have failures. I'd have a bad competition, but it didn't crush me. I knew this is what I need to go back and work on or change."

GOOD OR BAD VERSUS GOOD AND BAD

No one is perfect. You need to have a non-judgmental mindset. "Decide before you compete that you are going to evaluate your performance as having both good and bad aspects and NOT JUDGE your performance as good OR bad. When you judge you are not paying attention to the facts, so you are not learning anything." So, as Cain states, "Keep doing the good and learn from the bad."

EXCELLENT VERSUS PERFECT

Again, no one is perfect, so your goal should be to play as well and as consistently as you can. "Perfection is unattainable." Deep down inside most players competing are striving for perfection. However, the truth is that you never cross the finish line in your pursuit of perfection. But your pursuit for excellence is never ending. So compete only against yourself and let the end results take care of themselves. Compete against only yourself and not against the expectations of fans, parents, etc. Expectations are what Brain Cain refers to as the "mental emergency brake." Just as the primary purpose of an emergency brake on a car is to prevent movement, these mental emergency brakes hold you back.

LOSER OR LEARNER

Whether you lose a game or make a physical or mental mistake in the game, when you evaluate what happened, you must be rational and not emotional. "Emotion clouds reality. When you can remove emotion from your perception and see more of what is and less of what if, you will see more of the true picture." A good example of what Cain means is the following quote by David Ortiz of the Boston Red Sox. "On the day you feel your best, you can go 0 for 5. You go home and say, I feel like Superman, and I went 0 for 5. That tells you how tough this game is: On your best day you had a bad day." Then there is this quote from Skip Bertman, legendary couch of LSU: "You can play well and win. You can play well and lose. You can play lousy and win. You can play lousy and lose."

BITTER OR BETTER

Challenge yourself to get better. "Decide…that loss or lack of playing time or lack of success will drive you to get better." Get encouraged, not discouraged. Get better, not bitter. A great example is when Tom Brady decided to go to Michigan State. Before he even stepped foot on the campus the head coach who recruited him was fired and the assistant who recruited him left to go to another school. So not being the new coach's 'guy' he was really starting all over concerning where he fit in the scheme of things. By his sophomore year he was still low on the depth chart and even considered transferring to Cal. Instead he chose to stay and viewed the depth chart as a challenge.

He stayed because as he said, "In a team sport you gotta sacrifice what you want individual for what's best for the team... If I'm going to be the best, I've gotta beat the best, and if the best competition is at Michigan, then I gotta beat those guys out if I'm going to play. So, I just ended up starting to commit to being the best."

His commitment started with, as he said, taking more personal responsibility for his life. He was not going to be the victim. He realized he needed to make a shift in his mindset, from "complaining all the time that I wasn't getting what I wanted, to stop complaining and doing something about it." His mind shift went from complaining that he only had three reps—"how can I prove myself if the other guy is getting 30 reps and I'm only getting 3" to "If they only give you three reps in practice do the best you can with those three. If you do well with those three they will give you five. If you do well with those five they will give you ten reps...." The rest is history.

That's how Tom Brady handled his scrapes and bruises. What if it was you? What choice would you make? Bitter or Better?

FRUSTRATED OR FASCINATED

A challenge can be either frustrating or fascinating. It's an opportunity or a danger. In a previous section I mention that some people see taking a hot air balloon ride as a wonderful and exciting experience while some see themselves falling out of the basket—fun versus danger. When challenged only you control what type of attitude you will accept. Attitude is a choice! Turned on or turned off—fascinated or frustrated.

To illustrate, let's look at what occurred in the 2016 Masters Tournament. After 63 holes, Jordan Spieth, the current rising star in golf, was five strokes ahead with the last nine holes left to play. According to the TV color commentators, the match was over.

But as anyone who follows sports knows, nothing is a sure thing, or 'It ain't over 'til the fat lady sings." Well, the fat lady never sang! Spieth's round fell apart. He proceeded to drop six strokes on the next three holes with consecutive bogeys and a quadruple-bogey and essentially, according to all the experts, gave away the tournament to Danny Willett of England.

Now keep in mind that the Masters is one of the most prestigious events in sports, so much so that even non golfers will watch. So imagine what was written and discussed in the various sports pages and sport TV shows about his collapse. While it would be easy to use the word failure to describe the end result, let's look at Jordon Spieth's approach/attitude after those disastrous three holes, which by the way were referred to by one writer as "the longest 11 minutes of his career." Let's look at what was lost in all of what was said or written.

First, in golf, the winner of the previous hole gets to tee off first. Spieth's playing partner had birdied the hole that Spieth quadruple bogeyed and won the hole by 5 strokes. When they both reached the 13th tee, with a straight face, Spieth smiled and said, "Whose tee is it?" This would be like asking a player from a team who just beat you by 15 runs, 'Who won?"

Well, they both had a good laugh. And not only did he get off a good drive on that hole but he proceeded to birdie two of the next three holes! His use of humor gave him a shot at an improbable comeback victory. He just ran out of holes.

Imagine that! After everything that had just happened! Think of his mental fortitude. When asked about it during one of the interviews, he stated, "I was just trying to figure out a way to get it back.

I wanted to lighten the mood." When challenged, only you control what type of attitude you will accept. Attitude is a choice! Spieth chose humor. Would you? Would you be turned on or turned off—fascinated or frustrated?

Second, after the tournament he and some fellow golfers went on a mini vacation for a few weeks. When he came back, rather than go back on the tour right away, he decided to spend his time at the driving range working on his swing—to return it, as he said, "to the consistent level it was at during really the second half of the year when I struck the ball the best." But I think he could say it another way: "I decided to challenge myself to get better. I could be bitter but I chose to get better!"

Lastly, when he did decide to come back to the tour, he chose the Players Championship event. During an interview the day before the event, he was questioned about 'the collapse' on the 12th hole. "I didn't take that extra deep breath and really focus on my line," he said, referring to his initial tee shot. "Instead, I went up and I just put a quick swing on it." Asked about what happened when he put his next shot in the water, he stated that he felt he had the right club but at the last minute decided to hit a fade instead of a draw. "The swing just wasn't quite there to produce the right ball flight," he said. A great example of evaluating his performance and not judging his performance.

Recall what sports psychologist Brain Cain said: "Emotion clouds reality. When you can remove emotion from your perception and see more of what is and less of what if, you will see more of the true picture." Jordan Spieth decided to be rational and not emotional. In the aftermath, he looked back and saw what was. He saw that he got out of his normal routine on the tee shot and that he should have changed what club to use when he decided to hit a 'fade instead of a draw." He is a learner, not a loser.

So if you are determined to be successful in sports, then not only do you have to have that same level of determination but you also have to have that same level of control over your focus that you had when you learned how to ride your bike. While subconsciously you know it was worth experiencing some scrapes and bruises to learn how to ride your bike, in order to get better or play a position you have never played, then you have to *consciously* decide it's worth making errors. You know you will make mistakes, but you decide that your focus will be on learning. You know you will experience some scrapes and bruises. You decide you will associate failing with learning, not getting hurt.

In order to be as successful as you can with the abilities you have, you need to control your thought process. You have to accept that failure is positive feedback and a necessary component of success. Failing is moving forward. And doing so will help you overcome or prevent that dreaded disease called fear of failure.

Oh, by the way, Jordon Spieth won the 2016 Dean and Deluca tournament by 3 strokes. The 2016 Masters was played from April 4th through the 10th and the Dean and Deluca was played from May 26th through the 29th. So in just 8 short weeks he was a winner again!

SIGNIFICANT STAT

Because of the ongoing advancement in technology, the ability to be analytical in any sport has changed dramatically. By far, baseball is the leader in keeping records and using statistics. So much so that in 1971, the term *sabermetrics* was coined to describe the collection and summation of data from game activity. It actually stands for the Society for American Baseball Research. Need I remind you of the growing interest the baseball community has in things like launch angle, exit speed velocity, and bat speed when discussing and measuring offensive statistics?

From Webster's New World Dictionary, the definition of the word statistics is "numerical data assembled and classified so as to present significant information." The key word being "significant."

Major League Baseball's interest in using analytics has led them to their newest statistic called Weighted On-Base Average or wOBA. It's grown in importance because there's a feeling that it has more significance in measuring a hitter's overall offensive value than batting average, on-base percentage, and slugging percentage. It combines all the different aspects of hitting into one metric, weighting each of them in proportion to their actual run value. The significance of wOBA has reached the point where the King of Stats—the batting average—has diminished, at least in the eyes of team management.

While the importance of batting average has diminished at the pro level, that cannot be said at the non-professional level. Ask any high school baseball player how he's doing and the first thing he will mention is his batting average—provided it's a good one. Ask any father how their son is doing and I can assure you Dad's answer will include some mention of his batting average. After all, if he wants to prove to the questioner how good his son is, then certainly batting average will be proof enough.

Steve Springer, the author of *Quality At Bats* and someone who has spent 35 years in professional baseball as a player, agent, and scout, feels that "the batting average is the biggest trap in all sports." It is just one recorded measure of a player's success in baseball, and in the game of baseball there are actions performed by individuals that are an integral part of a team's success but that go unrecorded. I feel that these unrecorded actions are a better way to grade a player's success. In my world, a coach's world, these unrecorded actions are significant because it's a way to determine a player's production or run value to his team.

Individual actions can include moving a runner into scoring position or a sacrifice bunt or having a 9 pitch at bat. These are plays or actions that occur in a game that can ultimately help decide the outcome of the game. These are all things that are good for the team. But these success stories don't show up in the scorebook. They don't make it to the papers or get any airtime. There's no glamour in them. There's no notoriety. These actions do have significance, in the non-professional world, but apparently not enough to warrant being collected and recorded. Thus they don't receive the same appreciation as a stat like a batting average.

Part of the problem is today's media and what they focus on. For example, Sports Center on ESPN shows the home runs, the big base hit that scores runs, but it rarely shows how runners got into scoring position or even got on base. You never see the entire process of how teams score their runs because how runners got on or got into scoring position isn't dramatic. To use an ESPN vernacularism, these moments are not "Web Gems"! You don't hear ESPN's signature sound—Dah, Dah, Dunt—when they happen. They don't make the Top 10. And let's not forget that we live in a world where people are highly influenced by social media, thus increasing the significance of stats.

But the reality is that each individual on a team wants to win the game. So if the goal is to win games, then what is it that the team must do? The answer is easy—SCORE RUNS! The object of the game is to score runs. Bill James, an acclaimed baseball historian and statistician, states in his book, *The New Bill James Historical Baseball Abstract*, "A hitter's job is not to compile a high batting average. Hitting home runs is part of a hitter's job, hitting doubles is part of the job, getting on base is part of the job, driving in runs is part of the job, hitting singles is part of the job, stealing is part of the job—BUT WHAT IS THE JOB ITSELF? The job is to create runs. That is what all hitters are trying to do in every plate appearance. They are trying to create runs. The essential measure of a hitter's success is how many runs he has created."

If a team and the hitter's goal is to score runs, what must they do? The answer is simple: make things happen. But what actions must they take to make things happen? Put the ball in play! Make contact—get on base—move runners—any way you can. And make timely contact like it's the last inning, runner on third, no outs, need to put the ball in play time. Making contact is an individual action that plays an integral part in a team scoring runs. Exactly what a batting average does not do.

Let's look at what else a batting average does NOT do. When you calculate a batting average, it doesn't include plate appearances that result in walks, hit by pitch, sacrifice bunts or a sacrifice fly. All of these are individual actions that could help score runs. While this can certainly be considered a flaw in evaluating the value of a batting average, there are larger issues to consider.

A batting average doesn't tell who the better contact hitter is. It doesn't tell you who the best is at getting on base. It doesn't measure a player's frequency in reaching base. It doesn't measure how many runs he has created. And as we all know you can't score runs until runners get on base. Once they are on base you need to make things happen, like putting the ball in play—making contact—so that runners are moved and they end up scoring.

Speaking of just making contact, there was an interesting article written by sports writer Tom Verducci for *Sports Illustrated*. In it he described the approach the Boston Red Sox have taken concerning hitting. It's interesting because at the time that this was written, the 2017 season was described as the season with record rates of strikeouts and home runs. At the end of the season Boston was ranked as the best two strike hitting team and last in league home runs. And they had the most wins without a homerun. This tells me their emphasis was more on contact and not necessarily on power.

Apparently this approach started in the minor leagues. Theo Epstein, who at the time was the general manager, felt that on-base percentage and slugging percentage were more important than batting average. He wanted disciplined hitters rather than free-swingers. So they started using a player development system that emphasized what he called "selective aggressiveness" in which getting the right pitch is more important than power. He stated, "We want players who are good with pitch selection and attacking their pitch when they get it." In the article Red Sox President Dave Dombrowski is quoted as saying, "Instead of relying on the middle of the order (3-4-5 batters) the team relies on defense, base running and good at bats up and down the line up." In other words make contact.

Chili Davis, the hitting coach, mentioned that they don't have much use for metric stats like exit velocity, launch angles, etc. He states, "What we try to do is have a good approach at the plate." But a metric stat that matters most within the Red Sox farm system is QPA—quality plate appearance. They track the percentage of each hitter's plate appearances that meet their quality standard, regardless of the outcome, and give awards to the best performers.

By the way, the system must work pretty well since the Red Sox have won the World Series four times since taking this approach. Apparently they feel that not only is this 'non recorded stat' a positive reinforcement for the players but that QPA is more significant than the player's batting average because it's a measurement of a player's run creation value.

The following is a list of some contact "make things happen" actions that while they are positive actions for the team they have a negative or no effect on a player's batting average.

QUALITY PLATE APPEARANCE	PERFORMANCE—END RESULT
Ground ball out runner at third came home	Run scored
Ground out moved runner from 1st to 2nd	Put runner in scoring position
Reached base on error	Runner—possible run
Fly ball out to right field runner tags up	Moved runner—possible score
Struck out on 9 pitches	Worked the pitcher
Failed sacrifice bunt fielder throws ball away	Runner—possible Run
Line drive shot to short	Put 'good hitter' mindset in pitcher's head

Now, let's take it one step further. Keith Law, the ESPN senior baseball writer, goes into detail in his book *Smart Baseball* about four commonly used hitter-stats at the team level and their correlation to the teams runs scored per game. The four stats he looked at were batting average, on-base percentage, slugging percentage, and OPS (on base plus slugging). So as you can see by the following chart, batting average really isn't on top when it comes to scoring runs.

HITTER—TEAM STAT	CORRELATION TO TEAMS RUNS SCORED
On Base plus Slugging - OPS	0.936
Slugging percentage	0.903
On Base percentage - OBS	0.833
Batting Average	0.749

While three of the four hitter stats are ranked above batting average, notice that on-base percentage is significantly higher than batting average. Objectively this is important because as Law states, "On-base percentage is the most important for telling you about a hitter's ability to produce runs." It's a better measure of a hitter's and a team's performance. Proof of this statement is in the *Smart Baseball* book. "From 1901 to 2015, the team with the best OBP ...led in runs scored 58 percent of the time versus 53 percent for teams that led in batting average."

Most young and high school players probably focus too much on their batting average when they should be focusing on their actions that contribute to scoring runs. Players need to appreciate and acknowledge every action—whether it is or is not measured—with the same intensity. Now, don't misunderstand me. Batting average has value, but sometimes an unrecorded stat just might have more.

It might be time for a new statistic for the non-professional level. While it's not realistic to think that at the high school/youth level wOBA is possible, but it is realistic to come up with a way to measure a hitter's overall offensive value in scoring runs. This stat would reflect the batters' run scoring ratio. It could be called Scoring Batting Average—SBA—where you track the percentage of each hitter's plate appearances that helped score a run.

The following is how it could work. Keep in mind that this is only a suggestion. You should set up your own qualifying standard.

- Keep track of the number of plate appearances each batter has when runners are in scoring position—on second and/or third—not total at bats.

- Award a point to the batter if he makes contact that moves a runner into scoring position that eventually scores.

- Add those points to any RBIs the batter has to come up with total scored points.

- Divide the scored points number by the number of plate appearances with runners on.

For example:

- Batter A gets up 5 times but only 3 times was there a runner on base.

- One at bat he hits a ground ball to the second baseman which moves the runner from first to second. That runner eventually scores. Batter A has one point.

- One at bat he gets an RBI. Batter A has 2 points.

- One at bat he strikes out.

To determine his Scoring Batting Average, divide his 2 points by the 3 plate appearances that had runners on—his SBA is .667.

For example:

- Batter B gets up 5 times but only 3 times was there a runner on base.

- One at bat he strikes out.

- One at bat he hits into a double play.

- One at bat he hits the ball to the shortstop, who makes an error and the runner at second moves to third. That runner eventually scores. Batter B has one point.

To determine his Scoring Batting Average, divide his 1 'contact' hit by his 3 plate appearances that had runners on—his SBA is .333

A batting average also does not measure "clutch hitting." Currently there is no definitive way to measure clutch hitting, so whenever a player is tagged as a clutch hitter, it's purely subjective.

In fact ESPN aired a show called "Major League Baseball's In the Clutch" whereby the winners were selected by coaches, players, and sports writers. Interestingly though, there must be some relevance to clutch hitting because to this day, analysts continue to work on developing a formula that would measure "how much better or worse a player does in high leverage situations than he would have done in a context neutral environment." In other words it would be a measurement of a hitter's performance when faced with critical situations.

Now let's consider pressure situations. When you are up with the bases loaded, what's more important—your batting average or making contact? What's more important—making contact to drive in a run or improving your batting average? Is the pressure greater when you are up with the bases loaded in the bottom of the seventh or when no one on is on base in the second inning? Is the pressure greater when you are trying to move a runner over or when no one is on?

A good batting average does not equate to one's ability to handle the pressure in critical situations. It's a statement of hitting safely. But it's not a statement of when you hit safely. It doesn't tell you what impact, if any, a hit had on the game. When it comes to hitting under pressure, your batting average doesn't matter. It doesn't make you a clutch hitter. You can have a low batting average but still be a clutch hitter.

When you think about it, batting average is more of an individual statement and not a team statement. Would you rather have a high batting average or be highly committed to creating runs so that the team can win? Ever feel frustrated after a game because your team had a runner on third with less than two outs and no one made contact to tie or win the game? I know how a team player would respond to that question.

CONCLUSION

The following chart ranks the top 15 Major League players by batting average in 2019. It also ranks the top 15 players by wOBA ranking.

BA Ranking	Player	BA	w/OBA	w/OBA Ranking	Player	w/OBA Ranking	BA Ranking
1	Anderson	0.335		43	Yelich	1	3
2	Marte	0.329	0.405		Trout	2	
3	Yelich	0.329	0.442		Bregman	3	
4	LeMahieu	0.327		30	Cruz	4	14
5	Rendon	0.319	0.413		Bellinger	5	
6	McNeil	0.318		17	Rendon	6	
7	Moncada	0.315		23	Marte	7	
8	Arenado	0.315			Springer	8	
9	Reynolds	0.314		35	Soto	9	
10	Ushela	0.314		38	Arenado	10	8
11	Blackmon	0.314	0.387		Rizzo	11	
12	Brantley	0.311		40	Bogaerts	12	15
13	Devers	0.311		29	Freeman	13	
14	Cruz	0.311	0.418		Blackmon	14	11
15	Bogaerts	0.309	0.39		Canha	15	

Notice that 9 of the players in the batting average list don't make the wOBA listing. Or said another way, only 6 made it to the wOBA top 15 ranking. Now look at the names of the players who are not in the top 15 for batting average but are in the wOBA. How about Mike Trout or Anthony Rizzo? Remember, wOBA is a stat that measures actual run value, so if you had to pick one player for your team, who would you pick—Mike Trout or Tim Anderson? A player's run value, a stat that tells you how well a player contributes to scoring, is a significant stat.

Making contact or getting a hit with runners in scoring position has more significance than when no one is on. It's a good reason to focus on your QPA—Quality Plate Appearance average. Considering using SBA or any other system that reflects a batter's run-producing actions might be a better reason. It's a better measurement of a player's run production to the team and a gauge of how he responds in critical situations. And in a way, it can determine if a player is a clutch hitter. Trust me—the significance you give it will be appreciated by your teammates and your coach.

SLUMPS

The season starts and after three games Player A is 0 for 14 and has no batting average. Boy, he's in a big slump. Right? Before you agree, consider the following facts about his fourteen at-bats:

- Three of the at-bats are hard line drives that went right to the left fielder.

- Two are deep fly balls to the center fielder.

- Six are hard ground balls to the third baseman or shortstop; in one, the shortstop went into the hole and made a great throw.

- One at-bat is a strike out.

- Two are line drives right at the second baseman.

Knowing the facts, do you think that Player A is in a slump? You would be surprised by how many players do. The following is just one example of this type of thinking. It comes from *Baseball Excellence*, an online magazine I used to visit periodically. In the 'Ask the Coach" section, I came across this question by Shane from Utah:

"Hi, I'm writing to you because I am having a tough time hitting faster pitching. The first couple of games I was 6 for 8 with a grand slam, 2 triples and a double. But once faster pitchers started throwing

I'm only 1 for 3. I got a hit up the middle, struck out twice and walked. The odd thing I seemed to be in front of the pitches and I didn't feel comfortable at the plate. What can I do to adjust?"

So let's get this straight—After 3 games this player:

- is 7 for 11 (that's a .636 batting average).

- has an on base percentage of .727.

- has a slugging percentage of 1.454.

- got on base 50 percent of the time.

But after facing one pitcher who he has determined throws fast—he was 1 for 3 and the one hit was up the middle—he feels he needs to make adjustments. He does not understand that hitting has an innate high failure rate, but it's also the only sport activity that failing seven out of ten times is considered great.

This is why I contend that while slumps are real, in many cases, especially at the high school level, players think themselves into a slump. What happens to a player's batting average if he goes hitless a few games in a row, like my 0 for 14 example? It goes down. And whenever a sports reporter, coach, or fan is asked to measure a baseball player's overall performance, there is always one standard—and I mean always—mentioned as the qualifier: his batting average. It's a widely accepted indication of how good a player is.

This is a perception, not a reality. But perceptions can become realities, so for players who make that correlation, that a batting average defines a player, then a slump jeopardizes their perception of themselves as a player and, for some, the perception others have of them as a person. They do not separate the player from the person. To them it's one and the same. So after one or two "bad" outings, like Shane from Utah, they become preoccupied with their "failures" and overly concerned that they may repeat them in future competitions. Like rerunning an old movie, they replay the "bad" at bats over and over in their heads, and like a broken record, they constantly tell themselves, *I can't hit! It's awful! I stink!*

This bombardment of negativity has a domino effect—a chain reaction—on their mentality: A player starts questioning his abilities. Questioning leads to self-doubt. Self-doubt leads to an erosion of confidence. The player's loss of confidence takes him out of his comfort zone. And being out of his comfort zone is critical because being comfortable allows an athlete's talents to flow so that there is little or no interruption in his performance when he competes.

Self-control --------> Body control ---------> Skill control

The outcome of this domino effect is that the player panics. Instead of looking inward, they look outward. Instead of considering that the problem could be in their head, they conclude that it must be their body. It's not mental; it's physical. So what do they do? They start tinkering with their mechanics. Now, mechanics just might be the problem in a player's hitting difficulties. In his book *Sports Slump Busting,* Alan Goldberg, a sports psychologist, states, "Peak performance is a byproduct of your mind and body working together in perfect harmony. Instead of cooperating, your mind starts sabotaging your body."

Shane from Utah is a perfect example of Goldberg's statement. I find it interesting that he said "I didn't feel comfortable up at the plate" when he was talking about the third game. You have to assume he was comfortable up at the plate those first two games. What changed? Based on the limited information he gave, the only change was the type of pitching he faced. Want to bet he changed his approach to his at bats? I can almost hear him thinking, *Wow, this guy throws heat! I better be up there hacking! I'll never catch up to it.* Shane allowed his mind to sabotage his body. His body and mind were out of sync. Or as Alan Jaegar, a sport and fitness psychologist, states, "It's not your swing that changes between the lines."

It is not my intent to be unrealistic about slumps. If a player is striking out and rarely putting the ball in play, then he has a reason for concern. This is when players imagine they are in a slump. And when that happens they panic, opening the door for a real slump.

When you think you are in a slump, you may notice the following physical effects:

- tension and pressure, which cause your muscles to tighten, which affects how fluid your swing will be

- tightened facial muscles that control your eye movement, which causes rapid eye movement and makes it more difficult to see/focus on the ball

- a changed approach toward hitting

- "paralysis by analysis"

- chasing balls that you normally take

- over swinging, trying to do too much

This is why I say players think themselves into a slump. What's going on in their heads affects their mechanics. To sum up, your attitude moves you from an imagined slump to a reality. If you think you are in a slump, you probably are. Yes, slumps are real. And yes, mechanics might be the problem in a player's hitting difficulties but it might not.

You are responsible for your mental game. Your attitude determines if the imagined slump becomes a reality. You control your response to the situation. You feel the pressure—the pressure of a batting average that you or others think is acceptable; the pressure of having to get a hit in every game-winning situation; or the pressure of "I'm 0 for X number of at bats." You create the self-doubt by questioning your abilities. You make up your mind that you can't hit. And the moment you make a pre-performance decision like *I can't hit!* is the moment you have decided that you are in a slump. When you decide you are in a slump, guess what? You are! And the moment you become Shane from Utah and make pre-performance predictions—like you can't hit fastballs—you won't. What the mind thinks, the body will do—or in this case won't do! Perform the task—hitting a baseball. Henry Ford, founder of Ford Motors, once said, "Whether you think you can or think you can't, you're right!"

It's one thing not being successful because you don't have the ability or haven't practiced; it's quite another thing not being successful because you fail to make mental adjustments—like how much importance you put on your batting average. Steve Springer, the author of *Quality At Bats* and someone who has spent 35 years in professional baseball as a player, agent, and scout, states, "The batting average is the biggest trap in all sports." He feels that "players must redefine their definition of success from getting hits to hitting the ball hard and helping their team win." If you don't make mental adjustments you increase your chances of not achieving success. So before you and Shane start tinkering with your mechanics, consider tinkering with your mindset.

What determines a real slump and an imagined one is the quality of your plate appearances, not if you got a hit.

That's right—I said plate appearances. Now, as we all know, whenever the word slump is mentioned, one of the first solutions coaches mention is to use your quality at bat average as your measuring stick. You are instructed to analyze every at bat, determine if they were good or bad, count each good at bat as a base hit, and then divide that by your plate appearances. That's how you determine your quality at bat average.

While this is probably good advice, there are some issues with it. First, many players are not convinced of its value, for two reasons. In the baseball world, unlike batting average, quality at bat is not even a recorded stat. Apparently it's insignificant. It's never talked about; therefore, it must not be legitimate. It doesn't garnish the attention that the historically considered "King of Stats' has, so in the player's mind, there's no social appeal. Essentially it's not sexy.

Secondly, in my opinion, coaches don't do enough to explain the value of quality plate appearances to the players. They don't mention to the team things like "That bases loaded walk in the 7th inning was huge" or "Two of the seven runs scored can be attributed to X, Y, Z players' good at bats." The coaching staff unconsciously shows that they aren't convinced of the value of quality plate appearances, so the players are skeptical too.

And who determines the quality of the plate appearance? The quality standard, regardless of outcome, set by the players and coaches in many cases can be totally different.

Players want base hits and coaches want contact. Coaches like a ground ball that moves a runner into scoring position, while the player is ticked off because he didn't get a hit. In the player's mind, there is glamour in a base hit, but a ground ball out has a stigma to it. Let's face it, there are very few players who would grade that ground ball out as a quality plate appearance. The coach would, but they wouldn't. Again, it's not sexy. They feel it adds no value to their performance or to their ability as a player. And for some, it adds no value to them as a person. So players continue to allow their batting average to determine if they are in a slump.

A more definitive measuring stick to determine if you are in a slump is what I call your "quality plate performance average." Not your batting average. It's a better measurement of your performance value because hits alone aren't enough to judge the full scope of a hitter's contribution.

Not only does your quality plate performance average demonstrate your value, but more importantly, it demonstrates your value to the team. This can help how you feel about yourself as a player, a person, and a teammate. Every player on every team wants to think he is contributing to the team. A good quality plate appearance average does just that.

The problem with a batting average is that there are flaws in its value. A batting average doesn't show who the better contact hitter is. It doesn't show you who the best is at getting on base. It doesn't measure the player's frequency in reaching base. So why is that important? Remember, a team's goal is to produce runs. You can't score runs until runners get on base and then things happen that cause run production, one of which is putting the ball in play—making contact, getting on base—to make things happen.

When you calculate batting averages, you do not include plate appearances that result in walks, hit by pitch, sacrifice bunts, or a sacrifice fly—all of which are run-producing or runner-providing results which could lead to runs scored. So while we can all agree that those qualify as quality at bats, let's look at just some plate appearance results that are run-producing or runner-providing—quality at bats.

QUALITY PLATE APPEARANCE	PERFORMANCE—END RESULT
Ground ball out runner at third came home	Run scored
Ground out moved runner from 1st to 2nd	Put runner in scoring position
Reached base on error	Runner—possible run
Fly ball out to right field runner tags up	Moved runner—possible score
Struck out on 9 pitches	Worked the pitcher
Failed sacrifice bunt fielder throws ball away	Runner—possible Run
Line drive shot to short	Put 'good hitter' mindset in pitcher's head

So that you understand quality plate performance average versus batting average, let's look at the following hypothetical. A batter has 10 plate appearances. His performance is as follows: 3 hits—1 walk—1 sacrifice bunt—5 miscellaneous outs—no runs scored—no RBIs. To determine his batting average, because walks and sacrifice bunts do not count toward batting average, you would divide the 3 hits by his at bats—NOT HIS PLATE APPEARANCES—which in this case would be 8 not 10. Thus his batting average—the value of his performance—would be .375 (3 for 8).

Now assume the same batter gets up but his performance is as follows: 1 hit—1 walk—1 sacrifice bunt—7 miscellaneous outs with one run scored and one RBI. Now let's assume that of the 7 miscellaneous outs, one was a ball hit to the shortstop, who makes an error and the runner at second advances to third and scores because the next batter gets a base hit. And one of another outs was a ground ball to the second baseman—fielder's choice—which scored the runner on third. So of the seven outs, two can be considered run producing—quality plate appearances. To determine the player's quality plate performance average, you would divide the 10 plate appearances by his quality at bats, which in this case would be 5. Thus his plate appearance—the value of his performance—would be .500 (5 for 10). However, his batting average would be .100.

Remember, a team's goal is to produce runs. Making contact and on-base frequency play a big role in run production. So with that in mind, which player in my hypothetical offers greater team value? In essence which player performed the best for the team? Which stat—batting average or quality plate appearance average—is better for the team? Quality plate appearance average is the better stat because it serves the team, while a batting average only serves the player.

So make up your mind that you are going to avoid talking and ignore any conversations about batting average. Including your teammates'. Talking gets you thinking, and thinking about batting averages puts you in panic mode, which gets you thinking about slumps. Instead think about how much you help the team by hitting the ball hard, making consistent contact, getting on base—think *quality plate appearances average*. This should negate thoughts about slumps.

Let's go back to that Henry Ford quote: "Whether you think you can or think you can't, you are right." I would like to change his statement to: "Whether you think you are in a slump or think you are not in a slump, you are right."

Bad days are a normal part of every sport.

You are not going to have your best every day. Slumps are a part of baseball. They are inevitable for even the greatest players; a natural and unavoidable part of baseball. They are part of every player's season, especially in high school, where a season, on average, is a short 20 games. You need to accept the fact that, as Tony Gwynn, one-time star right fielder for the San Diego Padres, considered one of the best hitters in the 1990s, states, "every hitter on every level is going to struggle" at some point during his season.

Or as Derek Jeter, renowned New York Yankee, stated in an article published in the July 2011 issue of *Sports Illustrated* when asked if he ever doubted himself: "No question ….You have doubts… You cannot feel good. I hit .180 for two months [in 2004]…in May I was hitting .189 and there I was on the cover of *Sports Illustrated*. So there are times when you go, 'What is going on?' But you still have to try to be positive. Even if you didn't get any hits, you have to say, 'Well, I hit the ball hard,' or, 'Well, I laid off a tough pitch.' You know what I mean? 'I drew a walk.' Something positive. Otherwise, you'd go crazy."

You need to be realistic about your hitting abilities.

Everybody wants to be a .350-plus hitter, but even if everything happens just right, and you practice diligently every day, maybe the best you will achieve is a .275 batting average. Call it your God-given talent or Mother Nature or a fact of life, whatever you want; everybody just doesn't have the same abilities. Instead of concentrating on your batting average, consider other things. Like improving your bunting skills. Decide you are going to be the best bunter on the team, and help the team.

You have to be realistic about the caliber of the competition you are facing.

For example, as I'm writing this, the 2016 National League playoff games are being played. At this point the Chicago Cubs have already defeated the San Francisco Giants and are currently into the third game against the LA Dodgers. Anthony Rizzo of the Cubs is struggling. He ended the series with the Giants hitting .067 and after 2 games against the Dodgers he has not had a hit. He is 1 for 23! Based on his regular season stats he should have 7 hits. So why is it that a player who hit .292 for the season—which in pro baseball is very good—is not anywhere near his season average? The answer is that the postseason features the best teams with the best pitchers. Read the following description of what Rizzo has encountered: "The Cubs have drawn a particularly daunting gauntlet. Among the six starters they've faced: Kershaw, the best pitcher in the game; Bumgarner, one of the best postseason pitchers ever; and Johnny Cueto, who is coming off a Cy Young-worthy season."

While the physical aspects are obvious, there is a tactical aspect as well. An example of this is an up-and-coming star on the JV team at a high school team I coached, so in his junior year, playing for the varsity team, he had high expectations. About one-third of the way through the season he was not doing well and had become totally frustrated. The coaching staff explained to him that he was not yet used to this higher level of competition. It's not just the physical part—faster fast balls—but the tactical part as well. Varsity pitchers think more about what pitch to throw, when to throw, and where to throw, as opposed to the JV pitcher. He refused to accept this as an issue, struggled all year, and never came out to play his senior year.

As you move up in playing levels, the abilities—caliber—of the players change. Playing college baseball is harder than varsity high school, varsity high school is harder than JV, and JV is harder than Teener baseball. As you go up in levels, the game is played faster and at a level where routine plays are routinely made and "Web Gems" are made with more consistency. Not only do pitchers throw harder but they also have good command of 2 or 3 pitches. Your base swing, which has served you well up to this point, may not be good enough.

Get another opinion.

There is a section in the book *Sports Slump Busting* entitled "Eliminating Causes of the Slump." "Slump busting begins with the athlete or coach examining and then ruling out any physical…. reasons for the …bad play." So if you feel your attitude toward your hitting slipping, don't be the judge and jury. Get another opinion. Ask your coach for his evaluation. The quickest boost to your confidence may just be to know that the coach's opinion doesn't match yours. His opinion concerning the quality of your at bats may be totally different than yours. And by the way, he may even remind you that the team needs you on defense and that you are a good team player. Point being that there is more to the game than hitting. If your mindset is on your positive value to the team, it just may change your mindset on your abilities as a hitter.

Don't play "catch up" with your eyes.

Hitting is actually a visual skill, and you need to work on it because "you can't hit what you can't see." Review the two philosophies about what your eyes should be doing when you are in the batter's box on pages 188 and 189 in the Quicksand article. Hard focus vs. soft focus or scan and hunt—either method can help you see the ball better. Either way, when you are in the batter's box, get your eyes to the release point at the right time—when the pitcher is about to release the ball. If you shift your focus too soon, your eyes will focus on an object beyond the pitcher. When the ball does appear, your eyes must readjust or catch up, which takes time that you don't have. Your goal should be to have your eyes ahead of the ball. You should be tracking the ball to where it's going—not where it's been.

Do you have physical issues?

Slumps can be caused by physical problems—injuries, over training, or even vision problems. Slumps can be caused by technological problems, like a bat that is the wrong size or too heavy.

TAKE RESPONSIBILITY
FOR YOUR
ATTITUDE ADJUSTMENT

I find it interesting that when a coach or the local "guru" evaluates a player, when it comes to issues in mechanics, the player will ask for and willingly accept advice and suggested drills. So based on the coach's advice, in an attempt to fix the problems, the player goes off and does self-directed work at practice. And he does so with the expectation of a solution. Doesn't question it. But what happens when the outcome of the evaluation is that coach feels the player's problems are with his emotions and mental approach. It's certainly not the solution they were looking for. For some players the evaluation is critical, unfair, and unjustified. It's an attack on their self-image. Their feelings are hurt, so they go into denial and resist.

As former Oklahoma State baseball coach Gary Ward in the 2/2/2020 issue of *Collegiate Baseball* explained, the player "hides in his comfort zone and fights off the negative emotions of blame, shame, guilt, and seeks to rationalize away any accountability or responsibility for such an evaluation." What he is saying is that the player doesn't rationalize that the solution to his issues could be his attitude or emotions. So not only does he not accept it as a solution, but he won't take responsibility for it. Responsibility being the key word.

"Responsibility is the acceptance of our "selves" as the cause of our current (or past) situation, and it's our willingness to cope with the situation." To put this into 'English', our beliefs about a situation directly cause our feelings. Others do not cause our feelings—we cause them ourselves. So in order to cope with the situation it's your responsibility to be willing to make an adjustment to your thinking about the role the mental part of the game does have on your physical game.

Rather than go deeper into psychological thinking, the following story about Orel Hershiser is an attempt to illustrate what this all means.

Orel Hershiser played 18 years of Major League baseball with the LA Dodgers. In his biography, *Out of the Blue,* there is a section titled 'The Sermon on the Mound.' It tells of his troubles in the early days of his career as a relief pitcher. "I couldn't get anything going, couldn't maintain any consistency. I might get a guy or even two guys out, then I'd get too fine, too careful, and walk somebody. I'd get even more careful, and before you knew it, someone had doubled up the alley. I'd be yanked, out for not doing what I was paid to do, and then I'd sit, wondering what was happening to my brief career."

He goes on to say, "I was young and looked younger, and because I was thin and wore glasses, and because I was known as a Christian athlete, I got the feeling people assumed I had no guts. Hershiser was too passive, too nice, too mellow to get the job done."

His record was 2 wins, 2 losses with a 6.20 earned run average when Tommy Lasorda, the Dodgers Manager, called him into his office and proceeded to lace into him. "Hershiser, you're giving these hitters too much credit! You're telling yourself, 'If I throw this ball over the plate, they're gonna hit it out.' That is a negative approach to hitting! You don't believe in yourself! You're scared to pitch in the big leagues! Who do you think these hitters are, Babe Ruth? Babe Ruth's dead! Quit being so careful. Go after the hitter. Get ahead in the count. Don't be so fine with him and then find yourself forced to lay one in!"

Lasorda continued, "You gotta go out there and do it on the mound. Take charge! Make them hit your best stuff. Be aggressive! Be a bulldog out there. That's gonna be your new name: Bulldog. When we bring you in in the ninth to face Dale Murphy and he hears; 'Now pitching, Orel Hershiser, man, he can't wait till you get there! But if he hears, 'Now pitching, Bulldog Hershiser, he's thinking, *Oh no, who's that? Murphy's gonna be scared to death!*

"I want you to believe you are the best pitcher in baseball. I want you to look at that hitter and say, 'There's no way you can hit me.' You gotta believe you are superior to the hitter and that you can get anybody out who walks up there. Quit giving the hitter so much credit. You're better than these guys."

It was just a couple of days later that Hershiser was called upon in a difficult relief situation against the San Francisco Giants. As he got set to pitch to the first hitter, Lasorda yelled out, "C'mon, Bulldog! You can do it, Bulldog! You're my man, Bulldog!" Not only was Orel Hershiser successful that day, but that year, he became a premier pitcher, setting records and winning several World Series games. He did so because he was willing to make an adjustment—an attitude adjustment—about how he perceived himself. Instead of a passive, thin, nice guy he was an aggressive, tough-minded bulldog. It was his way of coping with his situation. Taking responsibility for his attitude had a direct bearing on his physical performance.

Now for those of you who underestimate the influence, or to what extent, that your attitude has on your performance, consider the following sequence of thoughts and ask yourself if at any time you have felt or thought the same way.

Watching an opposing pitcher warm up before the game, Player A is impressed with how fast and how strong he's throwing.

He remembers how good this pitcher is. He mentions this to his teammates as the pre-game jitters run through his body and it gets close to game time.

The game begins and the first batter goes down swinging for the first out. As the batter returns to the bench, Player A says to himself, *Boy, this guy really throws hard. It's going to be tough to get hits today. This guy is unhittable.* Player A is so impressed that he doesn't even hear the batter, who has just struck out, critique the pitcher as he returns to the bench.

The next batter gets a base hit, followed by the next batter's hard line drive down the left field line that scores a run and puts a runner on second with one out. Next batter hits a triple and after four batters have faced this hard-throwing pitcher the score is 4-0 with only one out. It's player A's turn at bat. As he approaches the plate he thinks, *Can't be throwing that hard. I've been making good contact all week.* The first pitch he faces he sends over the second baseman's head for a base hit. As he's standing on first base picking up signs from the third base coach, he leans over to the first base coach and says, "This guy's not that fast."

What type of an at-bat do you think Player A would have had if he didn't see his teammates' hard hit balls prior to his at-bat? As he approached the plate do you think he would be thinking, *Can't be throwing hard.* Do you really think he would have an attitude adjustment concerning facing the 'un-hittable' pitcher prior to stepping into the batter's box?

Player A's attitude changed because he had a reality check. He went from *probably won't hit this guy* to *hey, I can.*

His belief about the situation—facing this pitcher—had changed. He saw that the pitcher wasn't un-hittable.

And let's suppose the batters who hit before him did not get hits. Suppose they hit weak ground balls to the infield or struck out.

Do you think Player A would have changed his attitude as he got into the batter's box or do you think he would have reinforced his impression—his attitude—of how hard the pitcher threw?

Doubt, fear, worry, and tension are natural emotions, even logical, when it's performance time and especially when things aren't going well. However, remember, doubt, fear, worry, and tension are negative emotions—obstacles to your confidence. They usually take control of your attitude, making you question if you can hit the pitcher you are facing today. This is important to understand because as sports psychologist Ken Ravizza and Tom Hanson co-authors of *Heads Up Baseball* state; "Confidence is the goal of the mental game. If you are not in control of yourself, you aren't playing with confidence."

Now, more importantly, you have to realize that emotions are the result of your own thinking. No one is forcing you to think negatively. Nowhere in the Official Baseball Rulebook does it state: "If the pitcher has walked the bases loaded, he shall put himself in a tense and angered state." The last time I checked the Rulebook, it did not say, "If a batter has not hit safely in his last seven turns at bats, he must spend his time questioning whether or not he will ever get another hit."

You are responsible for controlling your attitude, so it's your responsibility to make the necessary attitude adjustments in the situation you are facing—if it's needed.

REJECTING RESPONSIBILITY

A player must take responsibility for his mental approach to the game (and his actions), but some players reject this responsibility. Why? Some possible reasons include:

- to avoid the pain of embarrassment after he has made a mistake or after a bad game;

- to protect his reputation, his image;

- to get sympathy ("Poor guy, it wasn't his fault");

- to avoid criticism from his parents, peers, or teammates;

- to protect his pride;

- his strong desire to feel approval by others.

For example, ever wonder why a pitcher throws his best stuff during warm-ups but when he crosses the white lines, he doesn't have it? What happens to this pitcher during the walk from the bullpen to the mound? The answer is too much wrong thinking, which establishes his attitude. Consider the following chart:

BULLPEN	GAME
No risk. No chance to fail.	Chance of bad day and embarrassment
No concern for impressing or pleasing others.	Desire to please and impress others
Will not be judged or criticized	Worry about what others think about him and his performance.
Easy to concentrate due to few distractions.	Many distractions. Thoughts about what few distractions. others expect of him, teammates and fans yelling, thoughts about opponents' intentions.

Just a game of catch. Thinking only about what and where to throw the ball.	Trying to decide what is the right pitch. Thoughts about the damage the hitter has done in the past.
No thoughts about the past, only about the next pitch.	Thoughts about bad calls, bad plays, bad pitches.

Now that you know why, you need to know *how* a player rejects responsibility. He takes the easy route. He makes excuses. He blames other people, circumstances, conditions, or unknown forces. Any of the following statements sound familiar?

- The umpire blew the first pitch.

- The sun was in my eyes.

- The wind was playing tricks with the ball.

- I can't pitch in cold weather.

- I thought the umpire said there were two outs.

- The coach doesn't put me in the right spot in the batting order.

He makes excuses so that he has an acceptable reason for his poor performance or the outcome of the game. Excuses ease his disappointment. Unfortunately, all this player is doing is fooling himself. He doesn't realize that the degree to which he holds himself accountable and responsible for his actions will be a major factor in determining how much he learns, improves and succeeds.

Believe it or not, nobody is perfect. We need to accept the fact that whenever we attempt to do something, because we are not perfect, there is the possibility and the probability that we are going to fail at times.

THE WINNING EDGE

Brian Tracy, author of several self-improvement books geared toward professional salesmen, states in one of his audiocassettes, "It's small differences in confidence and abilities that translate into enormous differences in results. One of the most important things that you can ever do is to identify the winning edges in your field, and then concentrate on becoming superior in those critical areas."

Tracy refers to it as "the winning edge concept." He believes that people who achieve far above the average are not necessarily smarter or better than the average person. Rather they have developed their talents and abilities in specific areas where it makes a difference. They develop the critical edge that gives them a decided advantage over the average person.

Successful people make it a habit of doing what unsuccessful people do not like to do or won't do. They discipline themselves to go beyond where the average person would stop because it's too difficult, too fatiguing, or too challenging.

So you have to be better at something that the others you are competing against don't have. You need a point of difference. Doing the little things, like working on your mental game, helps you do that.

Develop a critical edge that gives you an advantage over others.

Let's say you are trying out for second base. It's the first day of practice and the coach tells everyone to go to their position. You go over to second and realize there are three players trying out for your position. After the first week the coach concludes that when it comes to mechanics and physical performance, all three players are equals. But he is only keeping two, so one must go. How does he decide who to keep? As he continues to observe he notices that one of the players always puts his head down after he makes a mistake. The other two get right back into position, ready to make the next play. When he talks to him, the player says all the right things, but the coach doesn't like his body language.

You're not the one putting your head down. You are selected because you have a point of difference. Your body language, in this case, is that critical edge that gives you an advantage over others.

Identify a winning edge and then concentrate on becoming superior in that area.

Let's continue with my story about the second basemen. The season starts and while both of you would love to be a .350 plus hitter, the reality is that you are average hitters—somewhere in the .260 range. So what do you do? Well, you could dwell on your batting average or you could find something you can do that maybe the other player can't or isn't good at. You could identify bunting as a critical edge and concentrate on becoming the best bunter on the team. Becoming the best bunter puts you ahead of the other player. You now have a point of difference.

Go beyond where the average person would stop.

Somewhere out there on some ballpark, players are working on their physical game. And I mean all players. They all will go through the same drills the same way. After all, they have been doing it that way since they played in Little League. But how many of the players are working on their mental game? Probably not many, because it's not the norm.

Consider the following hypothesis: Because you have been struggling at the plate, you decide that your mental game and not your physical game could be the reason for your problem. So you decide to add some type of pre-pitch routine to your at bat:

- Just before stepping into the batter's box, take a breath.

- Put your back foot in and keep your front foot out of the batter's box.

- Look at the label on the bat and say to yourself—*I'm in control.*

- Now put your front foot into the batter's box and take two powerful swings.

You decide that from that point on during practice, you are going to work on it, and when you step into the batting cage, you will explain to the coach or player who is pitching what you are doing. Basically you are trying to simulate a game time at bat. You don't want to face the normal rapid-fire pitch-after-pitch approach.

Ask yourself how many of your teammates, if any, are doing this. And consider what type of response you might get from them. I mention this because once you go against the norm, you are opening the door for ridicule. Don't be surprised when they poke fun at you. They probably will because your pre-pitch routine is different. It makes you different. And let's face it, no one likes to be different.

It's important that you explain to the coaching staff the rationale behind your actions. If the coaching staff and you are on the same page, if the team leaders embrace it, you will be okay. But if they do not, then be prepared to be by yourself on this. You need to decide how you are going to react when someone yells at you because you are taking too much time in the cage. You need to decide who's in control. Your teammates or you? Are you your own man or a follower? You can control that. Dare to be great.

Remember Brian Tracy's message? People who are successful make it a habit to do what some people don't like to do. They "go beyond where the average person would stop." But the fact that you do try something, like a pre-pitch routine, and they don't is a sign that you are the one willing to go beyond the average person. You are working on the critical edge that gives you an advantage over them. That is your point of difference.

For those of you who think that the reward of working on the 'little things' like your mental game is not worth the effort, consider a horse that runs in a race, wins by a nose, and wins ten times the prize money of the horse that comes in second. Is the horse that comes in first ten times faster? Twice as fast? Ten percent faster? No, the horse that wins by a nose is only a nose faster. But that translates into ten times the prize money.

Or consider that in 2016, the average batting average in the Major Leagues was .250. In essence the player got 3 hits in 12 at bats and earned the median salary of $1.5 million. But a batter who hit .300 and got 4 hits out of 12 at bats earned closer to the salary average, which was $4.3 million. Think about it, a difference of almost 300 percent in salary for just one additional hit for every 12 at bats.

The competition increases greatly at each level. The competition for making the team or becoming a starter or for scholarship money is sharper than ever, especially with the fast growing number of sport specialization instructors that high school players are working with. Because of this, you need a point of difference. You have to be better at something that the others you are competing against don't have. You need a winning edge.

THINKING TOO MUCH

Why do you think a player like Tom Brady has won multiple championships? Let's face it, to make it into the pros, players have to have a certain skill set. But what sets Brady apart from his peers? If you ranked all professional quarterbacks based on their skill sets, everyone involved in football would agree that Brady probably doesn't lead in any of the categories.

So what makes Brady and better players different? A common answer from many sports psychologists is "mindset." They think differently. However, sports psychologist Dr. Stan Beecham disagrees. "The reality is *not* that they think differently.... It's the absence of cognition. It's the absence of emotion." He feels their advantage is that these players don't actually think about winning. They simply believe they're going to do well. They don't overwhelm themselves with thinking.

I'm sure you have heard expressions like 'He lets the game come to him,' 'he's on fire,' 'I'm in the zone' or 'he's playing unconscious." Sports psychologist Alan Jaeger spoke about these 'peak performance' statements made by players in the 2/25/05 issue of *Collegiate Baseball*. "What the athlete is really saying is that his natural talents and abilities are taking over without any interference from his mind because his mind is free of thought. This is a unique state of mind because the mind is used to thinking. It is not used to being silent and still, especially when there are distractions or consequences at stake."

What both sports psychologists are really saying is that the players, whether they know it or not, play at their best when they're not thinking too much. One of the biggest performance mistakes athletes at every level make is to think too much *right before* and *during* their performances. They need to just play and immerse themselves in the game and let the game dictate what they need to do. The more successful athletes should wait until after the game to analyze (not judge) their performance. Doing so will help clear their mind.

Now in all honesty I have no way of knowing what Tom Brady is or is not thinking. But I do know he is a very good football player, and I know you won't be good in this game without the ability to quickly bounce back from errors, miscues, lousy calls and strikeouts. Regardless of what you are thinking about, thinking too much is always hazardous to an athlete's performance health. It distracts your focus from the task at hand at that moment—the mental part of your game. It tightens your muscles, which slows your reflexes and reaction times—the physical part of the game.

A phenomenon that occurs in sports and is a great example of too much thinking is called "paralysis by analysis," when a player overanalyzes (or over thinks) a situation, a decision, or an action not taken, in effect paralyzing the outcome. It can also lead to hesitation and indecision. An article by a sports psychologist states, "When one's instinctive or intuitive athleticism is compromised by the analytical thought process, the athlete is no longer able to flow freely on autopilot."

So what are some of the triggering events that could result in paralysis by analysis?

- You focus too much on your mechanics. When this happens you are no longer able to be on autopilot. You lose fluidity.

- When the pressure is on and you focus too much on situations like the outcome of the game or making a play or getting a hit when it's needed or the error you made the last inning. You have taken yourself out of the present and back into the past or forward into the future.

- A few mistakes or one error or one bad at bat. When this happens a player has a tendency to press. He tries too hard, and fear of failure or fear of another mistake runs through his head.

- You compete for others and not yourself. You feel a need to please someone—your father, for example. You feel you have to prove yourself to someone and fear letting someone down.

Understand that when you are playing your best, you don't even realize what you are thinking because you play on autopilot. You are efficient, there seems to be little thought, the game is effortless, and you are completely absorbed in the task.

However, when there is a heightened awareness of "feeling" your mechanics or feeling pressure, the level of your self-consciousness about performing correctly rises. And when that happens, as Dr Jay-Lee Nair, a sports psychologist, states, "The mind is paralyzed in thought and you feel uncomfortable over every shot."

My favorite example of this is not even a baseball story. It's about a salesman who flies into New York City with a prospect list to sell a brand-new product. He's excited, can't wait. Monday comes and goes—no sales. But he's going to be there all week, so he pushes on. Same results on Tuesday. Same results Wednesday. By Thursday morning he dreads even getting up. But he does and by the end of the day, same results—no sales.

Dejectedly he goes back to his hotel room and calls his wife. He informs her of his lack of success—he's done, he's failed, and he's coming home. But to his surprise she tells him, "That's okay, honey, I just won the lottery and we are millionaires." Imagine how he felt after she told him that. He's so happy that he decides—you know what—instead of flying home Friday morning he's going to make those last few planned calls. Guess what happens? He makes a sale—on the very first call. Second call, another sale.

So what happened? Well, he knew he didn't have to make a sale. He was a millionaire! The pressure was gone, and so he didn't press; he let the call dictate to him what he needed to say or do. He went on autopilot. He was himself. He relaxed! He stopped thinking about the consequences if he failed. He basically followed the message that a famous Nike ad conveyed when they connected with Michael Jordon. JUST DO IT!

This reminds me of a situation I was directly involved in as a coach. I was attending a clinic where we were told that the next segment was about pitching and it was going to be conducted by the local 'star' who I'll call Mike. Mike was a young man who we all knew and followed as he made his way from a successful high school and college career into the pros. So of course I wanted to attend that session. Mike started out but within minutes you could see he was uncomfortable. He was hesitant with his information and at times would stare out into the audience. You could hear the gears in his head going. Finally he just blurted out, "I can't explain how to pitch—I JUST DO IT!"

Then there is the cat story in the "Control" article.

I was driving down a small road toward home when something darted out of the darkness onto the road in front of me. I slammed on my brakes and just missed a large cat that was chasing a field mouse. As I continued on my way I marveled about the cat and his pursuit. For that cat, nothing else in the world existed except for that mouse.

If I had not hit the brakes I would have run him over. But he tore after that mouse as if I didn't exist. Only after he had the mouse firmly clenched in his teeth did he acknowledge my existence before running off into the woods.

Was he thinking about the last three field mice that got away or what the other cats would say? Was he concerned about his form or how he looked? Was he worried about making a mistake?

The intent of the stories is to help you understand the important role your focus plays in determining your success. Gifted athlete or not, you need to control how your mind is functioning, And that starts by becoming conscious of your own thought process. Let muscle memory do its job. Go into 'let it happen' mode. Just do it! If cats can, so can you!

In closing I thought "The Frog and the Centipede" would be a fun way to explain paralysis by analysis. ENJOY!

THE FROG AND THE CENTIPEDE

One day a frog was sunning himself on a lily pad when a centipede came walking by. The frog was immediately entranced by the centipede's flowing and graceful movement across the pad. He marveled at what an amazing ability the insect had to both time and coordinate all of those legs so that the end result was so smooth and precise. While he was a great leaper and strong swimmer, the frog couldn't help but feel a little jealous of the centipede's skills. After all, his job was so easy, having to coordinate only two legs and two arms, while the centipede's was so much more complicated, having to balance one hundred.

Hoping to be enlightened by the insect's tremendous skill, the frog said to the centipede: "Kind sir. I am most impressed by your flowing athleticism and your ability to closely synchronize all those legs of yours. I must admit that I myself could never coordinate a hundred legs the fine way that you do. Would I be out of line if I asked you, how in the world do you do that?"

Hearing the compliment from the frog, the centipede stopped his movement and began to beam with pride. He had never bothered to think about how he moved because it was just something that he did naturally. He replied: "Why thank you sincerely, Mr. Frog. I do appreciate your kind feedback. However, I need to spend a moment thinking about how I move before I can share with you my secrets. But now that you mention it, I must modestly say that my ability to coordinate all of those legs at once is truly an amazing feat."

The centipede then began to think very hard about his hundred legs, the order that he had to move each one in, and how he timed these movements so precisely. The more he thought about it, the more he marveled at his own ability. However, the more he thought about it, the more complicated the whole process seemed, and he couldn't quite figure out exactly how he was able to do it.

Then he thought, *Perhaps if I walk a little bit, I can pay very close attention to how I move and then I will be able to more fully answer the frog's question.* So he explained his intention to the frog and then got up and began to move. However, no sooner had he taken one or two steps than his legs became entangled in each other and he tripped. Slightly embarrassed, he pulled himself back up and once again set out to try to figure out exactly how he was able to coordinate his movements. Once again his legs became entangled and he again fell to the pad.

Now the centipede's embarrassment merged with a growing sense of frustration. How was it even possible that he could trip? He had never once tripped in his life and here he had just tripped twice in a row! He quickly righted himself and tried to figure out how best to regain his balance and coordination. He wondered if he was moving his legs out of sequence, or maybe too fast, or perhaps, too slow. He thought about the order of his movement and whether he should start off with the feet on the left side of his body or the right side. However, the more he thought, the more confused he got. This time, after just one step, he went down hard on his face.

His embarrassment and frustration turned to panic. He began to wonder what might happen if he couldn't ever walk again without falling. He immediately got angry, chiding himself for not being able to do something as basic as walking. However, his frustration and anger did nothing to help him walk. In fact, those feelings seemed to make things much worse. The poor centipede was now an unco-ordinated mess, falling all around the lily pad. Meanwhile the frog looked on in curious amusement. Soon the centipede couldn't even stand up!

He quickly thought about what had gotten him into this mess in the first place and inwardly cursed the frog and his stupid question. He suddenly realized that his own self-consciousness about walking was the one thing that was preventing him from walking. His anger boiled over and he yelled at the frog, "With all due respect, Mr. Frog, don't ever ask me how I walk again. I do NOT know how I do it and I don't WANT TO KNOW!" Whereupon he got up without thinking and quickly and smoothly ran off the pad headed for home.

Moral of the story: When it comes to athletic performance, OVER THINKING is hazardous to your performance health!

TO SWING OR NOT
TO SWING—THAT IS
THE QUESTION

As we know, baseball is a leader in keeping records and using statistics. With that in mind, let's discuss some baseball issues utilizing analytics.

SWING AT FIRST PITCH

To the age-old question of whether or not to swing at the first pitch, there are two schools of thought. There are those who feel that the selective approach is the best. The advantage of this approach is that by taking the first pitch you can see what the pitcher's got. Hitting is timing, so by taking, you can gauge the speed and ball movement and be in a better position to time your swing on the next pitch. You also find out what pitch the pitcher has confidence in because pitchers tend to be creatures of habit. They usually throw what they feel is their best pitch on the first pitch.

Another advantage is that by taking the pitch, if it's a ball, you can then treat the next pitch the same as the first—have the same approach on the second pitch as the first so that you might be able to work yourself into a better hitter's count. And let's not forget the umpire. As we all know, as much as they shouldn't, each umpire has his own strike zone. You won't know what each individual umpire's strike zone is until you see some pitches. If they're erratic, then taking a first pitch might not be a gamble.

Then there are those who don't like this "be selective" approach. They feel that the hitter ends up taking too many pitches, which takes them out of "aggressive mode." The hitter ends up facing pitcher advantage counts too many times. They also feel that because the probability of a first pitch fast ball is so high, you should be swinging. Pitchers certainly want to throw a strike and because coaches instruct them to get ahead in the counts, they have a "first pitch, first strike should lead to first out" mentality. Thus proponents of first pitch swinging feel that they are going to be good ones to swing at.

So how good are they? For four seasons, Dean Stotz, Associate Head Coach at Stanford University, gathered data from every pitch thrown in every Stanford game using The Competitive Edge Decision Systems software entitled Chart Mine. As reported in the 1/4/02 issue of *The Collegiate Baseball*, 68 percent of the time with a 0-0 count the pitcher would throw a fastball. Interestingly enough the University of Delaware also conducted a similar study and came up with the same results.

But here's the catch. While this is certainly good information concerning the type of pitch to expect, it's not on location. You see, what the Stanford study also discovered was that only 40 percent of the time was the ball in the strike zone. In other words, 60 percent of the time the first pitch fastball was actually a ball—provided the batter did not swing! Within that 40 percent, was the first pitch on the plate within the real strike zone or was it a bad umpire-called strike?

TO SWING OR NOT TO SWING—
THAT IS THE QUESTION

Speaking of swinging, some interesting data that also came from the Stanford study was that 43 percent of the time batters swung and missed first pitch fastballs that WERE OUT OF THE STRIKE ZONE! Okay—that's the college level. What about at the pro level? Well, in a recent study on location of pitches by Major League pitchers, in 2018, they threw first pitch strikes 57 percent of the time. They missed 43 percent of the time. Now to be fair at this level it could be a purpose pitch—off the plate—to see if the batter is overly aggressive. Pitchers at this level know they can get away with wasting a pitch, so they purposely do not throw a strike, and the miss data is a little skewed. They do, however, miss a high number of times.

Those on the 'be selective' side need to realize that there are times when taking the first pitch swing approach is not the right thing to do—like when you are facing a control pitcher. He has proven that he's tough; he throws strikes. Or facing the "average" pitcher who is having his day—it's his World Series. If you run into these types of pitchers, concessions or adjustments are in order. In this case your plan should be to open your strike zone and work on putting the ball in play. Don't make a tough pitcher tougher by constantly being behind in the count! Being patient—looking for your pitch—is not realistic.

And let's not forget about the umpire. If in a game you observe that the umpire's strike zone is inconsistent, you are going to have put your personal strike zone aside and go with the flow. You also need to note if the umpire seems to fall in love with a certain pitch or location, because whether you agree with his strike zone or use your personal strike zone, that day the strike zone is what that umpire makes it. You just need to protect the plate.

For those of you who feel I'm overestimating the importance of an umpire's strike zone, Boston University did a study and concluded that in the Major Leagues in 2018, umpires made 34,294 incorrect ball and strike calls. That's 14 per game. Imagine the effect that had on the outcome of a game or players' stats. And this was at the professional level. Can you imagine what the numbers would be at the high school level?

No one is suggesting that you should never swing at the first pitch (unless instructed to 'take until you get a strike' by your coach). But being selective shouldn't be equated with standing there watching a centered, elevated fastball get called for strike one. At the same time while you should use calculated anticipation that the first pitch will be a fastball, you can't assume that it will be a strike. Don't put yourself in automatic swing mode. After all, the pitcher could decide to throw an off-speed pitch or throw a purpose pitch.

In the end, except for certain game situations, the approach you take is personal preference. There are pros and cons for either one. One thing I know is that players who are comfortable have better chances of succeeding, so if you prefer swinging at the very first pitch, then do so. And if you prefer being selective or patient, go for it. In the end your bat doesn't know what the count is. The count you choose to swing makes absolutely zero difference as to the outcome. The difference is the hitter—how well can he barrel up the pitch he chooses to swing at. A line drive on a 0-0 count flies just the same as a line drive on a 1-0 count or a 0-1 count. There's no magic to putting bat to ball on certain counts.

AUTOMATIC SWING SYNDROME

Not too many people know this, but there is a hideous disorder running rampant in baseball today, especially at the high school level. It's called the automatic swing syndrome, and it usually occurs when a batter gets a 2-0 count. Because he knows that he will probably get a fastball, the batter swings at the very next pitch. And that is what makes this such a horrible disease. It takes away your ability to see the ball first so that you can decide whether to swing or not swing. It prevents you from determining if it's your pitch. It's diabolical! No one knows why the disease forces you to swing every time you have a 2-0 count…

Seriously though, too many times, based on pitch count, hitters are making up their minds to swing BEFORE THEY SEE THE PITCH. The problem with this mentality is that the body will do what the mind tells it, and because the player has preconditioned his body to swing, it will swing—no matter what. That's why players are swinging at balls in the dirt, over their head, or at pitches where you have to ask yourself, "At what point did that pitch look good?" It's understandable to expect fastballs, probably strikes, on certain pitch counts—2-0 being one of them—but not only is it important to see the ball first; it's equally important to understand that sometimes it makes sense to take a pitch. Especially on the 2-0 count.

Let me repeat that. There are times it makes sense to take a 2-0 pitch. While everyone has their own opinion, the following chart sheds some interesting light on the debate on taking a pitch. This was a study done in 2009 by Dr. J. Eric Bickel from Competitive Edge Decision Systems, and Dean Stotz, Assistant Baseball Coach at Stanford University. The data is comprised of over 76,000 pitches and 20,000 plate appearances during a three-year period at Stanford. The chart is referred to as a 'Decision Table for Taking a Strike' with the understanding that your goal is to get on base—NOT TO GET A HIT.

0-2	0% (K)	36%	-36%	No
1-0	35% (1-1)	38%	-3%	No
1-1	25% (1-2)	36%	-11%	No
1-2	0% (K)	36%	-36%	No
2-0	44% (2-1)	39%	5%	Yes
2-1	31% (2-2)	37%	-6%	No
2-2	0% K	35%	-35%	No
3-0	64% (3-1)	38%	26%	Yes
3-1	48% (3-2)	39%	9%	Yes
3-2	0% (K)	36%	-36%	No

Pay particular attention to the 2-0 and also 3-1 and 3-0 counts. Notice on these counts there is a YES, signifying that you should take a pitch. Let me explain what the chart reveals:

- 44 percent of the batters with a 2-0 count who took a pitch eventually reached base, and 39 percent of the batters with a 2-0 count that put the ball in play reached first base. This means the batter who put the ball in play actually reduced his chances of reaching first base by 5 percent (as compared to taking a pitch).

- 64 percent of the batters with a 3-0 count who took a pitch eventually reached base, and 38 percent of the batters with a 3-0 count that put the ball in play reached first base. This means the batter who put the ball in play actually reduced his chances of reaching first base by 26 percent (as compared to taking a pitch).

- 48 percent of the batters with a 3-1 count who took a pitch eventually reached base, and 39 percent of the batters with a 3-1 count that put the ball in play reached first base. This means the batter who put the ball in play actually reduced his chances of reaching first base by 9 percent (as compared to taking a pitch).

The chart is titled "A Decision Table for Taking a Strike" **if your goal is to get on base**. So based on this data, on these three specific counts, you should take a pitch to increase your odds of getting on base.

While the chart reveals why you should take a pitch on these three specific counts, it doesn't tell WHEN. So when's when? The answer is when runners are needed, like early in the game when you want to be the first to score, or when you are down one and running out of innings to play, or when you are tied. Basically when there is no one in scoring position. Keep in mind that runners are in scoring position when they are on second or second and third.

I'm emphasizing the WHEN because interestingly enough, what the study also concluded was that if the goal is to score a run, then batters should NOT be taking a pitch. Once runners are in scoring position, what the team needs is to get them moving, and in order to do that the batter needs to make contact. The hitter's goal now changes from getting on base to making contact. Notice I did not say *get a hit* but rather *make contact*—put the ball in play.

The last time I checked, a team can't win or score runs if no one gets on base. And I know that anyone playing on a team—a good teammate—will do anything to help the team win. So in order to help the team win, everyone should take advantage of and accept this data.

For you doubters, consider the following, which was reported in the *Collegiate Baseball Magazine* 2/6/15 issue. According to Kenny Kendrena of Inside Edge, a company that specializes in precision statistics for professional baseball teams, data from all 2014 Major League Baseball games revealed that pitchers only hit their intended target 24 percent of the time. Inside Edge defines 'intended target' as either the catcher's glove did not move or it was within one baseball width from the glove. "Pitchers don't hit their intended spot as often as one would think." So think about it—if what would be considered elite pitchers hit their target only 24 percent of the time, then they miss their targets 76 percent of the time! If they are missing their target that often, what percentage ends up out of the strike zone?

If professional pitchers are missing that often, how often do you think a high school pitcher misses? Probably more than 76 percent of the time. This increases the odds that the first pitch might not be a strike.

Bottom line—be mentally awake at all times so that you are aware of the game situation, which will dictate what your goal should be when you are up at the plate. And if your goal is to get on base and you are faced with any one of those three counts, then relax. Use this information to your advantage. Wait for a pitch in your zone. The pressure is off because the odds are in your favor to get on base if you take the pitch. And even if the pitch is a called strike, you can still relax because 2-1, 3-1 or 3-2 counts are also fastball pitch counts, so using calculated anticipation, expecting one on the next pitch is a good idea. The odds are in your favor and not the pitcher's.

Based on the data, another conclusion the study by Dr. Bickel from Competitive Edge Decision Systems made was "batters do not seem to take 2-0 and especially 3-1 with enough frequency." In other words there are a lot of 'doubters' out there.

A good hitter understands and knows there are times he must adjust his mental approach.

PATIENT AT THE PLATE

If you have been around the game of baseball long enough, I'm sure you have heard the expression "Be patient at the plate." And if you were asked to describe a hitter who is "patient at the plate,' you could say he:

- doesn't do a lot of first pitch swinging.

- doesn't swing at pitches out of the strike zone.

- doesn't swing at strikes that he feels he can't hit consistently because of the pitch location.

- generally gets a lot of walks.

- is selective.

While these are good statements, to fully understand 'patient hitter', let's consider the actual definition of the word patient—being able to wait calmly for something desired. So what is it that the patient hitter desires? I would say he is calmly waiting for a pitch in his zone. A pitch that he feels is perfect for him—one he knows he can handle.

Also notice the definition mentions 'to wait calmly," or relax. This is the approach you should take on hitter advantage counts—0-0, 1-0, 2-0, 3-0 or 3-1. These are the pitch counts where the pressure is on the pitcher, not the batter. Technically the pressure is off, so relax. It's okay to patiently wait for a pitch you feel confident that you can handle.

Now let's consider some basic tenets of being patient at the plate.

The more pitches a pitcher throws, the more physically tired he will get. The more tired he gets, the less effective he will become and the sooner the opposing team has to change pitchers. In most cases this will mean a weaker pitcher.

Extending the count early in the game forces a starter to reveal all of his pitches. The sooner you learn what his go-to pitch is, the more it helps you when the pitch count you are facing is a pitcher's advantage—0-2, 1-2, 2-2 and 3-2. You can anticipate what pitch you will see instead of guessing.

Extending the count affects the pitcher mentally as well. It's called "getting into his head." When pitchers get bogged down in long at bats, they can become emotionally affected. Thoughts of doubt start creeping into their heads.

If you are patient at the plate, you have a better chance to get a pitch in your zone or a pitcher's "mistake" pitch. Hitting is so much about timing, pitch recognition, and knowing your strike zone.

If you are patient at the plate, you can work the pitch count to your advantage—a 'hitter's count' situation—2-0, 1-0, 3-1 and 2-1. The pitcher doesn't want to risk throwing another ball and falling further behind, so you can anticipate seeing a fastball—one probably on the plate—not an "on the corner" pitch. This is when you look for your pitch. If you get it, take a strong, aggressive swing, and remember, the next pitch might be a strike but it could be a pitcher's pitch—i.e., knee high outside corner strike. So be patient. You don't want to be swinging at his pitch.

At times being patient at the plate can pay off, maybe during the first two innings or once through the line-up or score situation. But how long you wait—how long you remain patient—is determined by the game situation, the pitcher's control, and the pitch count you are facing. You don't want to be overly selective—too patient.

Now for you batting average fanatics who are now in a panic about how taking a pitch affects their average, let's refer back to the Decision Table for Taking a Strike. I have added two columns: the batting average with the starting count, and the batting average with the new count. These batting averages come from a 23-year study compiled by Steve Vickery, coach at El Capitan High School in Lakeside, CA.

First look at the "take a pitch" to increase your odds of getting on base counts, which are 2-0, 3-0 and 3-1. Notice that if you take a pitch with a 2-0 count or a 3-0 count, it has no effect on your batting average. Only the 3-1 count does.

Next look at "be patient at the plate" counts, which are 0-0, 1-0, 2-0, 3-0 and 3-1. Again the only count that affects your batting average is 3-1.

Lastly look at the "first pitch swing" count, which is 0-0. There is no effect on your batting average if you end up at 1-0. And if you do the batting average at 1-0 it's the same as 0-0.

I realize that if you get to 0-1, there is a drastic change in your batting average. But you need to think team first and not yourself. There will be times when taking a pitch is more important for the team than your batting average. So focus on just making contact.

Current Count	Probability of Eventually Reaching Base by Taking Strike	Probability of Eventually Reaching Base by Putting Ball in Play	Difference	Take	Batting Average with starting count	Batting average with new count
0-0	32% (new count: 0-1)	37%	-5%	No	.383	.363 (0-1)
0-1	24% (0-2)	38%	-14%	No	.363	.190 (0-2)
0-2	0% (K)	36%	-36%	No	.190	.190
1-0	35% (1-1)	38%	-3%	No	.380	.381 (1-1)
1-1	25% (1-2)	36%	-11%	No	.381	.194 (1-2)
1-2	0% (K)	36%	-36%	No	.194	.194
2-0	44% (2-1)	39%	5%	Yes	.407	.398 (2-1)
2-1	31% (2-2)	37%	-6%	No	.398	.209 (2-2)
2-2	0% K	35%	-35%	No	.209	.209
3-0	64% (3-1)	38%	26%	Yes	.426	.426 (3-1)
3-1	48% (3-2)	39%	9%	Yes	.426	.219 (3-2)
3-2	0% (K)	36%	-36%	No	.219	.219

As stated earlier, when you go up to the plate you should be prepared to swing at every pitch. Your only decision should be to not swing. Your mental approach toward each at bat should be aggressive. "See the ball, swing aggressive." But this does not mean swing at everything. Do not have an 'automatic swing' mentality. You still need some degree of being selective but you don't want to be overly selective. See the ball first and then decide to swing or not swing.

Think Aggressive > See / Select > Be Aggressive

In order for this to work, you need to have balance between your aggression and your control. As H. A. Dorfman explains in *The Mental Keys to Hitting*, having balance between your aggression and your control is like driving a car. Every car has an accelerator—the gas pedal—and a control mechanism—the brake. The gas pedal represents aggressiveness and the brake represents control. By pressing down on the gas pedal, you will get to where you are going. And with the brake, you can get to where you are going in one piece. So just as there is a need for balance between gas pedal and brakes so that you can appropriately operate the car, there is a need for balance between aggressiveness and control to have success in the process of hitting.

WHY PLAYERS ARE NOT PATIENT AT THE PLATE

FEAR OF STRIKING OUT

Some players are impatient at the plate because their goal is to put the ball in play as soon as possible. And why is that? Because they are afraid they might strike out, especially if they have struck out in a prior at bat and/or are in a slump. It's personal. Striking out is embarrassing and sometimes even humiliating! Let me give you an example.

The score of the game is 2-2 when all of a sudden the team starts pounding the opposing pitcher. Everybody is ripping the ball. Runs are scored in bunches. The pitcher can't get anybody out. Players are high-fiving. Fans are going wild. So who wants to be the one who makes an out—possibly a strike out? The player doesn't want to be that guy, so he goes up 'hacking." And if he does strike out, how does he react? He trudges off to the bench—head down. When he gets to the bench he sits down by himself, shoulders drooped. The inning finally comes to an end and the team now takes the field. He slowly gets up, grabs his glove, and walks out to his position. He takes his between inning ground balls and just goes through the motions, emotionlessly throwing the ball over to first.

You would think that the world just came to an end. To this player it has, because he feels humiliated, foolish. The problem is that hitters with this mentality place too much emphasis on the significance of a strike out, especially at the high school level and younger. An example is the Shane from Utah story. He struck out twice against a fastball pitcher, the only fastball pitcher he had faced. What did he immediately do? He asked for advice on what adjustments he needed to make. At this point he had hit successfully 7 out of 11 times but because two of the four unsuccessful at bats were the dreaded strike out, he felt he had to make adjustments to his swing. I ask you, do you really think if all four of the unsuccessful at bats were ground ball or fly ball outs he would be making adjustments to his swing while he is batting 7 for 11? Of course not! In his mind a ground ball out or a fly ball out does not have the same significance as a strike out. A ground ball means "I made contact—I didn't fail." A strike out means "I failed."

Players associate a strike out too much with failing. In some players' minds, of all of the potential errors (a word players associate with failure) that can be made in a game, the strike out is the absolute worst thing that can happen. It's as if in the rule book there is a chart that lists all the possible errors that can happen in a game. Each one has an assigned point value. And right on top is *strike out*. Just below *strike out* is *passed ball*, and below that is *didn't back up the throw* and next there is *missed the cut off man*, etc.

Let's say there really was a list of physical errors.

Error/Failure	Result
	Runner moves into scoring position, runner moves to third, runner Scores
Fielding/Throwing Error	Runner moves into scoring position, runner moves to third, runner Scores
Walk	Runner on base, moves runners up, runner scores
Strike Out	An out

If I asked if these are positive or negative results, I'm absolutely certain that everyone would say negative. To be successful in sports (and life), you need to find a positive in a negative, so can you think of anything that could be considered a positive from these "errors"?

I can't think of anything good about the first three. So that leaves the fourth one—a strike out. What if in striking out, the batter makes the pitcher throw a lot of pitches? Is that a positive? What if he is the leadoff batter and it's the first inning of the game and he makes the pitcher throw so many pitches that he is forced to show all of his pitches? Is that a positive? Is it a positive if the first batter facing the relief pitcher, who has just been put into the game, forces him to throw a lot of pitches? What if in the process of striking out the batter the pitcher threw a curve ball down and away which was by the catcher and allowed the runner on first to move to second and into scoring position?

Now, don't misunderstand me. I'm not saying jump up and down with joy when you strike out. But if you want to improve your mental game, you need to find something positive from something that probably in your mind is perceived as a negative. So when you strike out, ask yourself, "Was it a quality at bat?" If it was, then mentally tip your hat to the pitcher and walk out of the batter box with pride. That's right—with pride! He got you this time, but it wasn't easy. And because it wasn't easy you had some success. You did not fail!

Okay, so what is a strike out? It's one out—that's it. Think about it. If you play this game one out at a time, then logically, if you play a seven-inning game, an out represents 1/21st or 4.7 percent of the total outs. So let's say the value of a strike out is 4.7 percent. Your next time up you hit a ground ball to the second baseman and he throws you out at first. What's the value of that out? Is it higher or lower than a strike out? Do you lose more points or runs for a strike out? Does the opposing team gain more points or runs from a strike out? Does the umpire take away points or runs for a strike out?

Obviously the answer is no. No matter how the opposing team gets you out, the value is a constant—one out. Remember, Babe Ruth once held the record for most homeruns but at the same time held the record for the most strikeouts. I don't remember reading anywhere that in one of his games, because he struck out, the home run he hit did not count.

Now the good news for these players is that the stigma of striking out has been diminishing due to a change in attitudes toward an at bat. The June 22, 2012 *Sports Illustrated* article titled "Whiffs of Success" states that the chances for a no hitter in this day and age is more likely because hitters are striking out at a record pace. As of this date, 19.6 percent of plate appearances ended up in a strike out. That's one in five. Ten years ago the average was 16.8 percent. You might think that the reason is better pitching, which would be logical, but the author feels differently. "The game has steadily evolved to select batters who trade contact for walks and power—call it 'Take and Rake' hitting. The Take refers to taking pitches to work the at bat into a walk or to wait until you get your pitch so that you can 'Rake,' which is baseball lingo for hitting the ball hard for power, all over the park.

The author feels that the stigma of striking out has been replaced with today's players' acceptance that when they strike out "they are no worse off than outs made on balls put in play." Batters are striking out more because the players now believe the payoff—walks and home runs—are worth the cost. An interesting stat from an article in the 10/7/19 issue of *Sports Illustrated* supports this statement. "Before 2016 there had never been a season in which more than 40 percent of runs came on homers. In 2019 45.2 percent of runs were driven in by 'dingers' (home runs). The trends of this season—more home runs, more strikeouts ..."

Note that both articles were referring to the professional level. But it's occurring at the college level as well. In the October 4, 2019 issue of *Collegiate Baseball* it was mentioned that "the highest amount of strike outs took place last season in NCAA Division I baseball over the past 50 years. Teams averaged a record 8.08 strike outs per nine innings as the quest to hit more home runs grew."

For those of you who think fear of a strikeout is a non-factor, consider the following statement by Dr. Peter Fadde when he was asked "What are some common mental mistakes players make?" Dr. Fadde is the chief science officer for Game Sense Sports, a science-based athlete performance company. "Batters fear striking out. In particular striking out looking is a pitcher's greatest weapon. If you can take that out of the equation, if you are not afraid of hitting with two strikes and not afraid of striking out, then you can take control of that situation. You can be in control." His statement confirms that an emotion, fear—the mental part of playing—has an effect on physical performance. In this case swinging early—not being patient.

FEAR OF FACING A THREATENING SITUATION

Another reason why players are not patient at the plate is due to what some coaches refer to as a lack of trust in themselves. They lack confidence. While I believe that is true, I prefer to call it a fear of facing a threatening situation. Their fear is going deep in the count and/or facing pitcher advantage counts. They don't believe—don't trust—they can handle a 1-2 or 0-2 count or don't want to be at 0-1. So they go up with the *swing at anything* mentality. Doing this, they hope, will prevent them from facing the threatening situation—a 0-1 or a 1-2 or 0-2 count.

Inside their head all they hear is "What if I strike out again! I don't think I can take it! I've got to hit that first pitch!" Imagine the pressure they put on themselves. In their mind they can't go deep in the count because they think it increases their chances of striking out! They are not confident about their ability to handle 0-1 or 1-2 or 0-2 counts, so there is a lot of first pitch swinging. Do you think players who think like this handle pressure well? How effective is their performance at the plate going to be?

Their concern with 0-2 and 1-2 counts are valid. I'm sure most strike outs happen on these counts. But interestingly their fear of getting to 0-1 means striking out is not valid. The following is a chart of the pitch counts they fear. The first column is from a 23-year study of high school players. The second one is from a 2009 study by Dr. J. Eric Bickel from Competitive Edge Decision Systems on a college team. The third column is Division 1 College stats for 2018, and the last one comes from a study done by Lee Judge, a sports writer for the *Kansas City Star* newspaper on Major League Baseball in 2018. I did this because I wanted to show a good range of baseball level of play.

Compare the batting average of a 0-0 count versus a 0-1 count for each level. Putting yourself down in the count 0-1—either by hacking away and missing, or by taking a first pitch strike—is only bad in that it gets you a step closer to a two-strike count. Notice that the 0-1 count batting average is not bad in and of itself. Granted, I don't know what the strike out rate is if you get to 0-1, but it looks like players who are putting the ball in play—getting hits—at 0-1 fare nearly as well as batters who put the ball in play on the first pitch. They overreact with their fear on that count. Being patient on the 0-0 count might not be a bad thing.

Pitch Count	High School	Inside Edge	D1 Baseball 2018	Judge MLB 2018
0-0	.383	.343	.358	.340
0-1	.363	.318	.346	.319
1-0	.380	.339	.363	.338

And look at the results of the 1-0 count. If you can get to that count, you're really facing a 0-0 count. Odds are high you will still see a fastball.

TOO ANXIOUS

Things aren't going well. It's been a while since you got a hit. As ex NY Mets player Todd Zeile explained when asked about his turnaround in September of 2001 on the Mets drive for a possible wild card spot for the National League playoffs, "When you go through a cold stretch, you have a tendency to try to get out of it now, now, now. So I was hitting the first thing that came over the plate, putting bad swings on the ball and getting myself out. I've always been a guy that takes the count deep....I had to get back to that".

But even when things are going well, a player can get too anxious. Derek Jeter states it this way. "When you are going good …. it's easy to lay off it. It's not often during the season that you're zoned in. You tend to get yourself out. You say to yourself, Okay, I'm going to jump on the first pitch, and you end up swinging at a bad pitch."

A mini article in *The Baseball News* July 2002 issue illustrates the point. The article, titled "Extreme Impatience," states, "Colorado Shortstop Juan Uribe tore it up in April hitting .373. Now he's all the way down in the .240's. The reason for his falling like an avalanche average: He swings at anything. Pitchers have gotten wise and no longer throw him anything in the strike zone. Rockies Manager Clint Hurdle told the *Denver Post*: 'Until he allows the pitcher to actually let go of the ball before he takes a whack at it, he's going to struggle.'"

Then there is Adrian Beltre, who at the time was playing third base for the Dodgers. As quoted from an issue of *Sports Illustrated*, "Third Baseman Adrian Beltre ripped three hits in a 16-3 shellacking of the Colorado Rockies last Saturday, but that followed a 1 for 34 meltdown during which he swung at 28 of 36 pitches in one swing." Think about that!! In 34 at bats there were only 8 pitches he didn't swing at!

These quotes are from players who played a long time ago, but that doesn't change the fact that all were professional major league players. The fastball, curve ball or changeup is no different than a fastball, curve, or change up in 2019. It's still major league pitching.

Then you have the situation where you have a coach, parent, or teammate yell out, "We got to hit! Come on! Let's go!" in the middle of the game. Or have you ever told yourself to 'go up there hacking'? On the surface that seems to be good advice. But these are statements that are usually made out of desperation. There is no direction in desperation statements. They are statements that create anxiety. And an anxious hitter is a scared hitter. A scared hitter focuses on what he is afraid of—issues like the embarrassment of striking out—and not on the task at hand. Which is seeing the ball.

THEY ARE SELFISH.

Let's face it—some players are only concerned about themselves. They are concerned only about their statistics. You know who they are. They know their batting average better than their name. They talk more about how many hits they got in a game than the details of the game. On the bus ride home, after a loss, while the rest of the team is upset, this kind of player is okay because he got his hit.

These players are easy to spot. Coach gives the batter the bunt sign. The batter's body language is such that everyone at the game knows he has just been asked to do something he doesn't want to do. So what happens? He makes a half-hearted bunt attempt, which usually results in a foul ball or a strike. Or it's late in a tied game and the coach tells everyone to take until they get a strike. Watch the body language. Listen to their whispers to their teammates when the coach turns his back or walks away after instructing everyone to take until he gets a strike.

These players are actually mad when the pitcher walks them. They throw their helmet after grounding out or striking out after forcing the pitcher to throw ten pitches. They go sulk on the bench when, during a blowout game, the coach replaces them with a bench player. Their batting average, their stats are more important. They don't understand or care that every player's at bat has value to a team's success. For them it's all about "me."

Some young players place too much emphasis on their personal image. They are now playing to be the star pitcher, the player with the most home runs, or a member of the State Championship team. Let's face it we live in a headline news society. ESPN's *Sports Center* is a good example of today's headline news formats. Young players see the highlights and the attention given to athletes in what is perceived as 'positive recognition events' such as a key base hit or home run or records being set or the accumulation of statistics. They want to be 'that guy." They want the applause.

They unwittingly think "being that guy" helps their image. But the problem with this mindset is that their focus actually adds pressure to the situation. And the applause is short lived. It will stop. For young players, at this stage of their life, they don't realize that achievements are soon forgotten. Awards end up tarnished. Life goes on.

WHAT COMES FIRST—THE CHICKEN OR THE EGG

What comes first, the chicken or the egg? It's impossible to decide which of the two related things happened first and then caused the other. But what the heck does this have to do with playing baseball?

In the section on the Components of an At Bat, I indicated that your beliefs shape your attitude and your beliefs shape your mindset. So where do your beliefs come from? Well, I think they come from your performance, and there definitely is a correlation between performance, beliefs, attitude, and mindset. A negative performance causes a negative belief, which affects your attitude and mindset. And a positive performance causes a positive belief, which affects your attitude and your mindset.

PERFORMANCE >>>>> BELIEF >>>>> ATTITUDE >>>>> MINDSET

Look at the following chart that lists examples of what I mean:

PERFORMANCE	BELIEF	ATTITUDE	MINDSET
3 strike outs	I can't hit	Doubt	Fear
0 - 4	Gotta Get a hit	Anxious	Threatened
3 hits	I'm hitting well	Confident	Relaxed

Now let's imagine any one of the three performances listed in that chart summarizes yesterday's results, and today is a new day. Starting fresh. No performance results yet. But because of what happened in the previous outing—your performance—good or bad—the beliefs, attitude, mindset listed in the chart pop into your head. The following chart illustrates what can happen:

MINDSET	BELIEF	ATTITUDE	PERFORMANCE
Fear	I can't hit	Doubt	3 strike outs
threatened	Gotta Get a hit	anxious	0 - 4
relaxed	I'm hitting well	confident	3 hits

MINDSET >>>>> BELIEF >>>>> ATTITUDE >>>>> PERFORMANCE

So I ask you, does your performance determine your mindset or does your mindset determine your performance? Does a negative performance cause a negative belief which affects your attitude and mindset? Or does a negative belief which affects your attitude and mindset cause a negative performance? Does a positive performance cause a positive belief which affects your attitude and your mindset? Or does a positive belief which affects your attitude and mindset cause a positive performance?

If you focus too much on past performance, it could have a direct bearing on your emotions and your mindset, which just might be the reason for the end result—positive or negative—of your next performance. Consider how players decide they are in a slump. They have several experiences where they fail or don't feel good about themselves. Their mind then turns those experiences into a belief that they can't hit or just are not hitting well. Then the hitter acts on those beliefs. And what are the signs of players acting on their beliefs? Well, they start swinging at pitches out of the strike zone or take pitches right over the plate or spend an inordinate amount of time on their mechanics. It essence it becomes a self-fulfilling prophecy.

Your mind takes individual experiences and generalizes them into a belief. Your beliefs come from your performance. This is why you need to disregard any past poor performances and encompass the positive ones. You need to play the game one pitch at a time and not based on past performances.

WHAT COMES FIRST— CONFIDENCE OR SUCCESS

Whenever successful sports figures or teams are asked why they were successful, a common answer is confidence. Which I'm sure is true. The more confident you feel the greater the odds of success. But what comes first, success or confidence? I'm sure most players feel that after they have success then they will have confidence. In other words, if you are successful you will be confident.

While this statement might be true, consider the following scenario: It's the first game of the season. You are the starting second baseman for the first time. You have always played in the outfield. You know going into the game that you have not yet made a play as a second baseman. From what do you draw to feel confident? After all, up to this point you have not experienced any success as a second baseman. So again, what comes first, success or confidence?

Confidence is defined as a belief in oneself, the conviction that one has the ability to meet challenges and be successful ...and the willingness to act accordingly. In other words it's a state of mind. I did some research on ways to be confident or boost your confidence in your everyday life. The following are some of the commonly mentioned suggestions:

• Knowledge – know your strengths and weaknesses

- Training

- Positive thinking – try to be cheerful

- Use criticism as a learning experience

- Realize mistakes are inevitable – especially when doing something new

While these are suggestions to improve confidence in everyday life there's no reason why they can't be applied to sports. As stated earlier, confidence is a state of mind. It is not a skill.

I forget where I read the following statement:"The development of confidence requires risk taking". It is an intriguing statement. When I first read it I wasn't quite sure what the sports psychologist meant. But the more I thought about it the bike riding experience I mention in the Scrapes and Bruises article turned on the light bulb in my head.

So to refresh your memory in that article I asked you to consider a child's mindset when he is trying to learn how to ride a bike. I mentioned that his initial response was fear of getting hurt but because of his determination to be successful he risks falling. He unconsciously built his confidence. The message the sport psychologist is sending is that if your determination is to improve a particular skill or weakness you have to conscientiously be willing to risk failing . Like falling off your bike.

Now practice is preparation time to work on your skills. It's your training ground. Coaches teach. It's where you discover your strengths and weaknesses. It's where you work on problem solving and decision making. It's learning time. But you need to think of it as preparation time for your confidence, as well as for your skills.

This is a good time to 'Dare to be great'! 'Go for it'! Willingly take risks, take chances, and make some changes, in your process of improving a specific skill or weakness. Accept the fact that you will make mistakes but as the mistakes diminish your confidence will grow. Just like the process of learning how to ride your bike. Practice is where you start to earn and develop your confidence so that at game time, because you got better in practice, when you have an opportunity to perform that skill, you won't consider it a risk. You believe you can meet the challenge. And as time goes on with game time success you will be building your confidence.

"What comes first, success or confidence" is just like that infamous question, "What comes first, the chicken or the egg?" It really can't be answered. It's impossible to say which of the two was first and which caused the other to happen.